THE TAO OF TRAILING

A GUIDE TO FINDING CONTOUR IN THE CHAOS OF SCENT DOGS

BY JEFF SCHETTLER

Grey Wolfe Publishing, LLC
PO Box 1088
Birmingham, Michigan 48009
www.GreyWolfePublishing.com

© 2015 Jeff Schettler
Published by Grey Wolfe Publishing, LLC
www.GreyWolfePublishing.com
All Rights Reserved

ISBN: 978-1628280654
Library of Congress Control Number: 2015931487

The Tao of Trailing

Jeff Schettler

Dedication

The Tao of Trailing is dedicated to:

Officer Jason Crisp & K9 Maros
End Of Watch: March 12th, 2014

For their ultimate sacrifice in the name of duty and community.

You will not be forgotten.

Acknowledgements

First and foremost I would like to thank my family for putting up with my endless days and nights in front of computer screen poking away at the trailing life and how best to spread the word. I know it seems at times that I am the proverbial K9 Don Quixote desperately trying to tilt windmills with a literary lance. But, I am telling you: There are dragons out there to slay...they're simply hidden most of the time...

A special thanks to my publisher, Diana Kathryn Plopa for all of her patience and advice on this project. Good books are not possible without good publishers! Thank you Earl W. Wolfe for helping me weave down the writer's highway of proper grammar and punctuation! Great editors are the shadow warriors of manuscript manufacturing. Without Earl none of this would have been possible.

And a heartfelt thanks to my Tao of Trailing readers and fellow K9 aficionados out there around the world: Ultimately, my books are all written for you.

初心

"In the beginners mind there are many possibilities. In the experts mind there are few."

~Shunryu Suzuki

Introduction: Reading K9

One might say that dogs cannot read, but in fact they can. Let's just imagine that a K9 following human scent is like a dog reading a book. The environment the K9 works in would be the pages, and the words are written by the scent it has to follow. A fresh track or trail would be easy to read: the black ink, freshly printed, would be clearly readable on the blank, white pages. However, blank, white pages are virtually not existent in reality. The pages are smudgy, filled with other words of multiple sizes, in numerous colors and various fonts. Many other scents are present, both from human and other sources, making it harder for the K9 to read the lines. As the track or trail gets older, the ink starts to fade. Now the K9 has to focus even more, as the words are written over by fresher scents and might even get lost in the blur of colors and words in different shapes and sizes. Matters are made worse by other factors. For example, words can be washed away by water or blown away by wind. And while the K9 does its best to keep up with the writing, the book is moved sideward, back and forth by the wind, right at the very moment the dog is trying to read the words. This altogether is what makes tracking/trailing one of the hardest among K9 tasks.

To complete the task, the K9 is armed with a sophisticated piece of equipment. A dog's nose is truly remarkable, ready to do just one thing: perceive scent. And it's incredibly efficient and effective in doing so. When breathing normally, only the striking scents are noticed. This becomes totally different as soon as the dog switches to sniffing mode. A continuous sequence of short bursts of air reaches deep inside the nose, where numerous olfactory sensor cells are waiting to analyze what is inhaled. At that very moment, dogs do what they do best: to search for, analyze and follow scent. That perhaps raises the question: if dogs are already fully capable of using their nose, why should we as humans teach a dog how to track or trail? We don't. The objective of training a K9 for tracking/trailing is not to teach the dog how to use its nose. It is to train the dog in using its nose to our advantage. A dog already knows how to read. We don't have to provide it with a 'how to'-manual that tells it how to follow human scent. The only thing we have to do is to apply proper tracking/trailing training. That's how we let the K9 grow stronger into its task of reading the words of the scent of a specific individual.

The key here is self-experience. In training, we create the ideal learning environment. We create the circumstances in which the K9 is able to learn by itself; how it can stick to that particular scent we would like it to follow, or how it could work out problems while following it. Then, we are able to gradually push the dog's boundaries step-by-step, until it has developed itself into a proficient tracking/trailing K9.

The story does not end there however. Not only is tracking/trailing a difficult task for the K9, the K9 handler awaits a challenging task too. To the K9, the book deals with the human scent trail. To the K9 handler, the K9 is the book to read. Reading a working K9, chasing scent in harsh conditions, is a hard task to do. The K9 dictates the words in a continuous flow of body language and subtle behavior, more often than not, at a breathtaking pace that's difficult to keep up with. It requires the handler's complete attention, as the K9's words might not be repeated. An important signal can be missed in the blink of an eye. The handler must be aware of the K9, who might react differently in different situations. The handler must be focused at all times, especially when following scent in a crowded, urban environment or when danger lies ahead. There are few situations in which reading a book from start to finish is more crucial.

Proper K9 training considers both ends of the long line. It deals with the K9 and the handler: the K9 team as a whole. It prepares the team for the challenges they face in the field. Yet, training a K9 team involves more than preparing K9 and handler for reality. The ultimate goal is to forge a bond between them, that makes them live through any situation they might encounter. Few are able to grasp the synergy that is necessary between K9 and handler, let alone the effort that is needed to build the mutual trust and understanding. It takes time, patience and careful observation to make a K9 team truly a team. Jeff Schettler is one of the few who is able to create the circumstances in which both K9 and handler are able to grow. Based on his knowledge, experience and practical insight, he has what it takes to build a K9 team.

Fortunately, training is not the only aspect of his K9 work. New and experienced handlers are in good hands when they read Schettler's writings. As *Tao of Trailing* lies before you, his fourth book on K9 trailing is finished. Once again, he takes us deep into the world of chasing scent, developing training, accurate handling and building a team. It has been worth waiting for.

~Cor Oldenburg and Cor Oldenburg Jr.
Beverwijk, the Netherlands

Cor Oldenburg is the founder and owner of the 'Speurhonden Instructie School', a Dutch organization specialized in training dogs for various tracking, detection and scent discrimination purposes. Based on his background in dog behavior and K9 tracking, he developed the 'practical tracking' training method. Over the years, this method proved to be suitable for professional K9's and handlers, as well as for hobbyists. Oldenburg has been trained and educated by many well-known and lesser known K9 trainers and instructors in Europe and the US. He is known and respected for his careful observations of dog behavior and the interaction between dogs and handlers.

Son of Cor Oldenburg, Cor jr. assists his father in the Speurhonden Instructie School. Starting as a track layer at young age, his tasks now involve training, education and writing articles for various journals. Cor studied at Wageningen University, from which he graduated with a thesis on generalization in wildlife detection dog training. Together, father and son wrote the book on practical tracking Het echte praktijkspeuren: voor de professional en recreant (in Dutch).

Contents

From the Author

Ronin and me on a normal patrol day in the City of Alameda.

The *Tao of Trailing* is my fourth and final installment on hunting humans with a trailing dog. These books included one autobiography and three books on training for the art of trailing. I started this process in writing without knowing what I was doing back in 2005 while on the mend from a couple of major surgeries that ended my big dog work for quite some time, and kept me very immobile over most days and some very long evenings. During that ordeal, I also went through the agony of losing my long time police bloodhound, Ronin, the subject of my first book, *Red Dog Rising*.

At the time that I went down physically and under the knife, Ronin was diagnosed with incurable cancer. Talk about a double whammy! All the way up to his last days, he only had one focus though, and that was his work, well, and his stuffed animals too. He liked those a lot. I missed him terribly and writing down some of his stories and casework were a kind of personal release for me.

The more I think about the whys and wherefores, maybe *The Tao Of Trailing* started quite a long time before I had my first working dog. I remember the very day that I knew with certainty where my own path lay. I was a streetwise kid on the verge of legal manhood and had experienced a life on some of the roughest streets in America. I came to a point in my life that if I did not change, I would probably die or go to jail. My life then was actually pretty exciting, and in many ways, quite fulfilling. (In hindsight, my daily choices were becoming increasingly poor and it was only a major shakeup that would provide a way to salvation.)

I knew I had to change instinctively but not with any pattern of experience, dramatic situation or epiphany to guide my mind set. You know how certain things make your life complicated and every waking morning brings another fruitless resolution to get your "collective shit" together? The resolutions never come to fruition, at least until enough "get your shit together" resolutions pile up and you have no choice but to step into them. That did not happen to me. I remember the day as if it was today and it was just not like that. The thought simply… WAS. It came to me and that was the beginning of it all and change occurred over night. So what was the reason? Was there something that guided me to a path that probably saved my life?

Yes, there was and as with all times in my life, it was because of a dog. Dogs have always been by my side and I know now they have always guided me. Perhaps not with Vulcan doggy mind-meld communication skills, but by their total accepting and guileless presence. The dog never judged me, but because of the dog, I really was destined to do right.

Belit was my first real, all-my-own, dog and constant companion. She was the reason I was homeless for a brief period and as was the reason why I changed my life for the better. I wrote about her, just a little in *Red Dog Rising*, but to be honest, an entire book could be written of our experiences together.

We were sitting side-by-side looking off into the sunset of a hazy Fall evening on a golden grassy mound of old valley earth, very close to my mother's apartment in San Ramon, California. What set this place apart from any other in the area was that it always struck me as nature's last stand in the wake of the human development sweeping the Tri—Valley area just east of the-San Francisco Bay Area, in the beginning of the 1980's. Malls and condos were encroaching on previously wild lands like never before.

Belit with my son Shayne in Germany.

This little spot right across from my mom's apartment was bypassed for some reason. Kind of like a single boulder in a rushing, foaming river standing fast in total rebellion. I felt like it won the battle and deserved a little more attention. Attention became fascination and the woods there attracted me like few other places, but always in the company of my ever—present companion, Belit. I explored every inch and knew each and every creature living in the wood.

We sat there, that evening, looking off into the western hills as they turned to gold— as only the California foothills can do in fall, and for once in my life, thought about what we might do in the future. What I might be when I was fifty and I wondered where would Belit and I be then? But that was silly, because she could not possibly live that long. I scratched the "fifty" thought almost as fast as I thought it, because the feeling of not having Belit in my life was paralyzing and not something a seventeen year old wanted to face at the time.

On the heels of thinking forward came the conclusion that it had to be something more than what I was doing now, and if only it might be with what my passion was at the time, animals or dogs in particular. Belit looked up at me at just that moment and with almost perfect timing blinked her eyes and smiled as only a dog can. I knew then what my path would be.

The "oldness" of that tiny hill and the wood is missing now. The boulder, though seemingly impervious, had finally turned to gravel in front of a human tide-like onslaught, replaced by nothing more than another apartment complex and a shopping mall. But my mind will always drift back to what it once was, what it still is, if only in my dreams; those dreams with that little Chesapeake Bay Retriever who helped make me what I am today. In my dreams, she runs there always and occasionally, on certain nights, we roam those woods together exploring and enjoying life as only a boy and his dog can do. God, what I would do if only to have that freedom and certainty in life like I did then.

My life became what I dreamed of with Belit that fall evening in 1981, and though I did not perfectly remember that as I wrote *Red Dog Rising* twenty-four years later, her life's lessons guided my hand just as much as those I learned with Ronin, my first working dog.

Red Dog was not initially written for publication. My first book did not hold fast to any rules of modern writing because the last thing I was thinking about was anyone reading it. I was able to lamely pour my soul into each of the chapters because I did not care who read them. I felt things and expressed them in words because I could not talk to anyone about them. This lack of communicative ability about what was going on inside me was nothing new in my life; it was just exacerbated by my condition at the time. I wanted my dog back and the only way I could really feel him again was to write about him.

My first foray into book writing was liberating because I simply did not give a damn. There is no better way to achieve something than not caring whether you succeed at it or not, all while still being passionate about it at the same time. This justification for writing in 2005 and 2006 was the key to trailing but I had no idea that I was practicing in prose what I had been working for all along at the end of a long lead and only occasionally succeeding! And to be honest with you, I was not even thinking of that at the time. *RDR* was written on many evenings on the back porch of my California home in Plymouth, Amador County. Willow Creek was a gorgeous setting in the golden foothills of the middle Sierra Nevadas. I had a glass of an old time resident's Cooper's Zinfandel on my right, a Gurkha Churchill Maduro to the left, and the Mother of all Canyon Oaks just above the MacBook screen. Couple all of that with a little post-surgery medication and I had a recipe for remembering the happier old times in my head and putting them on the computer in such a way that really helped me reconciling my loss of Ronin.

On the heels of *RDR* came *K9 Trailing: The Straightest Path*... kind of a no-nonsense training manual for solid foundation trailing work. *"The Path"* really came about because of the sheer number of schools where I began to teach and I was very sober while writing it. It was simply the easiest way to get the message across. I never intended to be a writer; as a matter of fact, I never even graduated ninth grade, and English was appalling to me. There must have been some kind of Karma because here I am now! One of the problems with *The Path* was that I wrote far more than could be contained in one volume. I not only touched on foundation work but also on tactics for police K9 handlers, and advanced trailing situations. I think I had an exfoliation of the mind and fingers for a while! What started out as a simple primer became a K9 equivalent of *War and Peace*…. really only from a word count perspective. I had to break it down into three volumes for simpler mind digestion. It would do me no good at all to put everyone to sleep.

My initial plan was to quickly follow up *The Straightest Path* with a more advanced book on urban applications and some actual case-scenario work that I experienced on the street as a K9 handler. I wrote some thoughts for the new book while I was writing my first books, but I put no effort into organizing or finalizing than at that time.

Well, reality in the form of recent K9 officer deaths while on high risk tracks kind of got in the way of that. I produced my first K9 Tactical Tracking course in 1998 and had been teaching it in small bits and pieces, but never on the scale of our basic training— for trailing courses. I regretted that lack of foresight when I learned about these tragic events. I truly felt that if I could have simply been more diligent in spreading the word about Proximity Alerts and how to deal with them, perhaps these deaths would not have occurred. I felt that I had no choice but to focus all of my energy on trying to prevent these things from happening in the future, if at all possible. With the help of some great tactical friends of mine: Frank Merritt, David Layne, Derreck Bachner, Bill Lewis II, and many others, my new book: *Tactical Tracker Teams; A Guide To High Risk Manhunts,* was completed and was on the shelves in March 2013

As I promised, I did not forget about my advanced trailing book. As a matter of fact, I was still typing away at parts of it while *TTT* was moving forward. The other interesting thing that happened was that I could not hold on so steadfastly to some of my early viewpoints. I think this was because of all the exposure I had to so many other handlers and their training techniques over the years since *RDR* was born. Things just did not always work exactly the way they seemed to back when I wrote the book. Sometimes having the opportunity to look at things from the outside—in can change ones perspective; and as every Fall leads to Winter, a new year and Spring, with new ideas, is always on the horizon. I think becoming balanced with something is much like the seasons and we must always prepare for newness.

My life now is consumed only by trailing, and I work with trailing dogs today far more than I ever did as a full time police K9 handler. Trailing is almost 24/7. I've grown as a handler and a trainer and I discovered better ways to do things now-than how I preached about them before. All true professions are based on evolution and growth. Anything else can only be considered as so much stagnation. I also realized that some things I wrote about in *The Path*—that seemed super obvious to me at the time—could have been explained in more depth. What I thought was self-explanatory really was not obvious for many people and some chapters deserved more attention. But that is the way of life I suppose. Live and learn. Of all things that I cherished the most post, *Path* publication was to watch some of my students become better handlers than ever I was and to have the opportunity to observe them teach their own styles of trailing.

I thought long and hard about the title for my fourth book, and unlike the previous three, I did not seek advice. I wanted this book to be an expression of what K9 trailing philosophy is about in just a few simple words. This expression had to be truly personal and based on my passion for this art. I looked back on the rest of my life and what shaped it: the mistakes I made as well as the successes. I realized that my philosophy on trailing strikes similar parallels to the martial arts that I have always practiced and my experience as a soldier in the United States Army. In both, I learned that rigidity to only one form of fighting was constraining and also limited winning. With true trailing there must be a balance and comfort with chaos because so much is out of our control. Of all the words that shaped my philosophy none struck truer than the words of Bruce Lee in his book: *The Tao of Jeet Kune Do*. Bruce wrote:

> *All fixed set patterns are incapable of adaptability or pliability. The truth is outside of all fixed patterns.*

If there is a truth to trailing it is a true dance with one's dog, then Mr. Lee's philosophy on martial prowess spoke volumes and inspired me.

My company patch is dedicated to my mentors as well as a symbol of a Tao philosophy in trailing.

Concentration on one form and the science of scent does one great service in debate, but does it truly create a condition of confidence in actual deployment? Perhaps it might be in the beginning but there must come a time when handlers should throw what they have learned to the wind and become flexible enough to adapt to each new situation as it appears. A truly successful handler will have the ability to anticipate the movements, thinking, or changes in the subject's physical or mental state based on the K9's body language reaction. For the reactions of the dog to scent stimuli while trailing are, in a way, a mirror to the actions of the subject; just not in a way the average person can grasp. This knowledge can only come through experience and failure. There is seldom a better way to learn and grow than to fail, and trailing handlers must anticipate and learn from failure. And most importantly, a truly masterful handler will live in the moment like the dog does because true trailing is instinctual and in the moment.

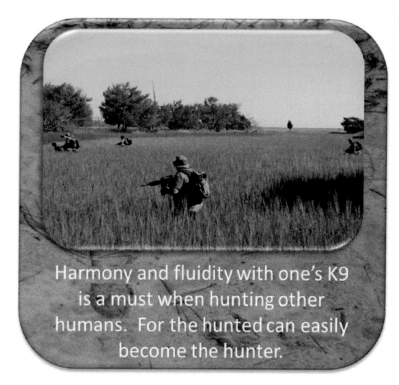

Harmony and fluidity with one's K9 is a must when hunting other humans. For the hunted can easily become the hunter.

I know *The Tao of Trailing* was originally supposed to be called "Advanced Trailing". Not only is advanced trailing obnoxiously boring, it is a horrible name for any book, especially this one, and I abandoned it as soon as I began to write again. This may disappoint some of my *Straightest Path* and *RDR* fans because I promised a primer on how to work a trailing dog in the most difficult situations of all: the City. As I began to put pen to paper.... er, finger tips to keyboard, the crux of my writing seemed to take a new path. It was almost in the same fashion as I wrote *Red Dog Rising*: at a whim, with a heartfelt urgency, and I really liked that feeling. I wrote what I felt, when I felt like writing. There was no rush, no schedule, and "No worry, Mon." Every chapter was written out of order, and now that I think about it, there was no outline or order. That stuff came later when thought, then word, coalesced into chapter and ultimately: book form. *The Tao of Trailing* will give a philosophical path to success without being a step-by-step training book. I realized that just like martial arts, the essence of trailing was truly in the act of self-expression and not simply following steps in a book. In order to really work the dog, the handler must be one with the dog.

Though I thought *K9 Trailing; The Straightest Path* was a great training manual... it was just that, a training manual. It was nuts and bolts and yes, though nuts and bolts are necessary to build the machine, there comes a time when a soul must be given to the gears, frame, and structure in order to give the machine life. And, if there is one thing, one thing above all other things, that I know now: trailing is an expression of life. It is as intricate and soulful as any form of music. It takes skill and conditioning as difficult as any martial art. My last book on trailing must be an expression of my passion for the life of trailing and not just a manual. The machine must have a soul.

I want you to feel what I feel behind the dog and hanging onto the long lead, for that is the soul of which I speak. That special tautness of a twenty-year old worn thirty-footer with a hound hell bent for the hunt on the buckle end. Understand what he is going to do by the toss of the head or set of tail, all while moving at a hunter's-mile feasting gait.

That visceral "knowing" that your course is true and nothing your quarry does will throw you off its scent: for that is true joy. The ending was sealed from the start; it is simply the game that remains, and in the end you will pine only for the game. When truly trailing without forethought, there is a sublimely perfect mindset that sends all caution to the wind; while pumping hunter's blood though veins already swollen with life. I am trying to describe it but I believe it can never be really written about and understood... it must be felt.

I want you to shiver at the first breath of cold air—with rain on the edge of your peripheral vision—while running through a place others would never tread—let alone run. Get dirty with the feel of loamy Mother Earth on your hands while your briar scarred trailing boots eat up the miles. Lose yourself to the hunt as your dog does, for it is this abandon they truly enjoy. The prey may be the target, but the passion for the hunt is the fiber of being that binds our dogs to the trail. The capture is nothing compared to the path; and those who truly learn this learn to fully live at least in one small facet of their time here. If your goal is oneness with your dog then you must learn to love the hunt as your dog does. In so doing, you will experience life in a way you never have before and finally find that balance to be one with your four legged partner.

The Tao of Trailing is this expression, this passion, this balance and love for the hunt that allows me to be one with the dogs I work. It is a release of thinking or reasoning while simply living for the joy of the hunt. If I can sum this book up in just a few words it is not "How to go" but rather '"How to LET go."

Jeff Schettler
Edisto Island, South Carolina

Chapter One
Scent Inventory: Starting The Trailing K9 Revisited

"To find the acorns the squirrel must first know the trees in the forest. Like the squirrel, the dog understands its prey and where it might have fled by first knowing the hunting ground and other creatures therein. If there is only one prey scent this task is not difficult. When there are many, it becomes more complicated and time must be spent in their separation."

I wrote about scent inventories in *K9 Trailing; The Straightest Path* and neglected to cover certain aspects that I believe were vital. I must apologize to the reader who perused this section and misused it due to this lack of detail. The following information might have proved helpful on the first go around. For my European students who are reading this for the first time, you are getting the amended version and will not suffer the confusion others perhaps have in the US.

The good news is that the scent inventory was designed primarily for contaminated areas and it works great there. Especially so in those areas where multiple people, animals, or things have happened after the subject of the search left the scene. The bad news is that the scent inventory practiced in a location with no contamination and only one trail out can be a waste of time.

The whole purpose of the scent inventory is to help the K9 wade through the morass of BS that is often present in a contaminated urban area. I developed my process to help my dog work out complicated scent problems in the middle of the San Francisco Bay Area; an area ripe with tons of people and low on vegetation. There was never just one trail out! So when I wrote about scent inventories and their purpose, my intent was to help new handlers work through contaminated areas, and I was not considering single, uncontaminated trails in the woods.

A patrol K9 handler walking on a scent inventory with his dog prior to the start of a trail.

The problem was that I was thinking that people would think like me when I wrote about the subject. I believed that the intent and purpose was self-evident. I did not consider that my recommendation would be taken so literally and for every condition. I guess this comes with being a newbie writer. I hope not to make the same mistake again and I do apologize to all of my early readers if my early writing on scent inventories caused any problems.

The scent inventory is meant to give the handler and K9 time to take in all of the sights, scents and sounds in the area of a search scene when such a scene is in a complicated and busy area. This is especially important when there are multiple, fresher scents over the top of the missing person trail. In the case of real missing person cases, the K9 team is often one of the last to arrive: usually because all other search resources and people are used first. When all else fails, the dog is called in.

The search scene: yard, house, and surrounding yards and houses may have been canvassed completely by foot troops and this means lots of fresh human scent and trails leading to and from to and from the place last seen. The K9's propensity is to tend towards fresh trails; often regardless of scent articles. I found, through experience, that when I gave my dog some time to walk around the scene prior to the start of our search, he seemed to have cataloged all of these odors in his own mind and would gravitate to the correct trail a little easier. On the other paw, when I jumped right into a search without this cataloging time, my dog had a tendency to jump to the fresher trails. In many cases, those trails belonged to other searchers who had checked the area before we got there. He would do this even when one of those searchers was part of my back-up entourage.

The other complicating factor with these contaminated scenes was that even if the dog did not jump to a fresher trail, the older, covered-up trail was often too difficult to immediately discover; there was simply too much cover scent. When my dog had a chance to circle outside of the contamination into "cleaner" areas and then move into the scene, he seemed to connect the dots from inside the contamination to outside quite a bit easier and we had more successful trails.

Basically, the purpose of the inventory was to allow my dog a chance to smell most everything in the area of the start of the search before we started. Hopefully that he would find our trail a bit easier; it usually worked very well. In other words, I gave him a chance to smell all of the ingredients of the hamburger before he looked for it!

The only place the scent inventory is a waste of time is when there is no contamination or where the contamination is so low or indistinct that the dog easily gravitates to the fresher, correct trail. Most important is the freshness or newness of the correct scent trail as it relates to the start. I found that if the trail that matched the scent article was strong and far fresher than any other scents in the starting area, my dog did not need the scent inventory.

I knew I was having some trouble communicating with some of my readers when I trained with them after they read *K9 Trailing; The Straightest Path*. I noticed this, in particular, after rereading the chapter on scent inventories or missing member. What I noticed was how the scent inventory or missing member applications were being made and perhaps misused. Probably the best way to explain and fix the problem was to outline what I watched and the measures I used to correct the concerns of these student/readers.

The most common improper use of the scent inventory that I have seen often went as follows:

The handler, carrying the scent article, would bring the dog out to the start of the trail. More often than not, the scent article would be in a very light plastic bag (more useful for poop disposal than for protection of a sensitive piece of evidence meant to target a very sensitive nose.) The bagged scent article was generally carried loosely in one hand, along with the loops of the long lead; his other hand holding the business end of the leash that was attached to the dog's collar.

Problem No. 1.

Once the dog got to the start of the trail, many times right on top of it, the handler would commence to harness the dog and add other items thought necessary for the dog and the trailing job. In the meantime, the dog would be frantically sniffing the start of the trail while being held back so the equipment could be properly put on...

Problem No. 2.

At this stage of the ritual the dog has detected the trail while the gear was being placed on its back. Because the scent article was in such close proximity to the nose of the dog and in a woefully improper container, the dog also knows the target scent of what it is that it is supposed to find... and then delay continues. The next step in the routine is the short circle around the start point and then we can show the dog the article...

Problem No. 3

Problems one and two are nothing more than impedance to trailing in some conditions. A highly motivated dog will certainly want to quickly get to work if it can detect and isolate the target scent upon arrival at the start. The dog will lose interest in the trail when the handler pulls it off of a perfectly good trail to do a circle around the start when the trail is the only one that exists. The dog's frustration continues when the handler then fumbles with equipment placement, and lastly, perform a ritual walk over the top of the single trail. When there is only one trail out or the trail is very fresh with no contamination, the "ritual" is a motivation destroyer and many dogs may shut down or simply take another trail when released.

The other big problem I see with many, who practice my scent inventory improperly, is the way the scent article is maintained. Instead of a sterile and relatively scent transfer—impervious bottle or other material, cheap and lightweight plastic bags are being used and carried right next to the dog's nose. Cheap bags and even good Ziploc bags leak scent. They do not maintain odor in a sterile condition. If you can smell recently collected dog poop through the plastic of the poop bag, does it not stand to reason that the dog can smell the scent article through this type of container as well? The dog has a far better sense of smell then we do and can detect minute levels of odor from phenomenal distances. If the handler holds the cheap bag with the scent article in it as he or she puts the harness on or other equipment, there is a very good chance that the dog already knows the scent. Many dogs have a short attention span and are sniffing for other stimulating things. This brings us the final problem and that is total lack of surprise for the dog.

I honestly believe the key to the scent article is when it is a surprise for the dog. If they find the scent article or the scent themselves and start a trail or if they see it from a distance and are excited about investigating it, they are more inclined to follow the matching scent trail if one exists. When the article is "found" by the dog, they seem to acquire the target trail with a high degree of accuracy. This is the reason for the method of scent article presentation that I used in *K9 Trailing; The Straightest Path*. The article has to be a surprise.

The unfortunate part of all three problems is that they were of my making. My short description of the scent inventory process in *K9 Trailing* was inadequate. The *Straightest Path* resulted in the creation of a "Ritual" simply for the sake of a ritual. I explained and diagramed the process quite well, but what I did not explain completely was the reason the process existed in the first place, and that it did not necessarily suit each and every condition. My scent inventory was taken literally and not in the spirit in which it was developed. My desire was to propose using the inventory to give my dog a better chance at finding one target scent amongst many fresher ones in a contaminated environment. My experience had always been primarily urban and I did not think outside the box to a rural condition where perhaps only one trail existed.

Primarily in Europe, but also in parts of the USA, my scent inventory was taken as gospel. It was practiced to the letter of the law, when no such law was ever intended. I had developed a method that worked for me in city situations and I tried to impart to the reader one of the several methods that I managed contamination.

First and foremost, there is no single "method" that works for all dogs: especially when that method is primarily made up of preparing my dog and myself with equipment for trailing and starting a dog on scent. Every dog and every condition is a little bit different and the best handlers are always those who have the ability to wade through a quagmire of difficult conditions and start their dogs minimum of fuss. This is what I really wanted to try to say. Find a way to create a clean slate for the dog so that when it comes into the scene of a missing person or a criminal it can isolate a single trail when that trail is covered over by lots of fresher trails and contamination. The start of a real search is chaotic; especially when that search involves emotionally charged situations such as missing children, homicide, or abduction. A handler has to have a way to come into these conditions and not be overwhelmed by them. If the handler is overwhelmed and confused, the dog will be equally so. What happens on the handler's end of the lead reactively occurs on the K9 end and this is often in the case of no trail or improper trail acquisition. The scent inventory was a way I worked through the chaos of these conditions.

Chapter Two
Failure

"Too often we seek only success in practice; believing that only success will produce perfection. This state of mind is driven by ego and not necessarily a formidable plan for perfection. In trailing, perfection does not exist because ultimately we are nothing more than an impediment to the dog in its action. Secondly, the nature of the hunt itself has a high degree of failure built in: for all of nature's top hunters will fail at finding prey the vast majority of the time. Failure does not deter the hunter. Failure only teaches the hunter that should it fail too often, it will die. Failure, therefore, is nature's best teacher."

When I began trailing I was taught and practiced guiding the dog to where I perceived that the scent laid. I was told that human scent did certain things and that it was my job to make sure the dog trailed there. If the dog did not, then I line checked or verbally corrected the dog to those places.

In those early years, I rarely questioned what I was told; believing that the trainers who taught me these things had the experience to prove what they were teaching was viable. I had no real background in general dog behavior and training, thus no basis for questioning anyway. My lack of questioning was exacerbated by one simple fact that, though small, was very powerful in my personal interaction with my trainers. I did not want to offend them because I felt these people might be a key to my working future and I wanted them on my side. Coming from an Army background, I learned that to succeed, I needed to play the game. I think this is a common feeling many new handlers share when trying to come up in a difficult field of work that their local agencies have not fully embraced yet. When one is attempting to start something new that nobody else is doing, there is a certain amount of friction experienced and it is difficult not to want to please everyone; simply to be accepted.

Though I learned many things from my trainers, some good and some bad, the most important thing I learned was not to subscribe to them exclusively. Though each one played a part in my success, and I give them credit for this success, there came a time when I had to take my own road. This is what I tell all of my students today. There will be a time they MUST outgrow me to continue along their own path to success. I am a motivator and an educator; I am not a perpetual fountain of knowledge.

Where I diverged from all my teachers in the past was in the areas of failure and the unknown. Where each mentor had their own technique or style, they all conformed to the same standard of known trails in practice, and especially in testing: Some marked their trails with flags, others walked the trail with the subject and then walked back, and many simply gave detailed instructions to the trail layer and watched their progress for as long as possible.

In the beginning, I believe it is important to have a rudimentary idea of where the trail is laid: simply to make sure that the dog does not get too far off, should it miss a turn or important section of the trail. This is one way to stop hunting behavior and encourage the dog to circle back to reacquire the trail. This is especially true of dogs trained to simply run ghost trails by handlers who were happy as long as the dog was moving. The dog must understand that it has to circle back on its own and locate the turn and not simply continue to run forward. Puppies trained from a very early age using the principals in this book and *K9 Trailing; The Straightest Path* will not have the ghost trail problem because they have little interest in moving forward if there is no scent there.

When I began to double blind test my dogs, (*Double Blind Testing*; Chapter Two), I learned that much of what I had done in the past for training was probably wrong. My beliefs in certain abilities of trailing dogs were completely dashed. In short, I discovered that I was leading or guiding my dog not just a little, but a lot. The first few tests were big with lots of problems, and for the most part, we failed them miserably. This forced me to start working smaller, double blind problems in order to dissect what was wrong and how to make it better. I failed many of these early tests too; even when they were small problems. What I discovered was that most of the failure was based on my guiding the dog with trailing lead pressure. This was directly related to my subconscious belief that I knew where the scent trail was, and because I was impatient with the dog's process. With each failure came new insight and with insight came small successes. Each insight encouraged more patience.

Each time I ran a trail where I had no idea of where the subject ran or ended up, I became more cognizant of what my dog was doing, for I had to rely solely on the dog's body language as a guide to the subject. There was nothing for me to do but watch closely—unless a track happened to be visible. In the beginning of my blind trailing paths, I made many errors and found that more often than not I had several factors that influenced trail difficulty:

1. The trail was too difficult for the dog at that stage of its training. In this condition, I was generally too impatient for bigger and better things and put the dog in a place it was not ready to be. This was the start of my philosophy of tiered training levels; Chapter Ten.

2. Patience for the dog. This was a hold out from my known trail training regimen that had made up so much of my former life. When the dog circled for what I perceived as too much time, I would mistake concentration on odor and K9 frantic effort at trying to untie the scent knot as distraction or loss of scent. I would then pull the dog off or unknowingly or incorrectly guide the dog in a new direction.

3. Bad lead handling. When the dog circled too fast or pulled at unexpected times, I tied the dog's legs up with the lead or line checked too hard causing the dog to come off. This usually happened because I was too busy looking at places where I thought the person went not where the dog was circling. I was not watching the precursor body language changes that indicated that the dog was about to bust a move.

4. Moving too fast in tough conditions. When we were working in variable or hard surfaces I ran too much and too fast resulting in a condition where I pushed the dog past turns too often. This situation seemed to be related to my intention at getting to the trail layer as soon as possible.

The common denominator for all four conditions was directly related to my overall impatience and desire to find the person as soon as possible. My impatience was directly related to my prior training and testing technique of known trails.

So why was I so impatient? I think it was directly related to always knowing where the subject walked. Having this knowledge inclined me to push the dog each and every time I perceived that it was off the trail or thought it too slow. Rather than allowing the dog to figure things out on its own, I used line checks and verbiage to move the dog along, simply to get moving. I had no idea at the time that I was missing so much wonderful body language that then explained all that I am learning today all that I am learning today.

I discovered that each and every time I pushed the dog or tried to guide it too much when the trail and ending were unknown; we failed, and the dog could often not recover easily. I discovered that I was the problem—more so than the dog. On the other hand, if the K9 overshot a turn on its own and worked back to it without assistance, it seemed to always recover and take up where it left off. The difference was the K9 learning through self-discovery versus me showing it what to do. Each and every time I took the dog off what it was doing—processing scent—it disconnected from the trail and focused on me. I broke the chain and interrupted the "three-tone missile lock" that I had before. The longer the focus on me and away from the scent trail, the less interest the dog will have for the trail—if it does happen to make it back. The best way to visualize this might be to consider a gas gauge with a needle going from full to empty on a gas guzzling the car... the more you press the gas, the quicker that needle hits "E"

Trailing Malinois working in front of a shopping center.

The interesting thing about double blind training is that it taught me that I could and would fail the more I interfered with the dog. It also taught me that failure was simply a part of trailing, or the nature of the hunt. It was the best teacher I could ever have, and if I did not embrace failure and consider him a friend, then I would never grow as a handler. You see, I really never failed when training as a young bloodhound handler. Each and every practice trail was always set up so I could pass it: because I always had an idea where the trail ended and, of course, always knew who the trail layer was.

Always knowing where the trail is and knowing with certainty what your runner looks like: all mixed in with a little bit of ego and you have a recipe for guiding your dog versus the dog guiding you. This is how it works:

You send out a friend to run a trail from one place that ends in front of Wal-Mart, with hundreds of people walking in and out. You are convinced that your dog is scent discriminating very well because it always had in the past—with all of your past known trails. Your dog runs the trail into the shopping mall on the way to Wal-Mart and as it encounters different people you either slow or pull back on the lead before your dog gets to the person. The dog naturally comes off the wrong person and continues the trail. Rather than nose low, the dog is running head high and looking left and right. As you come to the front of Wal-Mart, you spy your runner sitting on the brick wall of the planter next to the shopping carts. As your dog approaches the area and is close to the runner, you let the lead loose and magically your dog jumps into the lap of the runner and everyone is happy. The ability for your dog to scent discriminate has now been proven above and beyond all doubt. OR HAS IT?

Frankly, I think not. I believe that in these training scenarios the vast majority of the time the handler dictated the outcome through lead handling. This is always most evident when the trailing dog handler is around the distraction of people and constantly chokes up on the lead, stops, or pulls the dog back altogether. Yet, when the handler encounters the correct person, he or she suddenly, lets the lead go. The trailing lead is a communication tool as good as a human command.

Guiding with the lead during trailing is difficult to detect. It might be a small change such as sideward pressure from the handler standing off to one side.

To the practiced K9 trainer this can be sorely obvious. Many Master Patrol K9 Trainers, specialists in detection or other scent work, catch the line handling direction immediately. However, this seems lost on so many trailing dog trainers. The reason why it is obvious to seasoned patrol dog people is because of their generalist background in K9 training and dog behavior. They have years of experience watching K9s interact with their human partners and understand intimately how easy it is to guide a dog with a leash. *Search & Rescue handlers, (SAR)*, on the other hand, usually come from a non-professional K9 background without this experience and often do not see the guiding.

The reason why many single purpose trailing dog trainers do not catch the lead handling/guiding problem is because, in many cases, trailing was the first dog job they learned. They do not have much experience in other forms of scent detection such as narcotics or explosives. They simply never learned how easy it is to guide a dog with voice, stance, and especially lead handling. Furthermore, these people were often trained by other single purpose trailing dog handlers who, themselves, never had any generalist dog behavior or training experience. It is a perpetual problem that has been in existence for as long as trailing has been popular.

This is something that most people do not understand. With Patrol K9 or other forms of Military or Police K9 work, there is a selection process, testing, and lots of formal training for any aspiring dog handler. Becoming a trainer usually means many years of street experience and more training. Not everyone makes it. Becoming a trailing handler is something most civilians can do without any real formal training or testing. The same thing can be said about a trailing handler becoming a trailing trainer. Trailing is not a mainstream K9 discipline yet; though it should be. Right now, anyone can call himself or herself a trainer—with or without experience—and almost always without a selection process. There has to be a selection and testing process for new trailing trainers based on reality and the ability to understand how dogs work. In trailing search and rescue (SAR) work today, it seems the only thing someone needs to do to become a trainer is to host a seminar.

I know I digressed a bit with the last couple of paragraphs but I felt it was important because trailing handlers really need to have an understanding of the history of their discipline. Though the work has been around in the USA for over three-hundred years, it has never been standardized for modern law enforcement. This is kind of an oxymoron because trailing is the oldest American K9 job there is. The tide is turning and there will be a day that trailing sits side by side with all other police K9 work; but for now, it is still on the fringe.

I believe that all aspiring "Mantrailers" need to learn other K9 disciplines and become students of dog behavior in general. Through this knowledge they will understand how better to handle their dogs: not impede them, and especially not guide them.

So, let us go back to the scenario and not only make the trail unknown but the trail layer as well. Have someone else find a runner for you and have them set up the trail and not go with you when you work the dog. What most people will discover is that many of the dogs will not even make it to the front of Wal-Mart. Nor will they have a tendency to jump on the first person the loose leash allows them to. I believe anyone reading this book for the first time should try this scenario before assuming that his or her dog is trailing effectively in an urban environment or scent discriminating with any reliability. Failure will be the likely result and this is a good thing; for it is the failure that can pave the path to correction and make a better trailing dog team.

The problem, unfortunately, is that many people who fail at such a test often ignore the failure or blame it on another factor: the dog was not working properly: my dog was sick, the weather was too hot, my back-up did not warn me about the cars coming and I demotivated my dog because I moved too slow… etc., etc. This is ego talking. Rather than looking at the K9 work critically, we as handlers have a tendency to rationalize everything the dog does because we love them too much. In reality, they are an extension of what we perceive as our own abilities. We do not look at them as tools; we look at them as pets. This has to stop to become a true handler.

When the dog does not effectively work a problem out properly or fails to find the subject, it is important to understand why without bias. By testing with the unknown, we remove bias from the equation. When we test with known trails and trail layers, we automatically assume a biased position and lessen the chance for failure. This, in the long run, will lead to delusion about our own abilities.

Failure or the chance of failure must not be feared by the trailing dog handler because the failure can actually set him free from very confined ways of thinking and growth. Embracing failure and looking at the dog work with a critical mind will generally show the handler that they have moved too far too fast and missed critical associative steps in training. Every time we fail we truly learn because we do not want to fail again.

Most of my trailing trainers, in the past, believed that the dog must always have a positive ending or a find at the end of the trail to make sure it is motivated to trail the next time. In other words, we never really failed. Even if the dog was not working and got lost, we brought the trail layer back or walked the dog to the trail layer. At the time I thought this was the right thing to do and that the dog learned from this. In human terms this might be a teaching method; but for dogs, it is simply teaching them that, when they stop, the handler will lead them to the reward. Dogs are not dumb nor are they puritan in their approach to work. They will always take the easy way to reward even if it means not trailing. By leading the dog to the source we are literally teaching the dog that they do not need to trail.

Failure in trailing training, especially when failure is repetitious, is teaching us that what we are doing needs to be scaled back to something more effective. A tiered training ladder must be used from small to big, low to high, simple to advanced. Failure is a good thing because it will lead to a better way as long as the failure is not rationalized away.

Chapter Three
Double Blind Testing and Training

"An error does not become truth by reason of multiplied propagation, nor does truth become error because nobody sees it. Truth stands, even if there be no public support. It is self-sustained". ~Gandhi.

Trailing: There is no other K9 work that produces fewer results in actual deployment yet still maintains industry wide blind faith. The fact of the matter is that search and rescue-trailing dogs rarely find what they are looking for. Think about other types of life saving work that produce a similar success rate in real deployments. There are not many at all. When something does not work reliably, the method is abandoned. But not with trailing and I am not advocating abandoning trailing. I am an advocate of change based on reality and truth.

The truth in our industry is plain and extremely clear, but the problem is that our discipline, to a great extent, is blind to it. Trailing dogs are constantly touted and "certified" for their ability to run extremely aged trails—often in excess of twenty-four hours—and to scent-discriminate very accurately. The reality of the situation is that trailing dogs rarely find people on trails older than twenty-four hours, and K9 scent discrimination, though very possible, has proven to be less than reliable in actual scientific tests. When double blind testing is applied to trailing dogs in an attempt to validate the claims that are made in support of some of the more fantastical work that is claimed there, none of the claims hold water. The trailing dogs touted as having these amazing abilities never pass the tests. Yet, all of the training and "certification" for these claims continues and grows. Often the excuse for this is the "fact" that the dogs do so well in training and pass the tests and certifications reliably. The problem with the training and tests are they are based on known trails and the dogs are constantly being guided. This is extremely evident in video. Simply look at the trailing dogs in urban environments running head up and constantly on the lookout for the clue from the handler or subject of the search that they are close. Then look at the videos of dogs really working. The body language says it all.

The difference between a dog with scent "heads up" and the same dog without scent "heads up." Forward momentum does not necessarily mean the dog is trailing.

Yes, trailing dogs do find people from time to time with trails older than twenty-four hours but they are very rare. When this does happen, it is often based on air scent and proximity; not necessarily following aged odor over distance. Every now and then a dog or two actually follows an aged scent trail. Regardless of how the find is made, whether it is blind luck, trailing, or air scent, trailing usually gets the credit and the fantasy about aged trails is propagated yet once again. And more devout followers of the trailing faith are born and fantasy training techniques are passed on once again.

This is the crux of the problem. Too many of us blindly follow those methods of training that do nothing but guide the dog, and in so doing, guide the handler into a belief system that the dogs are miracle workers. This feels good, it's warm and fuzzy, but is it reality?

I advocate training and testing as it relates to the dogs true ability and the only way to discover that is through double blind testing. A double blind test is where nobody on the trail, other than the subject, knows where the trail is or where it ends. Furthermore, the test must be set up in such a way that the trail is not an air-scent problem. This means that consideration of geography and distance must be made in a knowledgeable way. When we do this, the reality is quite plain. Most GOOD dogs are reliable with trails that are no older than six to twelve hours and rarely, if ever, over twenty-four hours.

The argument is then made that we have to have dogs and training that are the equivalent of what we are deployed for: e.g. trails over twenty-four hours old. When considering this argument, one must look at why the argument is there to begin with. It is made because trailing dogs are called on as an afterthought and this is largely due to all of the fantasy claims and testing in our industry. We have created the deployment problem by saying we are capable of the fantastic! Trailing has been around historically on record since the 1300s, but it has not been until the 20th century that we see the change in deployment to incredibly aged trails. The reason for the change is media sensationalism of a few modern cases that received national attention. Suddenly, a new movement is made with all of the training to support it. But not once were scientific tests used to prove the training. Just blind faith. So, why the blind faith?

I think that is a simple question to answer as well. We all love our dogs and we all want to be heroes. If we can do something others cannot, we are looked upon for direction and training. We stretch the truth and the facts because we look better and people will like us. More importantly, they will call for our dogs. Many trainers preach the fantastic because it is the only way people will follow them. Some of the more dramatic offenders in our own arena are now facing or have faced prosecution not only in the courts but also by their peers. There is a book I highly recommend all trailing dog handlers read: *K9 Fraud!: Fraudulent Handling of Police Search Dogs*; Dr. Resi Gerritsen and Ruud Haak

We have done the public a disservice by allowing this delusion to continue as long as it has. The lack of honesty in our industry has hampered many real missing person cases. Some dogs literally led the investigation 180 degrees the wrong way. There has been too much blind faith in unverified K9 work. The lack of honesty in our industry is also creating some really bad trailing dogs that might otherwise, and with solid foundational training, be quite good.

And now we have another problem. Beginning about two years ago, I and only a very few others began to preach a double blind testing revolution for our trailing industry. At first, we were attacked and ridiculed en masse. Very few people wanted to listen. Times have finally changed quite a bit and there is a revolution taking place. Yet there are still many who not only ignore the truth but warp the message to suit their own needs. I am talking about the trainers and handlers who now have magically double-blind tested all of their dogs and, of course, have deluded themselves that the trailing results are comparable with proper double-blind testing results. The crime here is in the words being used, and not the message.

"If your adversaries are stronger than you, it is better to join the adversaries!" And nothing smacks more of the truth than this statement... but with some trainers and handlers, they are only words. They no more double blind test today than they did when they first started. These words are used simply to divert attention. It is easier to lie. There are MANY really great trainers and training programs out there.

There is no single method to make any one student a better handler. But, if I were to start

Starting a young bloodhound's trailing training in a wooded environment helps to create a very focused dog due to overall lack of distraction when the foundation for work is being laid.

this all again and from a place of no knowledge, the place from whence I came, the only advice I would give myself would be to ask anyone with "knowledge" the hard questions. If they could not demonstrate to me that they could personally do what they profess and do so in a true double blind test, I would not follow them. Ask the trainer if you can set up a trail for them based on what they are telling you and the only rules are that they do not know the location, the trail, or the subject of the trail. It might be interesting to see who steps up to the proverbial plate.

I've talked about double blind testing, but what about training? Double-Blind Training is just as important because it keeps the handler honest to the dog's ability and ensures that the handler does not guide the dog simply to get to the next tier of the training ladder. What I mean by this is that often times we handlers have a tendency to expect a finished product before the product has been earned or worked for. Excellent trailing dogs take time to produce. Dogs have the instinctual ability to do the job with no training, but do not have the instinctual versatility to do the job in every condition. The key to training a trailing dog is to have the trailing dog learn at its own speed. The dog should be slowly guided into new conditions that are tiered in such a way that the dog learns in manageable steps without confusion. Worse would be continuously allowing the dog to be running to an air scent.

Double blind trailing training is not for new handlers who have trouble reading dog body language; unless the handler is with an experienced handler or trainer with that ability. As with the training for the dog, double blind training for handlers should be done in tiers from simple to more complex too. The handler must have confidence in the dog and his or her own ability and that confidence can only come from past success. Start small and work towards increasingly more complex scenarios. If there is trouble along the way, as there invariably will be, step back and make sure that the prior condition is thoroughly trained for and easily worked without failure. I usually start with relatively easy trailing in soft surface conditions, in the woods with little to no human or animal distraction. Maybe a few turns with a distance of four hundred to six hundred yards. A good dog and handler should run a trail like this from start to finish and without deviation in about five to eight minutes. If this type of trail takes more than twenty minutes to complete it generally means that the dog was not working very well and has not been successfully trained for the condition yet.

Once the dog is showing exceptional ability to trail in the condition being trained for it is time to start training the condition double blind. Double blind training is nothing more than a double blind test. Send a runner out with instructions to run a practice trail in such a way that it mimics one of the known trailing models used before to condition the dog: no more and no less. The only thing now is that the way the runner ran the trail or where the runner went is unknown to anyone working with the dog. If a handler can run ten trails in such a fashion and successfully find the runner with little to no distraction or loss of the trail then the new condition has been successfully trained for. If, on the other hand, the majority of the double blind trailing trails are unsuccessful, it means that the training was not effective and there is a very good chance that the handler, knowing the trail conditions, was guiding the dog.

The ultimate benefit of double blind training and testing is that it is truly the best method to build 100% confidence in the trailing dog's ability to find the subject. It will also completely instill in the handler what his or her dog's limitations are. Knowing ones limitations is very important. This is not to say that we cannot learn to work past the limitations of the team. Proper deployment comes from understanding the possible versus the historically proven NOT possible.

Double blind work forces the handler to be more aware of what the dog is doing because there is nothing to fall back on, such as flag markers, if the dog seems unreadable. Flagged and marked trails, though extremely important in the early phases of training, are ultimately a "crutch" for the average handler. Once the handler is proficient with the basic mechanics of dog handling, this "crutch" may lead the handler to force the dog to work on top of the marked trail. In other words, he will be guiding the dog. Since all real searches are double blind. It makes sense that some portion of our training should mimic reality.

Chapter Four
Scent Article Starts; Revisited

"Imagine a plastic bag thrust into your face; worse yet, pulled over your head? How would you feel about it or any similar scent you might detect thereafter?"

I have long suspected that any attempt to force a scent article on a dog often leads to not only aversion of the article but also the trail related to it. I have seen this in double blind testing and simply through awareness of the dog's body language, which speaks volumes at all times.

After watching hundreds of dogs over the years, with handlers who use all manner of scent article presentation, the absolute worst of all that I have seen is the bag over the nose or head method. This is where the bag with a scent article in it, is placed over the muzzle or head of the dog, clasped to keep it as air tight as possible, and then released when the handler deems it an appropriate time relative to what he or she thinks is the amount of time necessary detect the scent in the bag. Whoever came up with this concept has no real knowledge of K9 scenting ability or how long, or with how little, a K9 might take scent. I am convinced that this procedure was developed because some K9 was obviously averse to a scent article. The trainer/handler probably never learned how to entice the dog to a scent article in the first place.

I can almost guarantee how this started, God knows how long ago. It was probably the handler who had been thrusting the article in the face of the dog over and over until the dog decided it did not like the process anymore and started to turn its head away whenever the bag was shoved in his face. The handler did not understand that pushing something into the face of an animal caused the aversion. He created even more problems when he decided more force was necessary and developed the bag over the head method. The handler knew that the dog liked the bag over the head method even less than the bag in the face and began to rationalize the reasons to make this method acceptable to others.

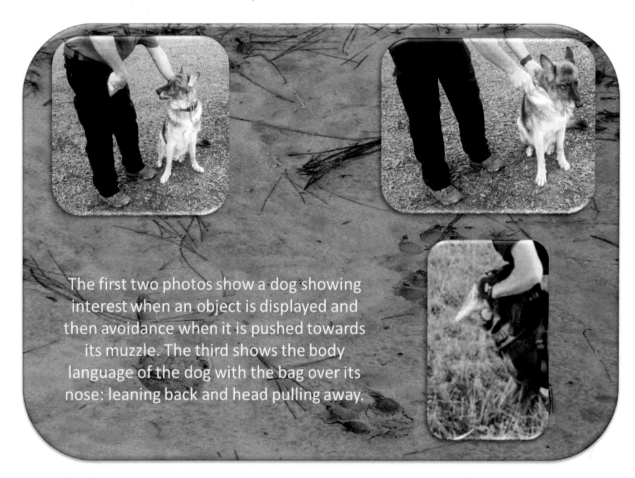

The first two photos show a dog showing interest when an object is displayed and then avoidance when it is pushed towards its muzzle. The third shows the body language of the dog with the bag over its nose: leaning back and head pulling away.

The rationalization goes like this: "I know if the dog has only the scent of the subject in its nose and that is all it can breathe, then I know my dog has target lock." Well, that is true when there might only be one trail present or if the subject trail is the freshest, because the dog defaults to instinctual trailing. In this case the article is really irrelevant anyway. Where this method suffers is when the trail is older than any other contaminating trails on top of it and there is no fear scent to follow. Practitioners of this method will state that their dogs easily pass these older contaminated tests even with this method of scent presentation. The facts they neglect to mention is that they have not double blind tested this method.

Worse, is that anyone worth their salt in K9 scent training understands intuitively that dogs need an amazingly small amount of odor to begin with for target acquisition. More importantly, if the dog discovered the scent on its own without influence, it tends to gravitate to that scent better than when it is shown the scent by a human.

My experience with double blind testing of the "bag over the head" method is that when the dog is offered several trails of equal age and the bag is thrust over the dog's head or nose to start on one of those trails, they have a tendency to not only shy away from the bag but also from the trail. In every trail I tested with this method, not once did the dog, (not mine but ones trained in this fashion), elect to follow the trail matching the scent article. In each, it appeared that they purposely avoided the matching trail. What I discovered was that the method was based on faulty human rationale of a K9 event. Worse, absolutely no K9 behavior response was considered when this was developed. It was a default because the dog was already adverse to the article to begin with. Force was met with more force.

The problem with this philosophy is that force is one of the worst ways to train or encourage a dog to be purposely selective in track or trail acquisition. Dogs follow trails or tracks due to primordial predisposition, and when something interrupts that thought process, such as a bag squeezed over the muzzle, proper track acquisition goes out the window.

I can belabor this point until Hell freezes over, but ultimately the only thing I can ask any offended party who reads this to do is to test this double blind in a contaminated, urban environment with the subject trail older than the contamination; then watch what happens.

I long suspected that my first trailing dog hated it when I tried to push something in his face unless it was food. Early on, I noted that he began to shy his head away whenever my hand brought the scent article towards his muzzle. It did not take long to understand why when I considered what it would be like or someone to do the same thing to me. I would not like it and neither did my dog.

I have long been a student of all things wild dog. I loved reading everything I could on the subjects of Coyotes and Wolves. I devoured books by David Mech and Barry Lopez as they gave me key insight into the ways wild dogs operating without human influence. Through these books I discovered the worlds of the wild wolf and coyote and sought them out in their own environment. After countless hours observing coyotes hunting, I learned very quickly how they best found scent and how they reacted to the trails relating the corresponding odor. I used what I learned from wild animals and applied it to my trade. So, how to make my canine more interested in the article? The answer was obvious; try to keep it away from him. My dog was so prey driven that anything that he could not get was a challenge that he had to overcome. He would work tirelessly at something simply to "get it". I took his weakness and applied it to my scent presentation. I would take my scent article and rather than thrusting it in his face, I would try to hold it away from him. If he could not air scent the article being held away from him, each and every time he would try to pull out of my grasp in an attempt to get to the article. My solution was at hand. Use the dog's natural drive to create a positive scent taking experience and I had a dog that liked the matching trail much better.

The way I did it on the street from that point on was to take the bag or bottle with the article in it and try to keep it away from Ronin from the outset. I would not let him anywhere near it, and the best thing was to keep it always in a wind unfriendly environment. If he air scented the article before I was ready, he did not want to smell it. If he had not smelled it yet, and it was held out away from his nose, he scrabbled across the sidewalk as fast as he could to get at it. Thus my first scent presentation method was developed. The problem with my "method" is though it was easy for me, a 220-pound weight lifter; it was not so easy for smaller people with equally powerful dogs. It was almost impossible for the average person to keep the bag away from big dogs.

Shortly after I wrote about my presentation method, I read a book by Dr. Leon Whitney. The book was written in 1937, shortly before World War II. Anyone reading this book needs to keep the context in mind that dog training in this era was a different 'animal' altogether. There are things in the book that I absolutely did not agree with, but on the same note, there were others that were eerily familiar.

A couple of things that I love about this book are the facts that for the first and only time that I know of, an author attempted to document the life and times of some of the earlier manhunters such as Captain V.G. Mullikan who was famous his manhunts just before and after the turn of the 19th century. Whitney and Mullikan are both lost to time and few recognize their names. This is a shame because these men, as well as those who came before them, are responsible for our modern trailing and tracking work. If you want to understand our discipline more then you must read everything that is available to you while it is still available. Our art is not new; it is very old with the beginning times, as we know them around 1307. The common denominator between the early writings and those current is they are few and far between. Devour them greedily while you have the opportunity.

The point of the Dr. Whitney reference was it was the first time I read anything from anyone about making the scent article a surprise. Nobody had ever taught me or showed me anything remotely like my method. There was no possible way that I could have been the first to understand basic dog behavior and article response so I was super excited to read Whitney's philosophy on the subject.

Desire to get to the article leads directly to desire for a matching trail.

What Dr. Whitney wrote was that he discovered when his hounds found the scent article on their own and without help, they tended to gravitate to the correct trail better. The big difference in how he did it and how I did it was he hid the article out of sight and wind scent of the dog and the article surprised the dog as it walked up on it. This is how my second process for starting a dog began.

When I read this for the first time I was amazed by how complicated I had made the process by holding the dog back and trying to stretch out and keep the scent article away from its nose in an attempt to entice the dog to investigate. In hind sight, the way I did it was great for super contaminated areas, but I was really making it too difficult. It was far easier to hide the article and let the dog find it on its own.

So, this is how I start all of our young pups now. They detect and find the article on their own and when they do, they are far more fired—up about a matching trail than any other way I could think about presenting scent. I have to be very careful about certain issues however:

1. The scent article must NOT be placed on a doggy pee spot or close proximity to other marking.

2. The scent article must be large enough if placed on the ground that it is the primary scent source. Cigarette butt sized objects are too small.

3. The article must be placed in such a location that the K9 cannot detect from long distances and determine the type of odor. If they can, they will often process the odor from a distance and then discount it.

4. If the area is contaminated, I like to use glass jars. They keep the scent contained, protected, and the bottle acts as a solar funnel. Outdoors, solar energy on the glass heats the object inside regardless of clouds and scent rises out of the jar.

5. Plastic bags are not good; they move with the wind and always fall over on their side. Furthermore, the temperature in the bag is so close to the ground that the ground scent, if there, is equally attractive.

When dogs find an article with a subject scent upon it and there is a corresponding scent trail leaving from that article, the dog will effortlessly respond to that trail odor. The beauty of this method—without a method—is that it is all dog and has nothing to do with the handler. The dog finds the article without assistance and discovers the matching trail without assistance. Short, sweet, and very straight to the point. This is the way of the dog and truly the way of hunting; uncomplicated, amazingly simple and sublime.

This series of photos show a sequence of events that entice the K9 to the article.

Chapter Five
Firetrails Revisited

"The observant handler will consider well the cat and mouse in all things trailing."

Runaway training or the term I use: "firetrail", has been around for about one hundred years or so and in writing since the mid-twentieth Century. A veterinarian by the name of Leon Whitney wrote about firetrails in 1953 in his book, *"Bloodhounds and How to Train Them"*. Dr. Whitney was a very influential dog trainer and breeder before and after WWII and was a prolific writer who was known for not only his

Leon F. Whitney DVM Author of the Book Bloodhounds And How To Train Them, Orange Judd Publishing 1947; was a student of one of the more obscure founding fathers of modern manhunting, Volney G. Mulliken. Author's photos from a first edition of Whitney's book.

Huge hunt drive in this K9.

book on bloodhounds and dog psychology but also for his articles in various magazines such as a 1937 issue of *Popular Science*. Whitney was taught by a very famous handler at the turn of the last century: Capt. Volney G. Mullikin. Mullikan was famous for many exploits—probably the most significant being his tracking of the Hatfield and McCoy families. Mullikan is also credited with a 300-hour-old trail but there is no verification that it was actually trailing. I have serious reservations about this claim, (and other things in Whitney's book). I mention it here because it is used so very much to profess the abilities of the bloodhound and what I consider to be an urban myth. Even though I question the veracity of the age, Mullikan's find and conviction rate is probably still one of the highest for a bloodhound handler; however, I digress.

I was taught about runaways when I first started by just about every one of my early trainers, the late Glenn Rimbey being probably the most influential and the biggest proponent of the process.

I now teach the firetrail but with my own spin on it. I mention the history here because I have heard some trainers making claims that this is a "new" method of training or their "own method" when in reality it has probably been around since the first bloodhound was used to hunt people... so at least one hundred years have passed. Frankly, what we do now is nothing more than a new spin on what a lot of people probably did long before we picked up a trailing lead.

I believe the basis for tracking and trailing is the excitement of the chase. It is the biological, Mother Nature given gift, the gene given to all Canids to help them hunt. Without the excitement and drive for the scent trail, the dog could not survive and the "trailing" gene would probably disappear.

The necessary steps for the fire trail layer are: tease with the reward, move away, present and drop the scent article, run out of sight immediately, hide, and reward happily.

I wrote an entire chapter on the process: Chapter 8 in *K9 Trailing; The Straightest Path*, that talks about the use of the firetrail to build the drive of the dog and establish the foundation for all future work. When building upon the natural skills the dog already has for trailing, we focus the trait by having a subject run from the dog while simultaneously dropping a "scent article" or large piece of clothing with the subject's scent all over it. The dog is torn between the dropped object it has not had a chance to smell yet and the fleeing subject. Once the subject has run a prescribed distance, the dog is released to get him or her. In most cases, the pup will sniff or even grab the clothing and then run after the subject. When the pup gets to the subject, it is rewarded profusely with whatever it likes the best such as food, ball, or tug toy. The puppy learns that there is a connection between the clothing/scent article, the running subject, and the reward. I feel it is important to revisit the method here because the philosophy still holds true to maintaining veteran trailing dogs' skills.

I have recently seen a new style of trailing training that steers completely away from Firetrails and the rationale. Though sound from a human perspective. It appears to me to lack simple understanding of dog motivators and overall drive. The rationale is that the dog will be too sight dependent and not use its nose. This might be the case if the training was conducted improperly, or with dogs predisposed to this condition. On the other hand, nose work is instinctual with dogs. When firetrails are used properly, most dogs will naturally start following the odor trail almost immediately. I have seen many dogs trained in this new style and feel that their overall drive tends to be lacking. Yes, they will work but they also have a tendency to distraction and poor scent trail discrimination.

I do runaways until the dog physically dies. From the day I get the pup to its last days, we do firetrails, not all of the time, but every now and then. I believe it is why dogs trail in the first place what they enjoy the most, and they seem to never get tired or bored with it. If they don't like firetrails to begin with, I really question the dogs' trailing ability to begin with and usually pass such a dog over when testing. I have heard many trainers and especially handlers espouse the "fact" that veteran dogs will get bored or tired of firetrails and it is the reason that their dogs won't do them or react poorly to fresh, short trails. I honestly believe this is rationalization for dogs that probably aren't too motivated to trail in the first place. It smacks more of human rationalization for a flaw than anything else. In my experience, the runaway is the essence of trailing life and the dogs love it forever. To say a good trailing dog will get bored with a runaway

Kooper is our 11 year old retired Trailing dog and even though he is getting old, he turns into a pup for the firetrail game! Short, sweet, and Koop is happy!

is like saying a good detection dog will get bored with its ball reward. The runaway is the trigger and subsequent catch is the prize burned indelibly in the dog's brain synopsis. Beyond a shadow of a doubt, each and every one of the top trailing dogs I have ever seen deployed all loved firetrails.

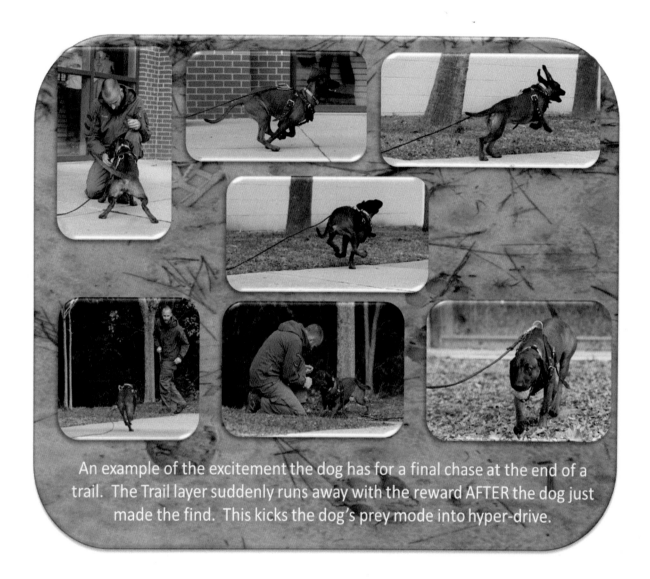

An example of the excitement the dog has for a final chase at the end of a trail. The Trail layer suddenly runs away with the reward AFTER the dog just made the find. This kicks the dog's prey mode into hyper-drive.

My first trailing bloodhound, Ronin, was my sounding board for trailing. He tolerated all of my mistakes and really trained me in how to work and read a dog. He walked his last runaway a distance of about twenty feet the day before he died. He was so happy about that runaway that the light in his eyes blazed with life and passion. For just a moment, he was a twelve-week-old puppy again. I knew then, more than ever, that the runaway was the reason for it all. The runaway is my tennis ball for all of our trailing dogs and I never end them.

Do I run firetrails with every training session? No; I believe in a variable reward training approach to increase drive and motivation while reducing the chances of handler cuing. But I do them a lot and for the life of the dog. I have also begun to use them for other purposes in training.

The runaway or firetrail is a huge part of the reward if not all of it. After working over a thousand trailing dogs over the years, I have come to the conclusion that we were totally missing the critical link when using firetrails by simply employing them as a trigger mechanism for physical reward such as food or toys. Yes, those items can be important for certain aspects of training but I think the firetrail coupled with the catch is the primary reward. We were focusing too much on the food or toys after the firetrail and did not consider the chase and catch may have had much more of an impact on the dog learning.

I first began to consider this when trying to get a normally food driven hound to take a treat after a good catch. At home and when simply being a dog, the female bloodhound would eat anything and everything, greedily looking for any handout. When on the trail, she was a different animal. Once she found the subject, firetrail or not, she would not take a treat, ball, or even praise. She only had one interest and that was the trail layer. I found that she was constantly alert for more movement from the subject; if that person happened to try to leave before we did, she would pounce on them as if the game had just began anew. It reminded me of the cat who gives up the mouse in its clutches only to swat and catch it again.

Example of K9 learning to follow ground odor by getting it closer to nose level by using tall grass.

I began to ponder the cat and the bloodhound. They both were very similar, albeit with different size prey but prey was the name of the game. I realized immediately that the game of catch and release simply fueled desire for the game to begin again or continue. Mother Nature had given us the training tool from the onset, we only understood part of it and more importantly, the reward was inside the dog all along. I now am constantly on the lookout for this type of dog. Bloodhound, Shepherd, or mutt really does not matter. I am looking for an obsessive-compulsive desire to chase people and not let them go. Interestingly, when I find these rare gems, not only are they always my best trailing dogs, but also they all have a similar lack of a huge desire for reward. Yes, most will take it but they would much rather have the subject try and run again; we need to harness that obsessive compulsion and build on it.

At my present training state, I employ the firetrail in the beginning, middle, and end of trails that require motivation to help the dog learn a problem. As with obedience, a cookie is often used to get the dog over a learning hump, such as the command to lie down heard for the first time. Nothing better than a snack then to get them to lower their posture and assume the position. Well, it is the same thing with a runaway firetrail when working in a difficult situation. It is often the grease that gets the dog's mind wheels moving in the right direction and quickly.

I covered Firetrails quite a bit in *K9 Trailing; The Straightest Path*, but I want to go over a few details that I should have written more about. When starting a new dog, never before introduced to this style of training, I recommend the following principals be followed closely. The elements to the Firetrail Principals are:

1. Animated runner or decoy
2. Large, strong scent article from the runner
3. Good location for ground scent work
4. Perfect reward timing

The first location to start training is soft surface and there are types of soft surface that tend to be better than others. I recommend areas with taller grass and shrubbery as close to the height of the dog's nose, while running, as possible. The reason for this is the runaway training, that we are going to start, causes the dogs to want to run heads up after the subject. By running through tall grass and shrubs, the trail layer will drop a lot of odor that will stay high and the physical contact will create a scent picture the dog cannot

Pic of a happy dog at the end of a trail.

ignore.   This is important because the subject will almost be immediately out of sight and the dog will be forced to use its nose.

I also like mornings and nights vs. daytime trails. Mornings and nights tend to keep scent lower to the ground. During the day, fresh trail scent rides high on thermals.

The scent picture is really the first consideration the handler has to have. This is because we want an easy transition from sight to scent and if the ground is chosen with care, the transition will be all the easier.   If the location is relatively hard and low—gravel, hard pack dirt, concrete—the dog will not gravitate to ground odor but instead look for the subject with its eyes, or try to wind him. Neither is desirable at this stage because we are trying to build a foundation on ground-based odor. The first trails are the start of that, and a good start is crucial to long-term success.

When building upon the natural skills the dog already has for trailing, we focus the trait by having a subject run from the dog while simultaneously dropping a "scent article" or large piece of clothing with the subjects scent all over it. The dog is torn between the dropped object it has not had a chance to smell yet and the fleeing subject. Once the subject has run a prescribed distance, the

A handler keeping the dog from spinning by straddling it.

Using obstacles such as trees and depressions restricts the dog's vision of the running tail layer.

dog is released to get him or her. In most cases, the K9 will sniff or even grab the clothing and then run after the subject. When the K9 gets to the subject, it is rewarded profusely with whatever it likes the best. In the game with a patrol dog, I like a good tug or Kong. A Kong is a rubber like toy commonly used in dog training. The K9 learns that there is a connection between the clothing/scent article, the running subject, and the reward.

Next, choose a reliable trail layer familiar with patrol K9s to run from the dog the first time or two. This will shape the drive of the dog to the work for future practice and actual deployment. It is very important that the trail layer or the subject, is animated enough to build this drive. A really good start with a subsequent runaway, followed by a timely reward will get your dog where it needs to be. I highly recommend subjects who have great track records as

High value rewards or rewards the dogs like best, are necessary to build drive and focus for most dogs: Dog liver pate in a tube, tennis ball, squeaky ball, and tug are just a few examples of what might make your dog's boat float.

decoys. These are the people who understand dog behavior and know how to get that little extra *uummph* out of the K9.

This is the basis for what we are about to do, but it is really not all that simple. In order to get the best results out of a runaway, it is really important that everyone knows what they are doing and when to do it. Timing is going to be critical from the time the subjects runs and drops the article to the time the dog is released, runs, and is rewarded. If at all possible, I recommend having a trainer very familiar with runaways present to help guide the first few of these "firetrails". It's not necessary but will help immensely. Once the handler has a few under his or her belt they are really rather simple—but the first few can be difficult.

If the location for the firetrail was successfully chosen along the lines I mentioned earlier, there is now only one thing missing. The start place for the dog must be in a place where it will only see the subject of the trail run for a short distance and then the trail layer is out of sight. Bushes or trees work great; better yet, walls or solid barriers. The dog should have a view of the subject as he or she runs for about ten to twenty yards and at this point, the subject must be out of sight. This will be the location that the dog will start to use its nose; hopefully.

To begin, the handler should have the dog completely harnessed up and ready to go. A stout patrol collar should also be on the dog with the long trailing lead looped in one hand and hooked to it by the snap. At this point, the handler should straddle the dog putting knees light but firmly into the flanks.

The trail layer now positions himself in front of the dog about ten to fifteen feet away and has a large piece of clothing in one hand and a reward such as a tug or a Kong in the other. The clothing item should be super-saturated with the subject's odor. Items like a well-worn sweatshirt, hat, or shoes are fantastic. From a reward perspective, I prefer to use something that the dog has a big hankering for, versus just any old toy. Believe it or not, some patrol dogs will prefer food, so if that floats the dog's boat, I recommend the handler try it. The trailing drive is closely linked to food from a genetic memory standpoint, and I find many dogs naturally gravitating to that reward system; even when during other exercises they might prefer a tug, ball, or Kong.

When the subject is properly positioned, the handler now unsnaps the long lead from the collar and snaps it firmly and with some vigor on the D-ring of the harness. I recommend the long lead be coiled in about two foot loops loosely held in the off hand and not thrown out in a line behind the handler. Keeping lead control while trailing in real cases—not sport—means managing the lead so people don't step on it or having it get stuck around trees, bushes, car tires, etc. Start the practice now and the new trailing handler will become better with each practice trail. The idea is to feed the line out as the dog moves forward and reel it in when the dog moves side-to-side or back towards the handler.

The game is about to begin and this simple but important step is the signal to the dog that trailing will soon begin. The snap on the harness D-ring is also the signal for the subject to go to work by moving a couple of feet towards the K9 offering first the scent article and then the reward, alternating until the dog's head is visibly reacting to the stimulation of both. This is why it is best to straddle the dog and keep it focused in one direction if possible. This simple process is often enough to put the dog into spin mode. We want the dogs focused on these two things that the subject has—at all times—and facing forward towards the trail layer. This last sentence is _crucial_:

Trailing incorporates the use of a scent article to target the K9 on one specific scent and this component keys the dog to the use of the article in starting this new job.

When the dog is straining at the lead and squealing ready to go, it is the signal for the subject to run the preplanned route; the first leg in view of the dog, the middle and the last legs out of sight. As a trail layer makes the turn around the blind corner for the dog, I like them to drag their feet a bit to stir up some good ground disturbance. This little spot of extra odor is often the only thing the dogs needs to go right to nose work vs. eyes and ears. The trail layer should run at least fifty yards or so and make one small

In the beginning, many puppies like to carry the article with them. This should not be immediately discouraged. We can take it away later. Now it is important because it marks the trail layer and is of high value to the puppy.

turn to another location that allows the runner to see the dog coming from a decent distance, and the handler to see the runner long before the dogs gets to this location. Once in place, the tail layer should prepare himself or herself for the coming of the dog by having the food, tug, Kong, or other item ready for presentation. The idea is to pay from the source as soon as the dog is close enough to the trail layer and knows exactly where they are. The runner should have the reward ready and toss it to the K9 as soon as the K9 registers the reward in the hand of the runner.

Once the handler is sure the runner is in place, he or she should allow the dog to pull towards the article and smell it. If the article was placed far enough away from the dog but in sight, this will happen almost automatically because the dog will have targeted the article as it relates to the runner and really needs to smell it. The K9 may want to mouth the article and that is just fine. Even carrying it as the dog runs on the trail is okay. If either occurs, DO NOT correct the dog…. just let them run with it. We can take this part away later. Right now fixation on the article is a good thing because it relates to the subject and the trail.

Once the dog takes scent or the article, the handler must allow the K9 to move and acquire the scent trail on its own without moving themselves. The human instinct will be to start running as soon as the dog takes scent but this is a muscle memory mistake and can create problems with unknown trails in the future when the direction of travel is unknown. The handler must try to allow the line to reel out quickly as the dog moves and be prepared for the end of the line: don't check the K9 too hard when this end is reached. It is best to start moving at the last couple of feet of line. The purpose of this step is to ensure the dog has a scent trail before the handler moves. On real cases where the direction of travel is unknown the dog must be given time to positively show with body language that it has detected a scent trail and is running with it before the handler moves. Moving prematurely will encourage the dog to move, perhaps in the wrong direction.

Because this trail is so fresh and so short, the dog will be working with a lot of air scent that is still swirling. This is one of the reasons I like using this method in the morning or at night. During hours of darkness, the scent has a tendency to drop much faster. In many cases the dog's head and nose may not even go to ground with these firetrails. Initially, the K9 will gravitate to the place last seen by sight and memory and only then start to uses its nose. This will be around the first blind corner. If the K9 drops its nose at the ground disturbance of the turn, half the battle has been won and the dog will probably use a lot of ground odor for the rest of this short trail. If not, the dog will probably attempt to use airborne scent to acquire the target. This may take a little time but there will be enough for the dog to work with. If the nose is not to the ground but they are running in the right direction, let them run. Forcing the nose to the ground with hand sweeps or line pulls is a mistake and, contrary to popular belief, will not necessarily cause the dog to find ground scent. It simply causes the dog to pay attention to the handler and momentarily—or permanently—forget about the runner. The dog must be allowed to figure this

The end phase of a firetrail when the puppy is running up to the trail layer.

problem out for itself. When the handler interrupts the dog in its dedicated effort to find the subject with unwanted help, the dog will not learn to find scent on its own. Humans have no idea where a concentration of human odor may be found on the ground or elsewhere. Only the dog does. Let the dog figure it out. I have a big problem with trainers who constantly try to tell handlers and dogs where human scent is the strongest. We simply do not have that capability and if we assume we do, it is time to put the harnesses on ourselves because the dog has become redundant.

Either by ground scent, air scent, or a combination of both, the K9 will find the subject and show strong interest when they get close. The body language will change to a "Proximity Alert" when the K9 detects odor fresh off the subject's body. These are the scent vapors directly emanating off the subject's body in large waves, almost like smoke from a military grade smoke bomb. Depending on the wind, this proximity alert can happen at quite long distances. When the K9 detects this, all of the body language will become intense with the nose and ears pointing towards the subject while simultaneously increasing speed. The handler must be prepared for the find at this time. Allow the dog to close the gap but be prepared to choke up on the line, slowing or stopping a short distance from the subject with a patrol K9. If working with a non-biting dog, let the K9 run in with abandon in this phase.

The trail layer should be ready for the dog at this moment and get its attention with movement of the hand containing the reward. As soon as the reward registers with the dog, the dog must be paid with it. A short toss from a few feet away is perfect. The handler must step in now and praise the dog with lots of love. I recommend that the handler really interact with the dog at this point with a good high voice and as much praise as possible. People can be horrible at this part of training and too reserved. All dogs love attention and praise; don't be stingy with it. Play this game up as much as possible and make the dog feel like it is the best dog on the planet. While the K9 is still really motivated and happy with the reward and praise, take the reward away and hand it back to the runner. It's time for another firetrail. Repeat this whole process three times and stop when the dog is at its peak by bringing it back to the car or kennel with the runner leading the way, just out of reach of the dog, holding the reward.

When training new puppies in trailing, I recommend the reader pick up a copy of my first training manual: *K9 Trailing; The Straightest Path*. Firetrails are an essential part for training all new trailing pups and I use them daily for the first couple of months in varying degrees of difficulty.

Trailing is a natural form of hunting for dogs unlike traditional sport tracking work. They usually take to it like ducks to water. I recommend running Firetrails for at least a week with adult dogs before starting the next phase of trailing training. Furthermore, don't ever stop them. The dogs love this work and the excitement of the hunt and watching the prey run, is like doggy crack. I run Firetrails with all of our dogs until their last working days. *Meaningless gifts are soon forgotten.*

Chapter Six
Reward and Timing

"All rewards must be given when earned. If a reward is given at any other time, the reward is meaningless and has no bearing on the task at hand."

Reward at the Completion of the Trail

As I wrote in the chapter on runaways and firetrails, I broached the subject that perhaps the runaway was the catalyst for trailing and the real "true" reward for dogs that are natural man trailers. The chase being the mental trigger that sets the trailing traits of the dog in motion. I find the best trailing dogs prefer a running target as reward above all others and the trail/chase is the excitement they really crave. This does not mean that dogs that like a ball or food more than the chase are not good trailing dogs; it simply means that the concept of catching running prey is the trigger for trailing in the vast majority of true hunting dogs. The handler can increase the overall prey and trailing drive by having the trail layer run from the dog as soon as the reward process is started. The dog thinks the food, ball, or whatever is being handed over and suddenly it runs away again.

I use the runaway/firetrail to start the process of trailing work with my working pups at our kennel. The excitement of the runaway is the fastest way to build a strong foundation and maintain a trail faithful K9. If a puppy has little to no interest in the runaway, I will always pass on the puppy as a trailing candidate. On the flip side, I do not use firetrails or runaways to motivate unmotivated dogs that have to constantly be re-encouraged to work. If they need a runaway every few days they simply do not like trailing all that much and are probably not suitable for the job. A runaway is the fastest way to get a dog into the trailing game and I do believe it is the basis for the trait of trailing. I do not think runaways should be a crutch for training unsuitable dogs. Unfortunately, there are some in the industry that use the runaway method as if they invented it and make it the primary way to work a trailing dog. This is primarily because runaways produce a fast result. From a student perspective, it is easy to train this way because most dogs will respond and if this is the only thing the dog does, and then it will always appear that the dog is working. The problems always occur when the handler has to move on to more complex problems of age and contamination. This is where the unmotivated dogs will shut down.

As soon as I get to the stage in training where I can start the puppy on the place that the subject was last seen, or with a scent article, without the puppy seeing the subject run or walk away first, I begin to implement runaways also at the end of the trail after the dog finds the subject at the end of the first trail. The purpose of this is to build upon the runaway start segment of training we just finished and further incite the K9 to higher levels of excitement at the end. When the subject flees shortly after being found, it creates a cat and mouse type reaction in the dog and encourages an instant prey response. This can often create over the top interest in trailing with the dog. This is how I do it:

To begin with, I believe in paying at the source as soon as the source is located with absolutely no hesitation or lag. I absolutely do not care about a subject identification, ID, for the first eight to ten months of the dogs trailing life. The ID is not important yet, the drive and focus is. Without drive and focus, a handler won't have subject identification on a real search to begin with because the person will not be found.

Paying at the source means this: As soon as the handler recognizes that the dog knows exactly where the subject is and it focused on that person, the dog is paid with the reward of choice, food, ball, tug, etc. In the beginning and usually with pups, I have the trail layer pay because they can see the focus of the dog better than the handler and they are in a better position to ensure that the reward is given at the proper time, and that is immediately. Handlers new to trailing, and even veterans, are often too slow with the paycheck when the dog finds the subject. They feel they have to be the person who pays and that the dog must exhibit a particular behavior prior to paying. We can change the vendor later and have the handler reward, but for now, correct timing is more important than a handler based reward system. Correct timing now is also far more important than an "alert" or unique behavior, such as sitting, that the handler wants to have the dog perform indicating that the correct person has been found.

Alerts

Not having an alert often times flies in the face of traditional trailing training I see on my travels. I often spend inordinate amounts of time explaining the reason why an alert is not so important in the beginning stages of trailing. Alerts seem to be super-engrained into the K9 training psyche in particular as it revolves around trailing in the Search & Rescue world. There are times that the first component of trailing that a new handler learns is to sense or to establish an alert with the handler: refining the action to state of perfection. The question I ask when faced with this predicament is: What matters said perfection of canine tricks when the drive for trailing and proper technique are missing? In other words, who cares what the dog looks like at the end of the trail if it can't get to the end in the first place? Why put the cart before the horse?

Unfortunately, handlers who spend too much time refining how the dog looks at the end of the trail often create dogs that have trouble trailing. It is not so much because the dog is learning an alert as it is related to the handler fixating the dog's focus on himself or herself, teaching the desired action, and not concentrating on the subject: trailing. The key to trailing and ultimately the alert is an unflagging desire to find and engage the subject of the search, not please the handler. We want the dog so enamored by the person it is looking for that it's only focus is that person and they do not take their eyes off that person. If the trail layer tries to move, the dog blocks them. If the trail layer runs away again, the dog is Hell bent for leather to catch him. When you establish this degree of need for the trail layer, you will have a dog that will use every hunting trait at its disposal to get the job done. You will also have a dog that easily adopts a specific body language alert later: simply so it can complete the sale and get paid. On the other hand if the handler focuses too much on a desired behavior before the drive is established, the handler will have a dog that is lackluster in performance and often very dependent on the handler to complete the trail for it.

When the dog finds the subject at the end of the trail and enjoys the happy and excited response, it will turn to look at the handler. It is expecting a paycheck and a command to sit. If the reward is not immediately available, it is too late. Postponing the reward will not be relevant to the trail or the subject. The relevancy of the reward now completely revolves around the handler and the dog believes that it is now being rewarded for switching focus from the subject of the search to the handler. This is a constant problem in narcotics and other detector dog training and deployment where we see dogs that are always looking over their shoulders for a reaction indicating they found the right thing. This is the beginning of false alerts triggered by handler body language. The problem with such alerts are that, once learned, they will not be forgotten. Though the dog can be retrained correctly, bad habits will never be completely forgotten and can rear their ugly heads when the chips are down. It is far better to establish the correct foundation, and the immediacy of the reward at the source will build this foundation. Reward after the fact can destroy it.

One of the biggest retraining issues I encounter with trailing dog handlers is the problem of dogs being far too dependent on the handlers. They are constantly looking for handler body language indicators that indicate that they made a correct trail turn. This happens for many reasons but is primarily related to handlers who guide their dogs too often to locations where they believe the scent is, or to the subject that they believe is the correct one. In essence, bad lead handling but also the handler showing the dog things when the dog should be doing that job. As soon as a handler disconnects the dog from focus on the trail/scent or subject to refocus on the handler, then the subject and the search are no longer on the dogs mind; the handler is. This is the problem. Unlike training humans, we cannot "show" dogs the proper reaction though physical guidance because they only learn to look to the human handler for the answer. We cannot lead by example with dogs. Dogs really need to learn on

Remember: Use the reward that the dogs like not just what you like!

their own through trial, error, and strong rewards with good timing. We can set up conditions that foster easier learning but we cannot guide the dog. When dogs figure problems out for themselves with a great reward at the immediate moment in time they discover the source of their search, they will remember any lessons learned on the path to that subject. On the other hand, if the handler points the dog to the source, the dog will learn nothing but to follow the pointing finger.

The key to reward and timing is to think like the dog and not the human. This is how I do it in the early stages of the dogs trailing life and in small bits and pieces throughout the rest of its life.

When the dog finds the person it is looking for at the end of the trail and was truly working the trail without being guided, the trail layer pays the dog immediately but just enough to agitate the dog for more. If the dog is food driven, give only a small amount forcing the dog to engage with the subject with more abandon. Then, when suddenly the trail layer runs off a short distance, say ten to twenty yards, taking the food with them. This will usually put the dog into hyper drive and it will squeal and jump in an attempt to follow. The handler should hold the dog back just long enough for the trail layer to get out a little bit ahead and then let the dog go. Simply drop the lead if it is safe to do so. The trail layer at this point needs to drop to the ground on all fours or sitting with the treat ready to offer as soon as the dog arrives. The same thing can be done with a ball or tug: give the dog the toy just long enough for it to think it won it and then the trail layer takes it back and runs away again.

This training process does a couple of things for the dog, and as far as I am concerned, they are two of the most important components of trailing. The subject should be of interest through subject/prey drive and subject/prey loyalty. The dog is motivated to find the subject above all things, and once the subject is found, the dog refuses to take its eyes off of them. Why? Because, in the past, the toy or food was stolen at the height of ecstasy and the dog, simply remembering the condition, does not want that to happen again. Do this a few times and you will have a dog that escorts the trail layer back home and will not let them alone. This is a manhunter. When considering trailing, one should also consider the cat and the mouse.

Reward in an Attempt to Fix a Problem

Occasionally, a dog shuts down on a problem for no apparent reason and it appears that it no longer has odor or is working it.   Do not bring a subject back to the point of the problem and reward the dog by using the runaway or firetrail game, or any other reward. There is an extremely good chance there will be no connection in the dogs mind of the original trail, the down time of the problem, and the subject coming back for the runaway game. There is simply is too much separation. The runaway game is a new event and it should be treated as such. Yes, the dog chases the subject with abandon, but they would do that with or without the memory of the subject of the search. So there is no way to prove the method to the problem solving. The gift given to the dog is now related to a new trail and not the original one. More importantly, any gift given at the moment the dog stops working may teach the dog that it only needs to stop working to be rewarded.

The issue really is in how dogs think. They are capable of many things and do calculate problems, but they are not linear thinkers based on time components like we are. They think in the moment. We have to think and create problem-solving components like the dog thinks; not how we would do it for ourselves. It is kind of like the old dog training problem: that dogs do not remember they pooped in the house in the morning when you punish them after you get home in the afternoon from work. Weird simile, I know, but go with it for a second. The problem is not that they forgot they pooped in the house, they remember that for ages, the problem is the punishment as it relates to the poop. It was in bad timing and had no relation to the infraction. In fact, because there was no timing, the handler is the problem now and not the poop; and will be considered as such in the future. Rewards must be viewed in much the same way.

When we reward dogs, and a runaway trail/reward in the beginning, middle, or end of a trail is a type of reward, we need to be very careful in the context in which dogs view the action. In this case, we have to be absolutely sure the dog is in the "moment" of the subject's trail or scent before we bring the subject or reward of the search back into the mix. If there is separation, then the reward could be meaningless. Worse, it was triggered by you and the dog learns that you created the reward. Now the dog is looking to you for guidance and may simply stop to trigger a response from you.

Trailing reward is no different than K9 Detection reward. The source odor must produce the reward for proper imprinting of a desired response. Good timing is critical!

Reward timing is one of the most essential components of good dog training; for all aspects of dog training. It is what separates great dog work from average. We have a model to look at in this case and it is our detection experts in the field. The name of the game is rewarding at the source: immediately when all the dogs attention is focused there. When we reward after disengagement, we teach the dog to always look to us for clues.

I often encounter this reward problem when training dog handlers in trailing. When dogs stop working for any reason, the solution I often see is the handler bringing the subject back to the dog and then rewarding the dog. Worse yet is to bring the dog to the subject and then reward the dog. This is akin to giving the dope dog the ball when he missed the dope in the cabinet or identified the truck door before you brought him up to it! From a correction standpoint, if the dog pooped in the house and you come home after work and punish him, you did nothing but confuse the dog. He was happy to see you when you came home, but you smacked his ass. It does matter that there was a problem and we certainly have to try and fix it, but this is not the way.

Dogs do not care when they lose the trail and stop working. If they get to the point where they appear to be distracted or have lost interest, I have news for you; they are off in another world now. Dogs do not get upset by losing the trail, and frankly, when it is obvious they lost it, they are usually investigating other odors by the time the handler recognizes the change. We care about the trail loss, we internalize it, and we often wear it on our emotional sleeve for all to see, but dogs really do not. They are onto the next thing if allowed to do so, and any canid emotional response will usually be interest in the new thing they just found: which has nothing to do with the trail. If a dog reacts badly to such a situation, it is often reaction to the handler's emotional response to "failure" and the fact that our dogs are very good at detecting and reacting accordingly. By rewarding during stoppage, we are usually feeding our fears and rationalization and not training the dog. Worse yet, it is very possible to condition the dog for a situation where they expect the handler to do the work and guide them in to the finish on a regular basis. I call this "Training The Handler."

This is what I would do if my dog lost a trail, stopped working, and we could not pick it up again after taking normal immediate remedial action: Take the harness off. DO NOT react in any way—hard part—and don't work the dog anymore. It's all good and there is NO PROBLEM with the dog. Come back later, maybe days later, and work the same problem with just THIS problem and no extra trail baggage such as distance, age, or other distractions. You absolutely have to consider that the issue that stopped the dog, depending on the type, was probably a temporary scent trail killer. The solution may not be running a dog through it during the problem, but rather picking up the trail later after the scent problem has dissipated. You can try to run a runaway trail through issues that stop our dogs. If the dog shows no scenting work during, and after, the hiccup may be too much of a problem for trailing and you simply have to wait until it is gone. You may just be teaching the dog to run through the problem. What happens if there is no trail on the other side on a real case? You simply ran the dog and the runaway training/ reward was meaningless.

When the trail is done, it's done.
Move on and do it again later
without hard feelings.

The Tao of Trailing

Chapter Seven
How Trailing Dogs Learn

"Once the fundamentals of handling and reading a trailing dog are discovered, it essential that the handler learn to find some contour in chaos and become comfortable there. Not everything can be controlled nor is the nature of scent truly knowable for us; this is the chaos of which I speak. Concentrate less on methods or patterns of training and more on interpreting the dog's language of trailing and reacting accordingly. Dogs follow scent seamlessly and with an amazing level of simplification. Yet, when learning trailing, we as handlers have this methodology mindset that by providing the dog a series of complicated patterns or processes to trail, we will somehow make them trail better. In essence, teach them to trail. Nothing could be further from the truth. The dog will trail without a method, a harness, without a lead, and definitely without the handler. It is better to learn awareness of the dog and how to move naturally with it. In the dogs' mind, simplicity and immediate timing will always eclipse complicated rules and patterns."

On Patterns and Methods

Too often in trailing we have to deal with training methods that revolve around human rationalization and human learning patterns vs. working with the dog's natural method of schooling itself. The reason for this is that trailing has far to many handlers with little or no other dog training experience prior to starting trailing. Trailing is considered a "Black Art" with many in the dog world because there are so many crazy training philosophies revolving around trailing and human scent with no real basis in successful practical application.

There is a ton of theory and hearsay about trailing, but very little in the way of quantifiable success in deployment. It is hard to get rock solid traditional K9 trainers behind trailing when these conditions exist. The problem we have is just like everything else in life; there is always an element of truth in just about every topic but the entirety of the topic rarely includes complete truth. In the case of trailing, the original philosophy is very sound but the message has been skewed by the many trailing participants who joined the ranks over the years with little to no prior experience in dog training. The reason for the influx was directly relative to skewed trailing work in the first place. In the latter part of the 20th century a few newsworthy trailing cases misrepresented trailing in such a way that they promised trailing dogs that could solve many day-old criminal cases and find people when all other methods failed. The excitement of this news coupled with the appearance of civilians performing these feats with normal dogs— with no formal K9 background—encouraged a riotous response in every-day people who wanted to get in on a potentially life-saving dog job. I know this because I was one of those people.

Most wanted to do it because of the genuine desire to help people, but a few jumped on the trailing express to become "experts" in the new wave of dog work, making it profitable for their egos and their bank accounts. The latter are the folks who advertise trailing as a "special" type of K9 deployment that only they can do and that the origins are a mystery. They capitalize on the human desire to have faith in the fantastic, on those who desperately need a miracle after the loss of a loved one, or weak people, needing a social lift that dog work gives them. Perhaps not lethal but misleading and harmful to real working K9's, the discipline of trailing, and to those who practice trailing with truth and integrity.

The training thread that connects many handlers on both sides of the fence is the thread of guiding. Everything the dog learns is due to the handler pointing to it with line handling or bad training techniques. The poorly trained trailing dogs become so dependent on the handler that they react to the slightest pressure changes of the lead to the harness or perceived body language changes in the handler. The connection becomes so good with time that the handler in most cases is not aware that they are guiding the dog, and to the average person with little or no experience observing the team, it appears magical.

The guiding problem begins very early in the training of the new trailing dog team and often with the help of trainers who, with all of the best intentions, exhibit the same bad behavior in training the team. It begins with insisting that the dog stays on what is perceived to be the scent trail of the subject because the trainer saw or knows where the trail layer subject travelled. In short, when the handler or trainer, believe that they know where the scent is and force the dog to work in that location then they are guiding the dog. The problem is that no human on the face of this planet can say with certainty that scent will be in any anticipated location while working in the field. We humans cannot detect scent in a trailing condition. Trail scent is not detectable by any of our human senses. Yet we still seem to be convinced that we know where it will be, and constantly try to teach our dogs that we know where it is better than they do. Our dogs may never believe we know better than they do but eventually they will go with our insistence that they follow.

Trailing right on top of the dog influences the dog and reduces independent reaction to scent. It is like when a person gets too close to you when speaking. You feel like moving. Dogs feel the same way.

When this happens too much, the dog will eventually become dependent on the handler to show them the trail, where it goes, and who the subject is. This learned behavior may never go away completely; even with solid training techniques applied later as remedial action. The handler showed the dog that there was a faster way to get to the reward and dogs, unlike us, will always choose the path of least resistance. If they learn the handler will lead the way, the dog will always default to this handler-based condition. Old dogs do not necessarily have the inability to learn new tricks, but they definitely never forget the bad tricks or training methods that rewarded them in the past.

The big mistake normally revolves around harder surfaces or surfaces that simply do not hold odor well. There are times even soft surfaces like dirt and gravel don't hold odor as well as one might expect. Trailing dog trainers and handlers mistakenly believe that there simply must be scent where the person walked, and when the dog moves to another location, the handler then corrects the dog with either line control, (pulling to the side, rear, or checking) or verbal corrections such as "get to work" or "leave it." A correction may be warranted if there is no body language that says *"trailing,"* but if the correction is based solely on the handler's perception of where he thinks the trail scent is—with no corroborating dog body language to that scent—the correction is, more than likely, wrong. This body language is not always shouted however; it is often subtle with variances related to ever changing conditions. Until a handler has seen many dogs in many conditions it will be impossible for that handler to understand this subtlety each and every time. The best intentions are often wrong in trailing because trailing is such a difficult discipline to master. All dog training is a never-ending education even for the trainer, but trailing takes it to a completely new level.

When we see subtle body language indicating that the dog has the scent, yet the handler corrects anyway, it is usually related to the handler defaulting to what his eyes tracked as the trail layer walked the path. This is insecurity and all handlers must control this emotion. It is worse when the trail layer does not do exactly what the handler asked him to do and the handler forces the dog to the area that was discussed but not necessarily walked upon. It does not take too many of these situations to teach the dog that it is better to follow the lead direction versus its natural instincts. This is especially true of soft dogs with lower drive and with K9's having a stronger than average concern for what the handler is doing. The latter are often dogs with very strong obedience training, at early ages, prior to trailing work being established. Some dogs are instinctively handler dependent from breeding and we see this with many lines of German Shepherds, Malinois, and Belgian Shepherds.

Motivation, reward, and learning by doing are the keys to dog training.

It is not so much the lead directing and verbal cues to encourage the dog to incorrect areas that hurts the dog and its learning what is expected of it. It is this incorrect handling coupled with a paycheck or reward at the end of the trail when everything before it was generated by the handler and not detected by the dog. The dog learns that it only must respond to the small lead corrections of the handler and then surge when it detects the looser lead indicating that the handler is now following; once it gets to the guided area.

Dogs learn human directed jobs best through the use of judiciously dispensed reward, motivation, and correction: all made with proper timing. A balance of all three is necessary for a balanced working dog.

Reward can happen at any stage of the trail, not only when the subject is found. Reward usually comes in the following forms for a trailing dog.

1. Handler following
2. Verbal Praise
3. Toy or food reward

Motivation is often related to encouragement through obstacles or conditions that create nervousness or fear.

1. Words of encouragement.
2. In the case of fear, leading by going in first.
3. Enticement through the obstacle.

Correction is based on handler— perceived improper K9 behavior while trailing, such as following the wrong trail or responding to a distraction.

1. Hard line check or snap
2. Verbal correction, "No", "leave it", etc.
3. Posting, not moving in the direction the dog wants to go

There is a proper time and place for all of these training components, but if the reward, motivation, or correction are not given with the correct timing or given in the wrong order, the consequences or learnt behavior may be opposite of what the handler expects. The bottom line, though, is the dog learns very quickly what the handler expects. If there is a repeated pattern of bad timing or application of the wrong training component, the learnt behavior will be incorrect trailing behavior, most often in the form of a guided dog that simply follows line and human body language cues.

I have found that dogs learn best in trailing when they learn a response based on planned conditions engineered to generate that response rather than "showing" the dog what proper response might be. Unlike humans, we cannot demonstrate the proper behavior, expect the dog to follow it, and then have them properly replicate our behavior. The reason for this is we are not dogs and do not have the traits or physical characteristics to exhibit proper behavior. As I wrote previously, dogs know how to trail already. They were born with the ability. They know how to follow scent better than we do because they are the part of the team that can detect scent. We are the part of the team that has the ability to decipher visually and cognitively the behavior and act accordingly. If we reverse the roles we will have an ineffective team.

I will cover this in detail in the chapter called Productive Sources. In short, creating conditions for K9 learning will be conditions that allow the dog to figure out each problem on its own without assistance. The linchpin is the creative condition that on one hand is not so simple that the dog simply cruises through it, but has a level of complication that forces the dog to think though the problem in a natural fashion and then successfully complete it.   The problem must be made up in a series of small steps that increase in difficulty without shutting the dog down or driving it to distraction.

Sometimes there may only be one step in the problem, and the step is worked over and over to the point of perfection. This should always be done over the course of days or weeks when excitement is high in the dog and it is fun. Other times the problem may have a number of steps but never so many that the dog falls apart or quits. This is the tough part because we humans have a tendency to overwork ourselves, and the learning curve, with the intent to get better faster. This is "learning" based on human ego, not canid learning.

Getting down and playing with the dog is absolutely crucial to build a feeling in the dog that they are the best thing in the world.

Play bowing is indicative of the fact that the dog is truly enjoying himself and the reward is significant.

Therein lies the rub. We cannot apply the human work ethic to dog training. When we do, we usually make the work too repetitive, in too short a time frame, demotivating the dog in the process. If a normally high-drive dog appears distracted or lost, it probably is, and the training problem is more than likely too complex or has been run too many times in a row. Train this way too often and the dog may actually be counter-conditioned and become adverse to the problem or the job altogether.

Dogs learn best when the training problem is motivating and fun. Excitement and enjoyment for the dog is paramount to get the most out of a training session. The handler must share this enjoyment if the dog is going to perform at its peak. Contrary to popular belief, the dog is not simply working for the reward. It is working because it likes to, and pleasing the handler is an important element. If the handler is happy and exhibits these feelings in voice and body language, the K9 will reciprocate. Remove the human element from the equation and the response will be reduced.

During schools and seminars, I spend a lot of time working with my male students on the human factor of dog motivation. Men more often than women seem to loathe exhibiting their true feelings before, during, and after the dogs work. Guys simply seem to have a problem with letting go or giving the perception of letting go. Getting a guy to get his girly voice on is like pulling teeth. Nothing is worse to male pride than being perceived as feminine and assuming a high pitched, excited voice coupled with sweet words of encouragement. This is just too much for macho men. Well, I've got news for you, dogs love that stuff. Nothing gets them going more than when their human exhibits loving behavior when they are getting ready to work or when the job was done successfully. When there is no emotion and no response other than a quick pat on the head and a low volume "good boy" it's almost like a lump of coal in the stocking on Christmas morning. The happiness has to go both ways. Guys, if you can't get your girly voice on and show some excitement for what your dog is doing, you are not getting the most out of your dog. It is that simple.

The co-component to fun when training dogs is repetition that is not taxing. As soon as the training regimen becomes tiresome and the dog seems distracted, the training has become a burden and less is learned. It is always best to work dogs in small blocks where the excitement level is very high. We want a dog that is lunging into the lead to do the job; not a dog that is lackluster and disinterested. If we see the latter manifested in doggy body language then it is normally a cue that we have trained too long on the particular task at hand.

My philosophy in dog training from obedience to trailing is to work the dog in increments that are always exciting and fun. I strive to work the dog to the peak of performance and then stop when it wants more. If we stop and the dog is squealing to continue, my timing for stoppage is correct. The other thing to consider is that every dog has a different max-training threshold. One dog may be good for an hour while another is best in a span of fifteen minutes. In other words, each and every dog will have a different training threshold that changes with variables such as the age of the dog, competence, drive, mental focus and health. Max-training threshold is never consistent and my cues are always the dog in the moment at that particular time. If I put my dog away when I feel it has done its absolute best, then I have reached the proper threshold. When I train in this manner, my dog will always come out of the box for the next session raring to go and at its peak level of interest in the training session. This timing is critical to enhance learning of new task and to expedite the entire training process.

Dogs, unlike people, do not learn a new job by example from a human. They may learn, perhaps, by watching another dog, but definitely not from the human. We see this error in staged detection dog work. The dog is led to the source, pointed to it, and the handler changes body posture or issues verbal commands to illicit a response from the dog in the form of an alert. There is no easier work for the dog than simply following the lead of the handler. This error, in essence, is no different than if the handler opened the cabinets, pulled out the dope, showed it to the dog, and said see? There it is! This type of incorrect detection work is alive and well in other forms of K9 work and it especially so in trailing. So how does one show a dog something he wants the dog to learn but in such a way that the dog does not follow the handler's lead? It is through the use of productive sources of odor for the dog. The dog learns where to look for scent based on past experience in similar conditions. Please see the chapter on productive sources.

Reward, motivation, and correction must all be used wisely and with good timing. The chapter on Reward and Timing will detail these elements completely, but we have to look at them here. If the dog finds the subject, gets no response from the handler, and looks back at them for direction, the timing for reward is now lost. This lack of handler reaction is most often related to handlers who demand a reward from the dog prior to establishing loyalty to the scent source. The dogs are trained to cue off the handler and not the source odor. In this case, it is the subject of the search or person who laid the trail.   In the early days of training, the source or trail layer pays and pays as soon as the dog knows with certainty exactly where the person is waiting. This is proper timing because dogs think in the moment and the paycheck must be given when the dog is in the moment of the initial find. If the timing for reward is given later, it is meaningless.

The same thing applies to correction. The dog may stop trailing because it detects another dog. This may be in the form of a "fire hydrant" previously marked with other dog urine. When our dog stops there and starts to perform the ritual of adding its watery comment to the post, the time for correction has been completely and forever lost. If the handler corrects after the fact or in midstream, the correction is absolutely meaningless. The new handler may wonder why but the veteran dog trainers knows immediately why. Timing! Dogs are not linear thinkers with the ability to process or think forwards and backwards in time like we do. They remember, but time forwards and backwards does not dilute the emotional response to a condition like it does with us. It is why they are always so very happy to see us each and every time they see us... fifteen minutes or fifteen days later.

If we correct the dog while it is peeing we are correcting the dog for peeing. We are not correcting the dog for the reason for peeing. And the reason is the most important component because if the dog does not understand what the reason for the correction is, it will continue to make the mistake over and over. In the aforementioned scenario, it was obvious that the reason for peeing was the dog's intent to mark or leave its spoor so other dogs will know it had been there at that particular spot. Consequently, the timing for correction must be at the time the dog initially detects the distraction source odor and begins to react to it. If correction is given at the time the dogs thinks: "Oh! That is a remarkable new dog odor on that fire hydrant and I think I am going to go over and sniff it!" Then, the timing is perfect for correction. The timing key is not necessarily knowing each and every time what the dog looks like when it detects other dog markings so much as in training scenarios that teach the dog that stopping at such markings is absolutely unacceptable.

In order to train for distraction it is important that the handler sets up scenarios and training sessions specifically with distraction in mind. In the beginning training sessions, each trail really should be nothing more than a subject trail with an artfully produced animal distraction cut somewhere in the middle of the trail that is visible to the handler from a distance. The handler must be able to see the distraction coming so that when the subsequent dog body language is observed; the correction can be given with absolute certainty and perfect timing. It is only with this method that the dog will learn that stopping and marking is unacceptable. Distraction training is a chapter unto itself and I have written extensively on the subject in my *Trailing Training Manual: K9 Trailing; The Straightest Path.*

There is no better training method than to have the dog learn a new task on its own with little to no help from the handler. The savvy trailing dog handler will do this by focusing on the following:

1. Harnessing the dog's innate drive for the job.
2. The use of productive sources of odor.
3. Losing the human instinct to guide or lead.
4. Never training past peak focus.
5. Ultimately, the proper implementation of correct timing for reward, motivation, and correction.

On paper, it seems step-by-step and relatively easy. In reality, this is not a seamless training philosophy that one can learn simply through reading. It is earned through years of mistakes and observation with trailing dogs.

The Tao of Trailing

Chapter Eight
Let Them Run Free

"Restrain the hand of a new painter and you will have no art. Hobble the feet of he who has yet to run and there will be no race. Harness and leash the mind and body of the young hunter and do not be surprised if you have no hunt."

     This chapter is about puppy trails or starting a young or green dog in trailing. My *Straightest Path* fans may wonder why I broach puppy trails once again, and I empathize, but bear with me on this one. If you read the *Path* and remember this topic, then you are probably a hardcore trailing and working dog junkie and there is no longer any hope for you. You are hooked and the trailing addiction is a tough one to break. And one of the symptoms of the trailing addiction is having multiple trailing dogs. You WILL start a new trailing dog one day, or perhaps many, and if you're really lucky, you read this chapter prior to starting that new dog!

I've always been a fan of making the first trails; especially for puppies, completely off lead. I want the dog to run as fast as they want to and more importantly make mistakes while doing it. If the drive is high enough and the trail was designed for success, the puppy will quickly try to correct any mistake it made such as missing a turn or overshooting the subject. This is the primary focus of this exercise. Once the pup understands the firetrail game and chases the trail layers with abandon, we make the trails a little bit more

When a puppy can run free to chase and catch freely it learns how to hunt naturally.

difficult. With this difficulty come the inevitable missed turns and overshoots. We want the mistakes as long as they are surmountable. The key to the level of complexity is really relative to the puppy's level of experience from repetition. A perfect example of progressive tiers of training could be the following:

First Firetrail Experience:

1. Pup has run 10 firetrails
2. Wooded or tall grass condition
3. Trailing length 50 meters straight
4. No turn, subject hidden behind tree, bush, etc.
5. All firetrails are successful
6. Time to progress

Second Tier:

1. Wooded or tall grass condition similar to the first 10 firetrails
2. First leg length is 50 meters straight
3. 90 degree turn at end of 50 meter leg
4. Leg after turn is 10 meters.

Most pups when faced with Tier Two will overshoot the 90-degree turn almost each and every time, and that is the plan. *If the pup nails the turn on the first go, it is a natural and it is time to make the tier more challenging.* Usually we see the pup run to the area where past experience has led to the subject and reward. When the subject is not there, most pups go into an almost hyper drive of panic. They start circling: hoping to find the trail layer hiding behind another bush. As they circle, they start to default to their gift of scent detection and in the vast majority of cases, immediately drop their noses and detect the ground disturbance scent and human odor that leaves the area of the turn. This is what we want... the nose drop and subsequent scent detection. Shortly after the nose drop, we want a quick end to the trail with a great paycheck.

A series of photos where a new trailing puppy encounters a turn for the first time. These photos capture the moment perfectly when the puppy overshoots the turn, circles back, and captures it through self-discovery. A lead on the puppy would be counterproductive to this action.

It is this second tier that sets the stage for all other problems and trails in the future. We want the dog to default or rely on its nose: not eyesight, sound, or handler guidance. The best way to create this change is to simply not be involved with the process other than setting up a well-planned trail, then allowing the dog to switch scenting on by itself. The lesson is learned completely and not forgotten when the pup wins this challenge on its own without your help. If you guide the dog to the run by walking with it, pointing to it, or moving the dog to that location or the subject, the puppy will learn nothing.

Worse yet is the training method of putting food on the turn or key place in the trail where we want the dog to move. This method is completely based on the human rationale that there should be human scent or the correct combinations of scent for the dog to make the turn at the place the food was dropped. The problem is no matter how hard we try, we really don't know the right place for this epiphany because we can't detect the scent in the first place. *Anyone who thinks they can needs to do the trailing instead of the dog.* The other problem, and the worst one, is if the puppy detects the food it will immediately disconnect from the subject and the trail and now focus on, and consume the food. If by chance the dog detects the trail or the subject after this, it has nothing to do with the beginning of the exercise. It is now a new event. In other words, we accomplish nothing, but, in error, teach the dog to look for food. I have seen this method used on a previously successfully trailing dog who worked naturally; effectively ruining it in the process. Once the dog is taught this method they never forget to look for food on the trail: whether it is on the scent trail or not.

What makes this training so incredibly successful is that the dog is doing all of the work and learning on its own without interference. It is learning from mistakes it makes in a condition where success is very possible as long as the dog defaults to its nose.

I am often told that true urban trailing dogs should be started on concrete immediately, or as soon as possible, avoiding the soft surface of grass and woods because this creates a condition of dependence on ground disturbance. This position is strong in the trailing world. I have found it prominent with mostly those who really have never worked trailing dogs professionally, or have never found missing persons or criminals with trailing dogs in an urban environment. Generally this position is postured by handlers and trainers who are great on theory but short on practical experience. I think it is very important to understand the origins of many theories about K9 work and this theory is really rooted in old school sport work.

To begin with, this ground disturbance theory comes from the original German sport dog training world: Schutzhund, where the dogs were trained almost exclusively on ground disturbance and were corrected if they deviated from it. There was not an early interest or test for human odor, blown, dropped, or otherwise—because the results seemed to speak for themselves, initially. There were sport trackers later who came up with an early 20th century test to prove that "tracking" dogs could not follow human odor and only followed ground disturbance. Frankly, this study did nothing but support how the dogs were trained to begin with. Very much the same methodology, for many dog tests, exists today. The testers are proving what they are theorizing by using a tool that can only prove their original theory because the tool was made that way to begin with. With the early Schutzhund test, Schutzhund ground-disturbance dogs were used to prove that only ground disturbance was used by the dogs for tracking. This is like saying that all fruits taste like an apple because the test model for taste was the apple. Unfortunately, with dogs, many scientists do not look outside the box for other sources of trained K9s and the results of their studies become canned. At times, this is planned, but mostly I see it simple ignorance about K9s, K9 behavior, and scent work.

I believe that putting trailing puppies on pavement or an urban environment too soon is a grave error and results in producing a guided, air scent dog. I see this problem all over the trailing community around the world. This is especially so in Europe where urban work is the focus for everyone due to the sheer mass of human population and the lack of public wild lands. The indicators of this are dogs who work primarily head up, looking around, mouth wide open and moving fast, and who are very sensitive to every time the handler puts pressure or directional guidance on the trailing lead. Videos speak volumes. When asked about this behavior almost all of the handlers say that their dogs trail heads up.

Well, I am sorry but dogs following ground scent in a difficult, contaminated condition do not trail heads up. This is a human rationalization for a problem that the handlers recognize but do not want to admit.

Where the heads up trailers always fail is when they are double blind tested. This is where nobody knows where the trail layer walked or is waiting and the distance is far enough that the dog cannot air scent to begin with. Interestingly, this also destroys the aged trail myths with the same dogs and handlers. The only times "heads up" dogs pass these tests are when the subject, trail, or end point is known and the dog is allowed to air scent when they get within proximity of the subject. The Google maps I see of "double-blind" trails, where the dog went completely the wrong way and still found the subject at the end, are always related to knowing the subject and getting within air scent range. Try this same test with an unknown subject and a real double blind test and the handler and the dog will fail every time.

Once a dog works this way it is almost impossible to make it a great trailing dog later. You can fix many of the problems, but for the most part, the sublimely perfect man trailer that could have been, has now been ruined by bad training.

The key to training puppies is in planning very small steps of puppy self-discovery in an environment where the puppy can succeed quickly using human scent as a guide. The puppy must have repeated success in varying distances and conditions where the human scent is strong and easy to follow. The puppy must perfect its skills and become missile locked only on one odor, ignoring all others. This condition can only be found in the woods or similar low distraction places that hold odor.

The reason why soft surface, woods or grass, are great for puppies is not really ground disturbance, although that is a component, but because the human scent drops and sticks close to where the subject walked or ran: allowing the puppy to follow odor better. An urban environment has too many distracting sights, scents, and sounds, but most importantly, the human scent blows too far away from the track and the dogs learn to simply run following the air scent. In other words, heads up behavior. This is great if you want a fresh air scent dog.

We will begin urban work but starting from scratch; with easy, low contamination, and few distractions. We do desensitize puppies to urban environments at the same time we train in easy places but this is a different deployment. Our free puppy videos show these steps well. Our mature dogs trained this way are finding missing people and criminals regularly in an urban environment and are the proof for our pudding recipe.

If you want a trailing dog that is very reliable in following ground scent on hard surfaces, then you must have a puppy that is very reliable in following ground scent in a soft, uncontaminated condition first. Do otherwise and you will have an air-scent guided dog. Perfect the basics, enjoy the moments of puppy self-discovery, and do not rush the process. The joy will be found in the path, not the ending. As a result, you will have a better trailing dog and know the truths of trailing.

There is a beautiful quote from the 1600's that I believe is very applicable here:

There are no secrets. Knowledge is open to all, but few truly want it. There is no need to hide things; most people go out of their way to avoid truth.
Leave the knowledge in the open and only the true warriors will find it.
~Miyamoto Musashi, The Book of Five Rings

Chapter Nine
Body Language Indicators

"The hunter's trail is a mirror of the prey. Truth in the reflection is not seeing oneself. He who understands this reflection so too understands trailing."

Trailing; Ground Odor without Air Scent
1. Head
2. Ears
3. Nose
4. Mouth
5. Gate
6. Posture
7. Tail

a. Trailing Behavior wind at the back
　　　b. Wind to the left or right
　　　c. Wind in the face

Distraction
1. Head pop
2. Fanning
3. Nose Plant
4. Tail Set
　　　a. Dominance factors as they relate to the tail

Proximity Scent Stages; Beginning to Final Proximity Alert Far
1. Head Set Change
2. Mouth
3. Ears
4. Speed Tail Set Change
5. Inability for handler to recognize due to lack of prior find subject

Proximity Alert Stages Prior to Final
1. Fluctuating head set
2. Trail to air scent flip flops
3. Intensity changes

Final Proximity Alert
1. Air scent mode
2. Focus on scent cone

Pool Scent; Subject Not Present
1. Slower speed
2. Increased animation
3. Lack of focus on one particular direction
4. Search for the exit trail

Contact Odor
1. Head pop
2. Slow speed
3. Panning
4. Tail Set
5. Focus on are not dog related

Lost Trail Behavior

1. Speed change
2. Head from low to high
3. Head into the wind
4. Tail set change
5. Tongue out with wide mouth
6. Ears perked forward
7. Eyes panning
8. Frequent nose returns to the ground
9. Followed by head panning after each
10. Looking or smelling the wind without scent

Trailing Ground Odor without Air Scent

Nose and Head Set

Good view of a dog's head following ground odor on soft surface. And, the same dog transitioning to hard surface next to the soft surface.

90% of the time, trailing ground-scent odor revolves around the dog with its nose in some proximity to the ground much of the time, if wind is not favorable to an air scent. I hear some handlers say that their dogs do not follow ground odor on the ground with their heads low in the fashion I describe. I have found through experience that most of these dogs are simply running with the handlers following until the subject is run into or the dog encounters the subject's air scent. Both are probable because the trails are generally known trails with these dogs. In these cases the dogs have simply learned through repetition and reward that if they simply run, the handler will guide them with lead handling to the subject.

The trailing head is usually hovering just off the ground from one to ten inches. The surface and environmental conditions create these distances not so much as the dogs working style. When the surface is grass or very low vegetation, the dog's nose will normally be just above the vegetation top. When the surface increases in height, so too does the dogs nose.

If the surface changes to a harder, dryer condition, the K9 nose often goes even lower if it is trying to detect ground odor. Basically, when the conditions tend to favor scent less and the odor is present on the ground, the nose goes closer to the ground, not further from it. The only time this changes is with radiating heat off the ground and when the wind shifts from the trail towards the dogs face. In these conditions the nose will trend higher.

Ear Set

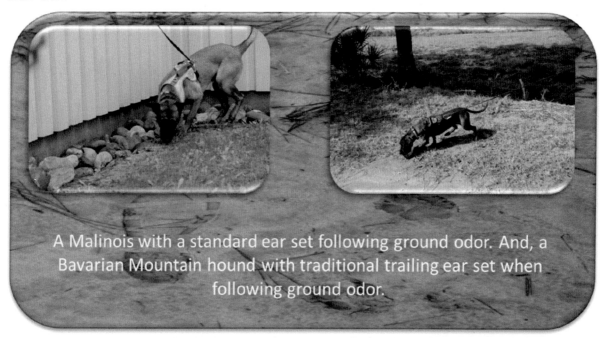

A Malinois with a standard ear set following ground odor. And, a Bavarian Mountain hound with traditional trailing ear set when following ground odor.

Ears are a variable body language indicator that fluctuates with just about every influence: visual, audible, and scent. With the pointy eared breeds the ears are like mini radars and incredibly important to pay attention to, especially when it comes to proximity alerts covered later in this chapter. The focus on this sub-chapter is trailing with general ground scent conditions.

With most dogs in normal trailing conditions, the best way to describe the ear set is relaxed. The ears have yet to tune themselves to anything in particular and they are in a resting phases, not so much reactive.

German Shepherds, Malinois, and other breeds with upright ears will generally have them spread to the sides and slightly back when trailing. I think the most important explanation however, is relaxed.

The floppy eared breeds have a similarly relaxed ear set, but of course, they are hanging down. The main thing to remember is that the ears are normally not flat, facing forward, or in a position of auditory attention, or seeking sound. They are usually flat hanging down or slightly back, hanging loosely.

Nose and Mouth

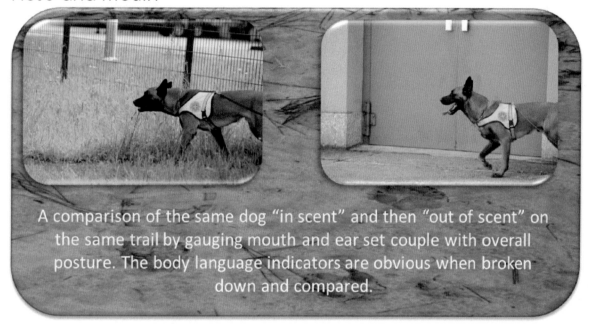

A comparison of the same dog "in scent" and then "out of scent" on the same trail by gauging mouth and ear set couple with overall posture. The body language indicators are obvious when broken down and compared.

Nose and mouth are operating simultaneously due to the relationship of taste and scent. Generally speaking, the nose operates best when the mouth is not wide open with the tongue lolling out the side. The dog can scent in this condition, but I do not believe that the nose is as strong or attentive as when the mouth is closed. The tongue will begin to come out and the mouth must open to help regulate body temperature as the dog's pace and intensity levels increase. However there is a significant difference between a working mouth and a resting mouth.

Gait and Posture

Gait and stance as they relate to positive ground scent trail change with every dog and breed, but they all share a commonality. These common denominators are: intensity, consistency, and focus to a direction or path. With the longer legged dogs there is a real hunched-over posture during movement as the dog tries to lower itself to the ground—thereby easing the stress on the neck. Shorter legged dogs need not articulate their bodies as much and seem to naturally have a much lower nose posture. I am sure this is why the early breeders of certain scent hounds accentuated short legs on some of the traditional scent-trailing dogs. Good examples of these are the Hanoverian Hound and Dachshund. These shorter legs do seem to assist in ground scenting posture but they have drawbacks as well when it comes to economy of movement in general.

Tail Set

The "Scorpion" tail so often seen in hound dogs on trail.

Is one of the best indicators for everything dog. I equate it to a naval ships series of signal flags on one end of the vessel that are used to communicate with other ships. The tails express interest, distraction, focus, fear, dominance, fight, and flight. Of all the indicators that I use, this one is perhaps the most expressive. When the tail moves I try to pay as much attention as I can.

Trailing tail really varies and the individual handler must strive to catalog all of the subtle tail variations for his or her own dog. I have found that many but not all bloodhounds have a tendency to have a curved over the top tail. This is almost like a scorpion tail with the stinger pointing towards the top of the back. This tail set is indicative of a strong subject scent and no indecision.

German shepherd tails are often held at mid-staff with a slight bow in the middle and the tip facing up but below the top of the back.

Very typical GSD Tail Set when following ground scent.

Many Labs and Malinois seem to wag their tails constantly when working and the degree of the wag coupled

A common flagging/ wagging tail of a Mailnois on trail.

with speed often indicates if the dog has subject odor or not. These can be some of the most difficult of all tails to evaluate, at least for me. Still, if the handler can video a good trailing tail often enough, I think it is possible to catalog a common tail set or movement.

I cannot begin to relate each and every tail set for this chapter, as I think I would be writing forever, because even with the breeds I mentioned, the tail set can change between individual dogs. Tail set, though, is often like a Geiger counter that detects radiation. If the radiation level is higher, the needle spikes, and as the radiation level drops, so too does the needle. Tail set will change with scent presence and intensity. The better the subject scent, the better the tail and easier it will be to read.

There is a point that this Geiger counter will drop even in strong scent conditions. This is when the dog is getting tired. If the work level is not compromised, the body language indicators are now less extreme versions of the original. This can be difficult for many handlers who have not trailed with their dogs on very long, arduous trails. They have never seen their dogs tired but still working sent well.

Once the K9 is trailing well in most conditions, it is important to build the dog's endurance; not only muscular and cardiovascular, but scent retention as well. Physical condition obviously comes first but the best long distance dog in the world will not be able to keep the olfactory capability at the physical conditioning rate without training for it. It is not simply a matter of having a dog that can run long distances without getting tired. It is also a matter of the dog maintaining a high degree of loyalty to the scent trail for long periods of time, over varied terrain, under duress from distraction, and physically tiring. Mental scent trail conditioning is a big part

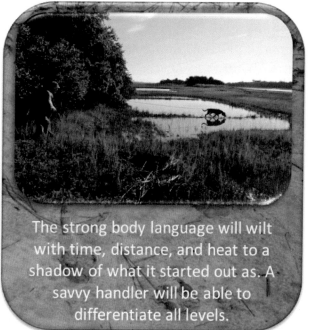

The strong body language will wilt with time, distance, and heat to a shadow of what it started out as. A savvy handler will be able to differentiate all levels.

of the overall trailing picture but it is often forgotten in the training regimen of most handlers I meet. The reason for this is too many times we have a tendency to run short, quick trails even after the dog is an effective man trailer. We do this because we get lazy. Olfactory training for distance must be treated like any other component of trailing training: Tiered Trailing Training, starting small and adding distance with complexity over time.

Trailing Behavior, Wind at the Back

Trailing body language with the wind at the back of the dog is probably the easiest to read because the dog may often stay very true to the original trail as long as the wind was at the trail layers back as well. The conditions will be very much as described above.

Wind From the Left or Right

When the wind is from the left or the right, the K9 will often run an almost zigzag pattern based on several factors:

1. Ground disturbance on good soft surface
2. Soft surface with tall vegetation
3. Smooth hard surface conditions
4. Age of the trail

When the dog is working a soft surface condition with tall vegetation, the dog will still often stay very close to the actual track of the trail layer. This is because the dog is following ground disturbance as well as the human scent that fell very close to the track. This is the strongest part of the trail for the dog to follow. Yes, there will be human scent that has blown past the track but that scent is not as strong. The vast majority of dogs gravitate to the strongest odor.

When the vegetation becomes shorter, there will be places that the dog shifts to the left or fight of the ground disturbance of the track to locate wind-drift human odor that has now becomes the strongest part of the trail. Where the human odor drifts is dependent upon wind speed and physical barriers that hold scent: such as taller grass, rocks or plants. This distance will not be too far from the track but there will be some divergence. The behavior change will be very subtle, and the only thing the handler may see is: instead of a relatively direct route, the dog's movement will meander left and right. The distance travelled on these angles will be relative to wind speed and where the taller vegetation or terrain is relative to the actual track. The left and right divergence may be several inches to several yards.

Smooth or hard surfaces with wind from the side can result in the dog travelling long distances to a productive source of human odor. In other words, places where that odor was trapped. Productive sources of odor include gutters, building edges, vegetation, and terrain elevation changes such as depressions and ridges. The left and right divergence will be more extreme and now the body language may really change other than directional panning. What I normally see with the vast majority of trailing dogs is the tail dropping slightly and the head comes up in a cast. The dog may put its nose into the wind trying to detect odor, but if the dog has been trained in productive sources, it will normally gravitate to those locations. The behavior may appear as if the dog does not have scent and, indeed, the dog may not. There may be a very big gap in useable odor for the dog and it is simply moving to the places where it might be found. The key is reading the dog when the scent is recovered, the head down position with all of the above body language indicators will apply once again.

The age of the trail can really affect not only the ground disturbance on soft surfaces but also the productive sources. The dog will stay strong and consistent with direction of travel as long as the scent remains strong. Ground disturbance odor as it relates to the human seems to expire first and the actual human odor of scent particles decomposing remains longer. This flies in the face of some ground disturbance tracking aficionados; however, it is my experience over thousands of trails. I have no science to back-up this claim, simply experience and observation. I do believe any practitioner of trailing, if tuned to their dogs trailing behavior, will have similar experiences.

As the trail ages, human scent will be destroyed and masked by contamination to the point that the dog simply cannot detect it. There is no rhyme or reason to this degradation and it is impossible for us humans to determine that rate of scent loss or when it will actually happen. Our Geiger counter of scent is the dog and it is the dog's body language that tells us if scent is present or not. The problem is that even though we have conditions that seem to create favorable conditions for scent, we cannot always count on them. There are times we can be completely surprised. This is why it is very important for all trailing handlers not to commit to a condition but rather to look to the body language of the dog as an indicator of the presence of human scent.

These are the occasions when the trailing handler will be sorely taxed in patience and powers of observation. There may be very large gaps of "no scent" and it becomes a matter of the dog and handler working together to find productive sources of odor that might still retain the target human scent.

Generally speaking, when the sun beats down on a surface and the temperature becomes elevated, scent loss occurs rapidly regardless of surface. Of course, hard surfaces will become voids sooner than a vegetative condition; however, heat and direct sunlight degrade scent on grass and bushes, too. The key to scent retention really is humidity and shade. Oftentimes, the dogs trailing behavior returns in the cooler, darker places along the trails. The fewer and farther between these places, the further between is the trailing behavior. Perfect examples are curb edges on a street or a building edge to the sidewalk. In the shade, these places are great human odor scent traps. In direct sunlight, they become far less productive. On a soft surface condition, short grass under direct sunlight may lose viability in a matter of thirty minutes, but when the grass is taller, the scent may last for hours due to the shade the longer blades of grass provide. The interesting thing is that when it becomes cooler and darker due to changing weather conditions, viable scent may return in places, but in a very degraded state. The ideal consistent aged scent trail condition is in the woods with little to no direct sunlight. Human scent trails in this condition may last in upwards of twenty-four hours.

Distraction

Distractions are the bane of all man trailers, and all man trailing dogs are susceptible to them to one degree or another. The degree to which a K9 responds to distraction in the form of odor is really relative to three major causative factors:

1. Exposure to distractions and proper correction techniques
2. Weakness or lack of trail while the dog is working
3. Intensity of the scent distractions.

All man trailers must be exposed to as many distractions as possible before actually working cases in the first place. This is simple common sense but often neglected. As puppies, our kennel-man trailers are exposed to six hundred new people and as many sights, sounds, and scents as possible in the first eight weeks of their lives with us. While we expose the pups to these new things, we determine the interest level each trailing candidate might have for humans, animals, and everything in between. We want to encourage lack of concern for everything without fostering excessive interest. We want a dog to be relatively fearless of all new things and, at the same time, not have excessive desire to investigate the new things once they are understood. Therefore, it is important to expose without encouraging contact too much. On the same note, negative trailing distractions include other dogs, cats, and any other animals. We do not encourage any of our dogs to seek out other dogs during environmental exposure training. When we observe body language indicators that the puppy has detected a animal distraction by scent, sight, or sound, we command them to "Leave It!" with a lead correction if necessary. From an early age the dog must understand that animals are verboten and they must leave them alone. If we can entrench this thought process in the puppies mind between the ages of eight and sixteen weeks of age, we will have an adult working dog that is less susceptible to distractions. We can never train distraction responses completely out of any puppy or adult dog, but we can decrease the dog's natural proclivity to investigate them. Dogs inherently investigate other dog odor out of the genetic requirement to do so. Reproduction, threat, and pack requirements dictate this response to a certain extent and our job as handlers is to mitigate it when they are with us. Our rule of thumb in dog training is that when the dogs are with us; attached to a lead or not, they are not allowed to investigate animals of any type. When they are not in our presence, what they do up to them. We have ample dog runs where all of our kennel dogs run and play together when they are not working.

This actually brings up another training component that we use to help reduce the level of distraction that our working dog candidates might have. We have a philosophy that other dogs are some of the best trainers of new dogs that there are. I believe there must be a level of dog-on-dog pack activity in the trailing candidate's life; starting at an early age all the way up to the point that they go to their new handler. What this means is that when the dog is not working, eating, or sleeping, it is with other age, demeanor, or size appropriate dogs in training. This is best in large dog runs with toys and other play stimulating items that encourage interaction and pack behavior. This interaction actually seems to reduce over-the-top reaction to other dog stimulation in the form of sight, sound, and especially scent, while working. In a way, it is almost like the dog trained in this fashion now has the attitude of "Been there, done that," and they simply don't have a huge interest in other dogs unless they are threats. Couple this attitude with a handler who does not tolerate reaction to other dog stimulation in the field and you will have a man trailer that is relatively immune to this huge problem.

Unfortunately, most people who get into man trailing for the first time, even after their second and third trailing dogs, still don't do this type of training. They will have problems with dogs that jump trail for animal odor or distractions. This part of the chapter should help these handlers immensely.

Extremely weak scent trails or trails that simply are gone, and the dog has given up, create conditions for dogs that will encourage them to jump to animal odor. The simple reason for this is the fact that the trail is fading or gone and now other things become more interesting in the dogs mind. When a handler pushes a dog in a no-scent or too-weak scent trail state for too long any trailing dog will be susceptible to other animal stimulators. The key is for the handler to understand that the trail is missing or degraded too much for the dog to properly work and that he should either find a productive source of correct odor or pull the dog from the mission. Only the handler can know this time by staying extremely attuned to the dog's body language. When the dog shows that it is losing trail or has lost it completely, the handler must understand how long his or her own dog will stay focused in this void state. Every dog has their own level of tolerance for this condition and it is the handler's job to be able to identify it, train for increasing amounts of time in it, and pull the dog when it is obvious the dog is about to forget what it is looking for. This time is what I call the "Dead Time". It is when the dog has exhausted its level of patience for the lack of trail and is now on the verge of detecting and following something else. Failure to recognize the Dead Time and too often allowing the dog to get distracted, in training, will create a dog that has been taught it is OK to detect and follow distractions. We can literally train our dogs to become more distracted by running too many trails where the dog has no scent and we just follow them while running or pushing the dog too far once it loses the correct trail. Any dog will jump to something else if continuously given the opportunity to do so.

The intensity of the distraction can be a problem regardless of how good the dog is. There are certain conditions that cause dogs problems and it is simply due to genetic hard wiring:

1. Female dogs that are ovulating and marking
2. Male dogs that are extremely dominant and marking
3. Extreme fear scent of another animal on the trail

These three conditions create a trail ripe for loss. Therefore, it is important for any man-trailing handler to recognize the body language indicators that scream these conditions. I encourage all handlers to set trails up with all of these problems in training so they can observe firsthand what is occurring and then take the appropriate counter measures to correct them. Generally, this means correcting the dog immediately for the reaction and then getting the dog past the problem as fast as possible. I do not recommend going backwards on the trail and starting again because the dog will simply encounter the problem once again. It is best to move past or off to the side far enough that the distracting scent is no longer detectable and then trying to pick up the correct subject trail once again. If the distraction is too strong and the dog will not go back to work, then the handler must now work on the distraction and do the correction away from trailing! If the dog is so distracted by an overwhelming scent that it refuses to go back to work, it will require a correction that may be too harsh to associate with trailing. We do not want the dog to think that trailing or the components thereof created the harsh correction. When I have such a condition I take the trailing harness and lead off for a future training session; strictly focusing on the dog ignoring the distraction.

Distraction body language indicators may change for each and every species of animal detected. For dogs that are a distraction, the man trailers' body language may change slightly for different dog situations such as male, female, dominance levels of both the mantrailer and the dog that is the distraction, etc. When a dog marks areas with urine or feces, the marking carries with it subtle and not so subtle messages that describe everything about the marking dog such as sex, dominance, health, friend, and foe. For dogs, smelling pee and poop is like reading a book about the marker. Consequently, there are accompanying body language changes from the man trailers as the dog initially detects the odor, locates its exact presence, and when it begins the translation process. The key to correction is doing the correcting at the detection phase as described completely in *K9 Trailing; The Straightest Path,* Chapter Eleven.

The first phase of detection is with the head pop. This is when everything changes with the dog and indicates initial detection. The dog smells the new dog odor and the head pops towards the direction of the scent cone from the source. Everything follows the head pop and the rest of the body language indicators begin to manifest themselves immediately.

When the dog locates the scent cone of the other dog scent source, its head will begin to pan back and forth at the edges of the scent cone starting wide and as it gets closer to the source, narrower. The dog will also slow its forward momentum significantly as it gets closer. Once the source is located exactly, the translating body language begins. This usually begins with a nose plant directly on top of the odor with the nose touching or hovering just above the source.

The next big change is the tail. Most dogs when detecting other dog odor for the first time will change tail set based on dominance and the condition of the other dog as indicated by its scent. Normally, the first reaction will be a drop in tail set. Most man trailers have an erect or higher tail set when trailing that varies with exertion and subject scent trail intensity. If there is a K9 speedometer for trailing, the tail is it. The better the subject trail conditions the higher the tail in many dogs. The tail drop as it relates to the distraction detection is not immediate. It can be actually a slow process and take several seconds.

The first tail change occurs as the dog head pops towards the distraction. Almost immediately, the average trailing K9 will lose trailing tail and it will begin to droop slightly. As the head pop turns to head panning, the tail will decrease even more. When the dog isolates the source odor and nose plants on it, the tail often drops to a completely flaccid state. In the case of German Shepherds that often trail with an arched up tail below the top of the back, we may even see the tail point towards the ground.

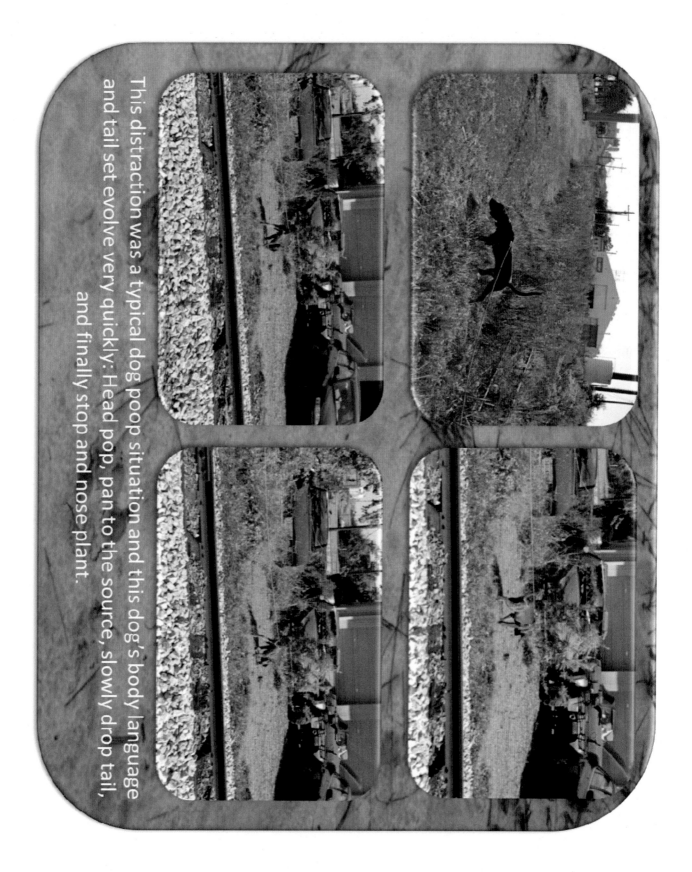

This distraction was a typical dog poop situation and this dog's body language and tail set evolve very quickly: Head pop, pan to the source, slowly drop tail, and finally stop and nose plant.

These three indicators taken together indicate a distraction of the dog order. The reason why I know this is really related to the tail set and dominance. Dominance, hierarchy, and pack behavior control everything in the dog's life and the detection of other dog spoor creates a condition in the sniffing dog that they simply cannot help. A Surprise encounter of a previously unknown dog while working or just out for a walk immediately creates a physiological response in all dogs on the receiving end. When the meeting is a surprise, the first reaction of most dogs is one of reservation. They do not immediately display aggression or dominance unless they happen to be on their own home turf. The reason for this is because dogs in most cases do not immediately want to fight. A fight in the wild with undomesticated canids and any significant injury that results because of that fight can mean death. Wild dogs do not seek out fights because death may be the end result.

Canis familiaris in all of its forms is not all that far removed from the wolf, especially when it comes to pack behavior, and *Meet & Greets* with other strange dogs. Most dogs do not have an immediate fight or flight response when they first detect another dog. What they have is a neutral response that may change as the interloper is investigated, usually from a distance. Consequently, the tail being the signal flag of communication for all dogs will, in most cases, stays low. In the case of scent, the olfactory system takes time to translate all that the spoor of the interloper has to offer. While this translation is occurring, the tail also stays down. Once the spoor is known, the tail may change as it relates to the dominance level of the detecting dog. Many high drive dogs will take a dominant, tail up stance and then mark.

I have found that dogs that immediately assume a completely dominant tail set as soon as they encounter any dog spoor, even without investigation are often dogs that have a predisposition to aggression and a general lack of regard for personal safety. This behavior is not normal and occurs in dogs today primarily due to breeding the behavior into certain lines.

The key to trailing without distraction problems is training the dog from a very early age to avoid distraction odor. If this is not done, distractions will be a part of trailing to a lesser or greater degree and in proportion to how well the handler detects distraction body language changes and how fast he or she gives a proper correction. The correction must be a command and not a plea. If the handler cannot take charge and correct distraction response, distractions will be a big part of every trail in training and at work. If distractions are a big part of training and a constant problem, then the dog is simply not an appropriate tool for real life trails.

Most dogs will have different body language responses to other animals such as deer, raccoons, cats, etc. It is really impossible to go into each of these critters because every dog will have a different response. Observant handlers will often have the ability to translate their own dog's body language to each of these creatures with experience. However, a big part of that experience must include correction. Other animals are not allowed in the trailing dog's repertoire... ever!

As with all trailing training, I highly recommend video recording of all training trails. If you want to know what your dog looks like when it encounters distraction scent, record it.

Proximity Alert Changes; Far Too Final.

The proximity alert is often the last scent many handlers will see. This is often due to their inability to decipher it and the impatience that comes with the lack of understanding. Proximity alerts on many trails are mistaken for distractions when the subject is not immediately found after the alert. The problem really is lack of patience and the fact that proximity alert training is lacking in most trailing training programs. The proximity alert issue is that when the dog encounters fresh human scent that is swirling in small amounts and landing somewhere on the trail, the dog will probably abandon the older scent trail for the fresher swirled scent, even if it is in very small pockets. This is natural for any dog because they always default to fresher odor. If the search of the proximity scent area by the dog drags the handler too far away from the trail, the handler stands a very good chance of forgetting where it was. Generally dogs can work these problems out for themselves if they are off lead. The problem is always the handler who restrains the dogs once the frustration sets in. For a complete introduction to proximity scent, please refer to *K9 Trailing; The Straightest Path*; Chapter Four and *Tactical Tracker Teams*; Chapter Four.

The first proximity alerts are often nothing more than small, subtle changes that are very easy to miss unless video recordings are poured over on a regular basis. They can also occur hundreds of yards away from the target. If the target is stationary, small pockets of fresher scent will often swirl and land in the area of the dog on the trail, dependent on shifting wind patterns. When this occurs and the fresh scent is very minimal, the dog will react with some of the following behavior changes:

1. Trailing ground odor with head in the primary down position
2. Head tosses up, mouth closed as the nose samples the wind.
3. Ears may perk towards the scent pocket
4. Tail may become more erect
5. Speed will increase slightly
6. If no more fresh scent is to be found on the wind, nose goes back down to the trail

Sequence of photos showing the K9 from the trail layer's view using a zoom lens from approximately 200 yards away.

There are two strong alerts where the dog tastes scent on the wind, but it comes from the side; and the final alert when the dog focuses on the direction to the source. Interestingly, the wind was at the dog's back at ground level.

Typical Pointy Ears showing intermediate level alerts. The ears show how they are trying to triangulate the source.

These alerts may come in a string of little fresh scent knots starting from a very long distance and only lasting for seconds. These little proximity alerts are the first signals to the handler to pay more attention and in the case of a tactical team on a felony search, to be more careful. Not necessarily a time to stop but a time to be wary. The problem with many new to trailing proximity alerts is that they may over react to these first changes and shut the dog down too early. Do this too often when there may be ten or more such reactions in a row, and it is very easy for the handler to start losing faith in the alert and when a strong, danger close alert occurs, it is often missed. Proximity alert training for felony trails is not a one-time affair. It should be a regular, weekly component of police K9 training.

It is very important to understand that these first alerts are due to small or minute amounts of fresh scent without a pool or scent cone. There is not a way to isolate them and detect the source from a distance just yet.

These scent knots on the wind will increase in size and intensity with simultaneously decreasing distance as the dog gets closer to the subject. This may not be the case if the wind shifts and no longer swirls towards the dog. If the wind is strong and consistently moving away from the dog, the alerts may stop altogether and the dog may trail almost right on top of the subject until the small side of the scent pool is encountered.

The next or intermediate proximity alerts are those that simply last longer and encompass more air or ground space. These are no longer little knots of fresh scent but fairly large pockets. They may vary in size from just a few yards in diameter to twenty-five or more. These alerts are marked by significant body language changes on par with those mentioned above but more extreme. Instead of a small nose pop into the air and quick head to the ground back to trail, the dog will actively begin to try and gain an active air scent by detecting the scent cone. The problem is that the scent cone may still not be available due to wind or distance. The scent pool of the subject is close enough now that even with shifting wind, there will more pockets simply due to the closed distance. In these cases the dogs will actively search with more intensity and speed. In the case of dogs predisposed to visual and auditory cues, the K9 may entirely switch to air scent, sight and sound mode. These are often the German Shepherds and Malinois. This body language is almost impossible to miss if a handler has had a chance to catalog it before. And ideally, this is the time to stop the team, get up next to the dog and be patient. Watch the nose and when the wind shifts just right, the dogs will probably point in the direction of the subject. These distances are usually within twenty-five to one hundred yards from K9 to subject dependent on wind direction and speed and they indicate Danger Close in high-risk felony trails.

The last phase of the proximity alert is normally when the team is too close if it is a high-risk search. This is when the dog detects the immediate scent pool of the subject or the scent cone of fresh human scent in the form of gasses emitting from the body. This is what most people refer to as "Air Scent".

Pool Scent: Subject Not Present

I cover this extensively in my chapter on pool scent. Pool scent is the fresh or old/ past odor of the subject that has collected in a location in various levels of concentration based on the time the subject spent in that area and his or her activity. This chapter is also the largest chapter in the current book because it is so important. Scent pools are the single factor that results in more loss of trail than any other. For many handlers this is primarily due to their impatience and lack of understanding. I will go over the major body language indicators here briefly, but for a detailed accounting of pool scents and how K9's might respond to them I highly recommend perusing Chapter Thirteen: *Scent Pools; Drowning Prevention.*

When a trailing dog is working primarily ground scent in traditional trailing conditions the nose is down towards the ground for the most part. If the dog's head is up above chest level it is probably air scenting, the trail scent is blowing towards the dog from the trail in front of it, or the dog is not working; it's really that simple. Pool scent, when the subject is not present, is most often a ground scent condition unless things have been

Bayischer Gebirgshweisshund working a scent pool caused by a leaf blower. The dog suddenly pauses when the scent is no longer consistent and now spread out. She circled perusing the pool until the edge is encountered with the exit trail.

touched by the subject above ground level or the subject was just in the area and the thermals are causing scent to drift. The dog's nose will stay closer to the ground now more than ever. The big changes are intensity and speed. This is also another time to be very patient.

Scent pools can distract from the scent trail due to the sheer concentration of odor over a given space. Depending on how long the subject was present in that space will determine how long the dog must work the area to discover the exit trail. With large, intense pools, the dog really has to work towards the edge of the pool to find this exit. This might take some time if the pool is one hundred yards across.

The body language for most dogs in scent pools stays fairly consistent.

1. Intensity change as the dog leaves the relatively weak scent trail to the stronger scent pool.
2. K9 will switch from consistent direction of travel to a left, right, and circling behavior.
3. Tail may become more erect and wag.
4. K9 may pause and hover over certain places for abnormally long periods of time.

While working the scent pool I find it extremely important to allow the dog as much freedom as possible, and try my utmost not to line check. Line checks in scent pools can take the dog off crucial parts of the pool that might very well lead to the exit trail. If your dog is in a scent pool:

1. Take your time!
2. Don't line check!
3. Don't talk to the dog!
4. Pay attention to spots the dogs hovers over: prints, evidence, etc., may be right under your dog's nose.
5. Be patient above all things!

Contact Odor

Contact odor is often confused with distraction odor because the dog body language is often very similar. If the dog is relatively distraction proof then we are golden, but if the K9 has problems with other animal odor then the handler must really be very cognizant of slight behavior changes and the only way to really do this is with a lot of video recording. I cannot begin to try and catalog the differences here because all dogs have their own unique reactions to other animals and I would be writing a never-ending book. The other issue is that I believe distractions are a mission-ending problem with some trailing dogs and should be rectified prior to actual-deployment on real cases.

Subject contact odor is the scent of the human body in the form of cells and oils that attach to object touched or handled by the subject.

Contact body language is also a big part of scent pools and is described in that chapter even further but we really need to go over some of the changes here:

1. Head pop towards the object
2. Nose pans to the scent source
3. Nose hovers over the object
4. Tail stay in a trailing tail set or wags

The head pop, coupled with the panning and nose plant are frustrates most people and the feeling that the issue is distraction. They often don't look at the entire picture and if they correct at this juncture, an immediate trail loss after the correction may quickly occur.

One of the key components of comparing the two in my mind was always the location the dog was sniffing. If the location was the low hanging, extra-long end of a bush and it was stained or wet; I was dealing with dog pee. On the other hand, if the spot was at the top of the bush. Lets' say thigh or at the hand level of someone walking, then your dog is smelling contact odor of the person who touched the plant.

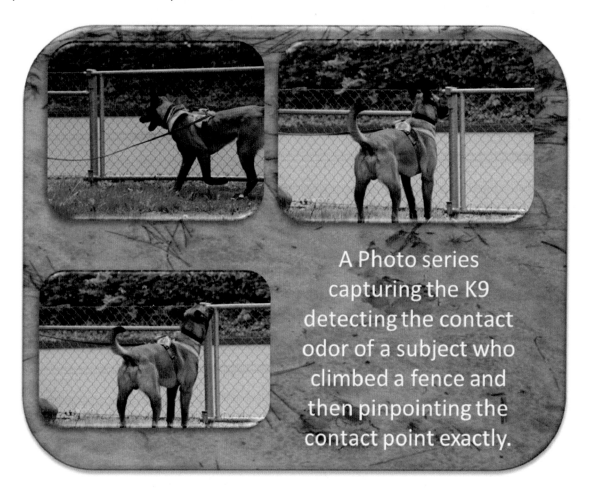

A Photo series capturing the K9 detecting the contact odor of a subject who climbed a fence and then pinpointing the contact point exactly.

Pair this location with a slight tail wag and I am positive I have my subject. Dogs normally do not wag their tails at other unknown animal scents. The reaction is generally dominant, submissive, or neutral. A wagging tail is a happy tail and that means that it matches something the dog knows. The trail and the article are known scents and if a friend or family member had a hot chance in Antarctica of touching that tall bush on our trail then I have my man.

Lost Trail Behavior

K9 Doc detecting leg contact odor of a subject who climbed over this log.

"Lost person" behavior is often missed because many handlers simply have no concept that the trail was lost in the first place. It is easy to just run with the dog. And a dog that runs enough with the handler until it air scents it will quickly learn that it does not need to work until it gets close. Running for the sake of running is rewarding. The handler running behind is the reward. I cover this in other chapters, but suffice it to say this is a huge problem with trailing and tracking. Dogs are great observers of handler behavior. They may learn that there is no need to follow scent because the handler will guide them. They will then manipulate this response over and over. If the pattern of training began this way, the dog will never show lost trail behavior because it had no scent trail to begin with and the handler simply believes the dogs is always working.

Loss of trail behavior happens when a previously well-worked trail becomes too thin to work or disappears altogether due to a missed turn or other circumstances. When the dog was previously working trailing scent, the lost trail behavior is obvious.

With almost all scent trails, the dogs are usually working scent forward. What I mean by this is they seem to process not only the odor that is directly in front of their noses but also the odor that is further in front of them but in smaller quantities. I can only equate it to how people hunt. Not only is the human hunter very aware of the tracks at his feet, he is also evaluating the upcoming terrain and how it relates to those tracks as well. The interpretation is visual but I think it is exactly how dogs process scent. An astute handler will see small changes in body language that dictate a change in the trail is forthcoming. This body language may foretell a change in terrain, turns, or other trail factors. This language is important to understand because if the dog moves too far past the change, and no more trail is found, it may not be able to find its way back to the change. This is especially true on concrete. The dogs follow odor on hard surfaces as well as they do on soft. It is not a matter of the nose; it is a matter of the condition and exposure. The scent on a hard surface may simply blow so far past a turn that the dog may miss the turn because it is following blown scent too far and it cannot find its way back. The issue is not keeping the dog closer to the trail from a human perspective, because the trail is what the dog follows. We will never be able to say where stronger scent is because we cannot know this. The dog is simply using its natural instinct to follow scent and that will always depend on the strength of the odor. We cannot teach a dog to follow a track when its instincts say that the track is not where the person walked. The key to solving the problem is exposure to the condition. When that is not enough, the handler must see the subtle changes that say the problem occurred in the first place and get the dog back to that area if it cannot do this on its own.

When a trailing dog begins to lose trailing odor, the first changes noticed may actually be preparatory changes or proximity alerts to the change in condition. For example, prior to a soft surface change to concrete, the dog's head may pop up to sample the wind due to swirling scent from the hard surface coming back to the soft surface trail. Similar changes often occur due to turns or other trail factors. Again, the key to the solution is in this early read.

Preparatory Changes

1. Head up sampling the wind, but drops back to trail sent on ground
2. Pace slows
3. Tail may drop slightly

Lost Trail

1. Head comes up, nose into the wind trying to air scent
2. Tail stays low
3. Mouth stays open and breathing become more labored
4. Ears may perk towards any sound or sight
5. K9 may circle back to ground scent
6. Lots of attention paid to any residual ground odor discovered. The dog may work these spots furiously because they are all that is left; circling again and again over the exact same spots.

I truly believe in the art of training for K9 self-discovery in all things, especially lost trail recovery. There is no way for humans to show the dog where to recover a scent trail and not have the dog switch focus onto the handler. This is the moment the dog shuts on the self-discovery process, when the handler steps in and tries to point something out. The other problem is we really do not know where scent is in the first place. If we stop the dog in mid-search and move it to a place we believe has scent and there is none, we are distracting the dog from its job and our direction has now become the focus of the dog. Nothing could be worse from a K9 training perspective.

Generally speaking, if my dog is circling and hunting for a lost trail with intensity, I let it work for as long as it wants. I do not let my impatience override the dogs hunt for the discovery. This can be really hard for many handlers who want their dogs to be successful immediately. Active hunting for a blown turn that takes several minutes is often too much time for many handlers. They begin to intervene with line checks and attempts to move the dog into what they believe are areas for better scent. I am all for helping a dog to a productive source, but I only do this when it appears that the dog is unable to perform this task on its own. My preference is for the dog to learn productive sources of odor on its own because I know that this lesson will be well learned. On the other hand, every time I help the dog to what I think might be a productive source two things can happen: first, I could be wrong and there is no scent; or second, there is scent and the dog learned that I will help it every time the going gets tough. Both are huge problems.

I prefer to only help the dogs to productive sources of odor on real deployments. In training I try to avoid helping at all costs. If my training creates trail loss problems that force me to guide the dog, then the scenario or problems are too much for the dog at that level of training. I need to step back to a problem that allows for self-discovery.

A great example of a subtle body language K9 in good scent from curb to the middle of a parking lot and loosing the scent picture as the trail migrates to the main road.

Chapter Ten
Scent: Productive Sources

*"The Leaves of Fall collect where few care to look. This is where the wind stops after the swirl.
It is also here the dog will find scent."*

*In the beginning, scent sources in difficult environs must be within easy grasp. For a young
dog, an excessively long hunt for the scent source will often produce trails other than those the
handler might seek. These sources must not be "given" through presentation but rather learned
by the dog itself and through natural selection. Therein lie the Dilemma and the Key to all things
dog training: to teach without teaching, to assist without assisting. When the dog learns on its
own, without help, or guidance, the lesson becomes hardwired. When the source is presented,
the dog will always look to the handler for presentation because the handler became the
solution."*

Productive Sources of odor or scent are those types of places that the dog learned from past experience and exposure, and provided the scent it had been looking for.

When I first began to work with trailing dogs I was told and taught that I must teach dogs to trail. And, as if I was teaching a human child, I went through the repetitive gyrations of showing the dog where I thought scent was and attempted to direct a response relative to that location. The basic understanding, that I failed to grasp at the time, was that the dog already knew what scent is and there was no way I would ever be able to duplicate that ability. Furthermore, if I could, I would not need the dog. So why now was I trying to show one of the world's best scenting creatures what scent was and where it might be found? It was Human arrogance, first and foremost. We as a species tend to believe that we are the enlighteners of the planet and when given the chance, will try to teach a rock how to sit still.

As humans use their eyes, so too do dogs use their noses. I often have my students try a simple exercise where they are to suddenly turn 180 degrees around and within a one second glance, attempt to catalog everything they see before turning back to the front. When they turn back around they must recount all that they noticed during their once second view. We humans have a dramatic ability to detect and catalog a myriad of items with such a short look. Of course, those with trained eyes can do this exercise with an amazing degree of accuracy; however, even untrained observers have an innate ability to detect and catalog a number of things without any practice at all. Our intuitive strength comes from our ability to see and see things very well; however, this ability has a flaw.

We humans can determine a huge number of things at a glance. If we are looking at our fellowman, for example, we can determine friend from foe, intent or lack thereof, age, infirmity, flamboyance and a number of other human indicators we often take for granted. It is why we go to such extremes to often cover up or hide our natural selves. There is something to say for the term: First Impressions are the most important. We internalize so very much from that first glance of our fellow man, and history has shown that the fates of many have been decided upon with less.

I think dogs have this same ability but from an olfactory standpoint with one enormous difference. Instead of a glance and with little more than a quick whiff, dogs can determine the same things as we humans but with far more honesty and, perhaps, more detail. Dogs don't only see in terms of black, white, and shades of grey, they smell things this way also. Whereas black, white, and grey often disallow great detail in vision, the tables seem to be turned when it comes to scent. Scent, unlike visual appearance, cannot be made to be to be what it is not. Scent, may be covered up or destroyed but it cannot be falsified. With a dog's nose, it is either there or it is not. It is what it is or it is not. Unlike our own human physical appearance as seen by the human eye, scent cannot be made to "be" something else as so much make up. Another dog cannot

The Tao of Trailing Jeff Schettler

hide its age or "appearance" with scent and at a scent glance, one dog may know another completely.

I believe the flaw in our human sight is the flaw of honesty. If it were not, make-up would not be on the shelf of the vast majority of western department stores. The arts of camouflage and concealment are the disciplines of the sniper and the better he is at his art, the better his chance of success and survival on the human battlefield. Camouflage and concealment are not possible with scent, and depending on the conditions, the sniper would be plainly visible to the dog no matter his attention to detail in the practice of his craft. By scent, the sniper might as well be wearing a Santa Clause suit.

We humans know that our ability to discern the truth can be compromised by camouflage. We often council ourselves to always look past the first glance, because what we perceived initially may not be the truth. Yet, after all of this, we still seem to plant ourselves firmly in the realm of scent at first thought and as if we can detect it. If we cannot detect it, how can we honestly know what it is doing and how the dog works with it? The truth of the matter is we cannot. Until the day comes where we can detect and utilize scent as the dog does, we will never be wholly in the dog's world. Therefore, I believe it is crucial for any aspiring K9 handler to stop worrying about what scent might do and how long it lasts. Time spent on reading rather than deciphering will result in a better pay-off in the end. Our strength is our ability to see, then interpret. The dog's strength is the ability to detect scent and follow it. The marriage of the two abilities is the key to trailing.

That being said, in training, after much time and experience under ones belt working trailing dogs, a good handler will have a basic understanding of where each dog appears to obtain scent. We know these places due to the level of animation in our dogs; the stronger the behavior change, the better the scent picture for the dog. By learning and cataloging these locations, a handler has the ability to put together of list of strong productive sources of odor to help facilitate training in new conditions. More importantly, the dog will also remember these types of places in future searches in new conditions.

To understand productive sources of human odor, it is important to understand that scent is in the form of gases and particulates that may or may not stay airborne. Depending on the time of day and the environmental conditions, human scent can drop to the ground quickly and stay in the relative location the human walked. With other conditions, that same scent may blow and drift for many yards, perhaps hundreds. Where the dog trails is completely relative to where the scent might be and this may not necessarily be where the handler believes it to be.

In my book *K9 Trailing; The Straightest Path,* I wrote that scent has a habit of collecting in the areas that air currents blow it. Another way to consider scent is like water pooling, collecting, and eddying as it would in the backwaters in a stream or river. The main current of the river causes the debris in it to rush headlong towards the ocean. As the river bends and encounters obstacles, portions of the stream collect and swirl due to the effect of the change in direction cause by the obstacle. These places are also where debris, insects, and other elements fall and collect. It is why these places are where the trout congregate while waiting for a meal of a larval nymph or mayfly caught in a whirlpool, looking delectable and ripe enough for a sip from the surface.

The woods are a constant source of pools and eddies waiting for scent to whirlpool and collect. In the woods, everything stops scent from blowing and the gaseous and airborne particulates have a tendency to stay where they fall. Not so much in the city. And it is why a dog that was trained primarily for the soft surfaces of the woods will always have trouble in the city. The productive sources of odor in the woods are literally from tree to tree. The productive sources of scent in the city may be at the individual trees, if one can find them, but most likely, in the dark corners between buildings and in the middle of alley ways where the wind seems to stop. Think of scent in the city as leaves in the fall, and when you do, you will know the productive sources of scent in the city.

Training for productive sources starts in the woods where it is easy and scent is simple to discover. This is the "time of the puppy" or new dogs fresh to trailing, for these dogs are the most impatient and subject to distraction. We build focus by drilling in areas of strong productive sources, and over time, wean the dogs down to minimum production. The dog understands instinctively that when scent is scarce, it must now locate scent in other places and have the patience to hunt for it. This hunting is not willy-nilly, but instead, directed by past experience of good productive sources found in past work and similar situations.

When I start young dogs or new dogs in trailing, I like to begin in areas where there is a lot of vegetation, the taller the better. Scent gravitates to moist areas and woods thick with plant growth are perfect receptacles. Human scent will stick to places on vegetation that have been touched or handled, such as tall grass and bushes. It will also fall very close to the actual human track because taller, moister surfaces will block or stop scent from spreading out due to wind or simple movement.

Taller vegetation and wet bottom areas are great productive sources.

The act of walking down a barren, concrete sidewalk in the city may mean that scent blows and collects fifty yards or more away from the actual track. In the woods, due to the blocking forces of nature, the scent will move very little. When scent is very close to the location that the subject human travelled, the young dog will have less trouble in following it and stand less chance of becoming distracted.

Productive Sources of Odor: Wooded Environment

1. Hardwoods forests with low pine tree population. Loamy earth with lots of thick leaves is better than beds of pine needles.
2. Narrow, slow moving streams, depressions. Scent gravitates to the water.
3. Alternating small changes of elevation. Scent gravitates to the base
4. Muddy areas with thick vegetation

I do believe that all dogs must be trained and practice in the areas that they must work, but city trailing should never be the first step. The productive sources of odor in the city are fewer and farther apart. Young or new dogs, forced to work in these conditions, may become distracted or handler dependent. They simply could not find the odor themselves in the training time conducive to their cognitive skills. The first step should be thick, vegetative conditions with areas of strong odor to build drive for the job and encourage complete focus. It is only after the drive and focus have been completely established that we can start branching out to more difficult locations. Of all places where tiered training methods are applicable, productive source training is the most important. The time necessary for each step is relative to the dog's innate drive, manufactured drive, and overall scenting ability. Some dogs simply have better drive and scent trailing ability than others.

Generally speaking, we take our pups from the woods to the city at about 16 weeks of age and after about 8 weeks of training in the woods, fields, and other strong areas of scent. However, even the rural areas are tiered. It is hard for a new puppy to go from thick woods to open, short grass. The scent simply has blown too far in the short grass conditions. So, when we move from the woods for the first time, we will go to more open areas with taller vegetation as back stops:, trailing next to them. The dog gets used to discovering blown scent on shorter grass but has a wall of vegetation relatively close that the scent trail holds to.

Productive Sources of Odor; Soft Surface, Open Areas

1. Smaller fields with tall grass, avoid grass over the top of the dog's head to reduce bounding or hopping.

2. Fields of grass with a section of taller grass next to the shorter. Start at the edge of short to tall. Scent will collect well there.

3. Fields of shorter grass with walls of vegetation in the forms of plants and bushes. Run the trail next to the brush line and slowly move out more towards the open field.

I take this same philosophy and apply it to the urban condition. Once the dog has progressed in varying conditions of vegetation with little to no distraction, I move them to similar areas but now with distraction: human and animal. I want the focus of the dog at its peak when encountering distractions for the first time. When the distraction attracts the dog more than the scent source, the training condition is flawed and this is normally because the source odor is too weak or spaced apart with large gaps of no source odor.

The key to distraction training is the dog understanding that distracting scent is simply not allowed in any form. This begins with early puppyhood. In our kennels and with all working puppy candidates, none are ever allowed to respond to animal odor when the pup is with a handler. If it appears through body language that the puppy is detecting a distraction by scent, the puppy is corrected verbally. If there is no response, then a lead correction follows. Distraction training may be found in *K9 Trailing; The Straightest Path, Chapter Ten.*

The third training phase is moving into a more urban environment. Like the woods, the first new environment must have stronger productive sources of odor and less distraction. It is almost like taking one step forward and a couple back. Even though you are progressing in location complexity, in order to deal with the location in a very strong way, the complexity must be tiered from easy to more difficult. It might be very tempting to take the dog, after doing exceedingly well in a soft surface environment with lots of human and animal distraction, and feel that it is now Ok to work with similar distractions in an urban situation. This is rarely, if ever, a good move. Most new trailing dogs faced with such a drastic change in new conditions will revert to heads up, eyes open, and air scent to close the trailing deal. Do this too many times and it is very possible to ruin a completely good trailing dog.

Ideally, my first urban areas are nothing more than woods or fields on the edge of humanity. I like these places because though we may have some human and domestic animal activity, it is usually low. The fringe of all the city activity is present and in the dogs mind but always on the peripheral edge. The dog will stay motivated and focused with little to no gap in trailing behavior when scent is strong and easy to detect. Run these types of trails to the point of perfection and then slowly ease in closer to the city center. Concentrate on soft surfaces along the way to increased contamination, so by the time you get there, the dog will remain solid. The frustration for the dog comes with major hard surface changes coupled with contamination. When the dog loses subject scent for too long of a period of time, as is apt to happen in the city center with primarily concrete surfaces, it is easy for the dog to become distracted and switch scents. In order to get to the major surface changes coupled with large amounts of contamination and have reliable work, the dog must have had success at all other levels and conditions prior to this exposure. This process is not fast nor is it necessarily easy. There are times that the team has to step back to easier conditions in order to become more reliable. Reliability is always the determining factor. If reliability drops off it is generally a case of the team moving too far too fast.

Once we start moving to hard surfaces in the city, the ability for the dog to maintain consistent scent is diminished. How much is lost is proportionate to the extremes in weather conditions and contamination. The worse the conditions, the more difficult or impossible, the scent might be to acquire. There are times that the conditions are too bad for any dog. Never mind age; the trail might be only twenty minutes old and from a scent perspective, it is nothing more than an instant dead end or brick wall. Part of working a good trailing dog in an urban environment is understanding that the trail might not always be there and it is perfectly fine to call the search when it is clear the dogs has no matching scent trail.

I start with this condition in a section about productive sources of odor in an urban environment because even with the best conditions, there are times that trailing dogs have too much difficulty putting the scent pieces together. This happens even when productive sources of odor are in abundance. There are times that the scent has just moved away too far on thermals, by wind, traffic or simply been covered up too much by contamination. The scent is sometimes destroyed or warped by human made chemical conditions. Productive sources in heavily contaminated busy city streets are not as productive as similar sources in a less busy area. It is important to keep this in mind so as not to "force" the dog to work something that is not there. This training problem can create a ghost-trailing dog.

Productive Sources: Urban Environment, City Streets: Little to No Vegetation

1. Curbs, where the street meets the sidewalk. These places are natural scent gravitation areas because of wind and vehicle traffic. Just like the rushing stream, where debris in the current often moves to the edges of the riverbank where it becomes trapped. An example of this in trailing is when the subject walks in the middle of the road but the dog ends up working the subject scent in the gutter at the edge of the road.

2. Building edges and particularly small alleyways or gaps between buildings. The best locations at buildings are where one might see leaves and other wind-blown debris pile up. These places are natural wind vortexes and allow for the debris to fall out and collect. As the leaves collect, so too does blown scent.

3. Human made planters and patches of grass. These are as good in the city as they can be in the woods. The only negative factor might be that these green places are also

the places other dogs like to mark. Though a great place for odor to collect, it is also a great place of distraction. Though the dog may gravitate to the greenery in order to obtain subject scent, it may get stuck there on other dog scent or spoor. Correction and motivation may have to occur simultaneously in this condition in order to get the dog back on "track".

4. Parking lot tire blocks and concrete dividers. These places are great especially when they have grass on them. Scent will collect against the edges and on top on the grass in a big way. Parking lots in shopping centers often times have a lot of these and they are arranged in natural funnels and directions of travel thus creating a way for the dog to learn on its own where scent might be and how to follow it. I use these places in a progressively tiered way starting with small gaps of open concrete with many tire stops or concrete dividers.

5. I prefer the dividers that have greenery in them for young pups because scent sticks there very nicely. These islands are like little oases in the weak subject scent desert that shopping center parking lots tend to be. Start with quite a few islands spaced within easy scent reach of the dogs. As the dog becomes more accustomed to working this environment and becomes proficient, start reducing the number of islands and increasing the space between them. This method of training will teach the dog that the scent trail may go missing and the dog must hunt for productive sources

Typical urban productive sources...where the leaves lay.

The Tao of Trailing   Jeff Schettler

in order to locate it again. Island hopping will also teach the dog to keep its nose closer to the ground during the hunt in order to locate the scent faster.

6. Cobblestones, paver paved roads, gravel, and ground brickwork. These types of paths are fantastic for dogs that are naturally going nose to ground in an effort to obtain scent. The small gaps and cracks between the cobblestones, bricks, and pavers are almost permanent sources of odor for as long and the odor stays viable. These sources are not so much subject to wind and traffic because the scent is imbedded in the crevices and has few places to move to. The great thing about these sources is that they can often be almost in the tracks of the subject and that allows for very accurate subject trailing. Cracks and crevices are good sources of odor, but they are minimal sources and require greater effort and concentration on the part of the dog. The dog is forced to move slower and with more precision in order to follow the trail. It is very difficult for the dog to go heads up on such a scent trail because the odor is too low and not circulating.

7. Driveways, exits, and entrances, off major roads and thoroughfares. These places are just like small streams that branch off the main river. Scent naturally gravitates to these areas because of natural and traffic driven wind vortexes that pool the scent off the main path and to the edges of the driveway. Again, this is similar to a watery whirlpool at the intersection of the main river and the tributary.

When using productive sources of odor in training, the handler must determine the sources before-hand and set them up in such a way that the K9 naturally gravitates to them when scent becomes less or lost on the open space of concrete. Scent is usually on the concrete but is such low quantities that the dogs tend to go heads up with the intent to air scent. We want them to seek ground odor but many dogs simply do not want to do this unless the scent conditions are very strong. This problem is because of their impatience to locate the subject and moving too fast. When the dog moves too quickly on hard surface, it may easily pass over a weak human scent trail without detecting it. So we use this air scent instinct to our advantage to stimulate attention to ground odor by the use of productive scent sources or scent islands close enough to the original trail that the dog worked previously well. These scent islands are close enough when the dog can detect the scent from this location at a distance. The distance is relative to wind direction as well as physical distance.

Some dogs have an amazing ability to detect trail and productive sources from a very long way off, but in the early stages, we do not want to risk trail loss coupled with lower drive due to distraction. We want the dog at its peak work ethic when the trail transitions from relatively easy conditions where the dog is working well nose down. At this transition phase, the dog will normally venture off the better surface with the good trail in the direction the scent drifted on the hard surface. Interestingly, there is often a proximity alert to the changing scent condition of the hard surface before it gets there. If the scent does not last long, most dogs go heads up into the wind in an attempt to locate the trail. As the dog runs into the wind and no trail is detected, the dog will then circle back to the good trail and try to reacquire. If the wind is correct, the dog may detect the productive source scent island at this point. It could be shortly after venturing off the good trail and into the "void" or it might be as the dog circles back into the wind; heading back to good trail it just left.

When the dog goes heads up for an air scent that is not there, usually there is corresponding body language change that says this plainly. Most but not all dogs will have a corresponding tail set change, usually lower as the head goes up and the scent is not found. When the dog circles back to the scent, the head goes back down to the trail and the tail rises back to where it was. This is usually accompanied by a head pop in the direction of the trail and an earnest following of the trail, perhaps in a back track direction, at a slower pace.

Trail loss at Hard Surface

1. Change of scent condition detected prior to surface change. Head may start to pop up and down prior to the change.

2. At surface change head goes up and into the wind and tail may drop

3. Dog may follow direction of blown scent on hard surface

4. If trail is not detected, the K9 will usually circle back to the original trail on the soft surface it just left.

5. Upon arrival, nose will drop back to the ground: nose searching for the trail

6. When scent trail is detected, head pops in the direction of the scent and tail rises.

7. After a short distance, dog may back track and eventually head back to where the scent was lost.

When the dog detects this productive source from a distance and on its own and at any stage in the first circuit, the condition was set up properly and the dog will really learn from it. This is because there was no handler interaction or direction. The best dog lessons learned are when they are learned without human assistance.

Though the dog wind-scented the productive source from a distance, it will immediately go back to ground odor upon arrival and work this location with vigor and intensity. In a way, it seems that the dogs almost panic a little when they lose the easy trail and when they encounter it again; they work it harder because of the earlier loss. This is the behavior we want to see in order to build the transition drive from easy soft surface trails with copious quantities of scent to low scent levels on concrete. The dog must have the desire to hunt for it and there is no better way than to capitalize on momentary panic from loss and then quick reacquisition where the dog immediately goes right back to nose to ground.

In that gap between trail and new productive source, (if no scent is present or not enough for the dog to react to), and the dog detects the new productive source from a distance, there will be a change from no-scent body language to scent-at-a-distance body language. It often manifests itself in this manner.

Typical scattering scent at an intersection and the body language of a very good trailing dog loosing it and circling back to a good productive source.

Productive Source Detected From a Distance

1. Heads up into the wind, tail drop.
2. Dog begins to circle back to the trail.
3. As the dog circles, it detects scent from a distance.
4. Raised nose jerks or pops in that direction with the nose out stretched.
5. Tail raises back to interest level some even curl over the top.
6. Body follows nose and tail towards wind detected productive source.
7. Upon reaching source, nose drops and dog works ground area tightly.
8. When exit trail is detected, head pops in that direction, body and tail follow.

Because of the gap in the trail, when the dog finds the trail again, the body language is often more intense as if the dog is becoming more possessive of the trail.

As we space the productive sources further apart, yet the trails are equally successful for the dog without assistance from the handler, the dog will learn that it pays to keep the nose closer to the ground. The dog will naturally realize that the scent did not disappear, it simply became more scare and in smaller quantities. Slowing down naturally and paying attention to detail will pay off for the dogs, but they need to learn this incrementally with a natural progression of steps that produce success.

When productive sources are planned out well, with good distances and tiered progression, good hard surface trailers begin to understand that the scent is not necessarily missing on the concrete, but just moved and become scarce. When this lesson is learned without human interference, dogs seem to naturally understand that they must slow down, and patience becomes a natural component of hard surface work.

A very normal reaction to an intersection and scent that has blown away coupled with its detection on the other side of the road at a good productive source.

Chapter Eleven
Tiered Training Transitions

"Seeking the top of the ladder without steps often results in a fall."

      This chapter revolves a lot around police K9 deployment and it first appeared as an article in *K9 Cop Magazine; Small Unit Tactical Tracking Part Two,* specifically for the purpose of providing basic information on producing a tiered training-trailing program that was as effective as it was realistic.   Realism in the world of trailing is a must if the team has a frog's hair chance of being really effective.   For the Search and Rescue Handler, some of the talk about tactics may not mean a lot but the message of this chapter is still critical for any trailing dog handler who plans to work or is working real cases.

      In the case of tracking and trailing, double blind training means that the handler and anyone with him do not know where the trail goes or ends. Anything else is canned, leading to programmed response. More importantly, it leads to guiding the dog; often when the dog knows exactly what it is doing and the handler does not. The problem with running too many known trails is the problem of track walking. This is the condition where the handler walks and leads the dog on the path they perceive to be correct. The problem is that human scent is often not in these perceived locations and humans simply do not have the ability to detect and determine where scent is to begin with. If we did we would not need the dog. Walk too many tracks with no scent and you can ruin a perfectly good trailing/ tracking dog.

In order to combat the chaos of the street, we have to bring chaos to training. This means realism and consequences. There must be both in order to truly learn life and death conditions and how to weave through them as safely as possible. If we always know the outcome of our training scenarios we simply become too complacent. If we only train when the conditions are good and favorable, we become at risk when conditions degrade. On the street, the consequences of making a mistake with a felony subject could mean your death. In staged training the consequences of making mistakes are usually nothing more than talking about it at the end of training over a beer. There has to be more at stake in training than a politically correct discussion and a beer. Simply put, tactical tracking requires a high degree of roughing it.

Location, Location, Location

The first part of reality based training for trailing work is to get rid of the fenced training area that you go to over and over again. You know the place with all of the grass, no distractions, and all of the known hiding spots. The problem with these types of locations is that the dogs know them better than you do and they really do not need to work to find what they are looking for.

Once the rudimentary skills of tracking/trailing are discovered, all training should be conducted in similar places to where you work. If you work in a busy urban beat with lots of houses, privacy fences, concrete streets, and people on every corner, training in a plowed cornfield or grass football gridiron becomes meaningless. You might start in a grassy field, but if you are not prepared for the street you have no business trailing there. This is tantamount to having a new police recruit on his or her first day of the academy work a real bank robbery. That would not happen in the normal course of police business, and plowed cornfields should not happen in the normal course of police trailing/ tracking training. Simply put, where you work is where you train. Get your dog familiar with the geography of your beat during trailing training and you will go a long way to capturing suspects there later.

Working in real conditions does not mean that we start at the peak of the day when there are massive amounts of distractions and the weather is not conducive to training; e.g. hot and dry. The best time to introduce the K9 to trailing in an urban environment is during the later evening or early morning hours when the citizenry is less of an impact. The proper *Tiered Ladder of Progressive Training* should be environmental exposure in times of relatively low human activity with low levels of complexity. If the business park district is a frequent place of felony tracks, the worst time to train for that place—when just beginning—is during the middle of the day when everything is open and at full tilt operation. The first exposure should be after hours with little or no distracting humans and by running short trails with relatively easy productive sources of odor. The human distraction odor in the area is what I refer to as "grey odor" or scent that though olfactory "visible" to the dog is really peripheral; with the training subject scent eclipsing the grey because it is fresher. As the K9 gets better with trailing in relatively easy conditions the conditions should become more challenging.

Get Rid of the Bite Sleeve

Too much police patrol tracking/ trailing training I see revolves around going to a relatively clean area and throwing a tracklayer out there hiding behind a building wearing a bite sleeve. The dog runs one hundred yards and around the corner of the building, right up to the bite, and the training is done. Does this sound familiar? How often does that happen on the street? More importantly, what happens when the dog runs around the corner into the presence of a couple of uninvolved civilians out for a stroll? You and I both know what is going to happen and this is the problem with always trailing into a bite sleeve. The bite can turn on and off in real conditions fairly easily so I do not see the need for a bite at the end of every track. If the bite is used a motivator or reward for the track, the dog will generally become quite the opportunist. Because the "reward" is the bite, the K9 will have a propensity to bite given the first opportunity, and this often means anyone the dog runs into. This is a very bad training method and fraught with liability. The key to good training is ensuring the K9 is truly scent discriminating and not jumping tracks to a target of opportunity.

After working with patrol dogs and tracking/ trailing training for fifteen years, I have discovered that the average patrol K9 digs biting and they rarely have to be encouraged to do so. As a matter of fact, I see more problems with call-offs than I do with initiating the bite. So why is the bite so often used for tracking training? I think the answer is simple: Motivation, Testosterone, and Myths about tracking.

1. Many handlers and trainers without much experience working and training trailing/ tracking dogs look at the bite as the fastest way to get the K9 to track and then use it as a crutch. The bite is so exciting for the dog that it is the quickest way to elicit a response.

2. The second reason, testosterone, is related to that of the handler or trainer. Though bite work/ apprehension often results in some of the least amount of yearly deployments, it is often the single most trained for deployment. Of course training is

a requirement for the liability aspect of it, but frankly, I think that one of the big reasons people work so much with apprehension training is that is fun and exciting. Unfortunately, if you make the bite the reward, with all of your tracking/ trailing training you may very well end up with an indiscriminate biter in the middle of your real trails; this means biting almost anyone in the way and that is a liability no department should have. I believe that an indiscriminate biter on the track should not be specifically left to the felony tracks but should not track at all. The danger is far too great to the public.

3. The third reason is often the most misunderstood, and in reality a myth: The dog will protect the handler on the track. I have covered this many times in the past, in various articles for our host *K9 Cop Magazine* and in my book *Tactical Tracker Teams*, but I have to go over it here once again. The simple fact of the matter is that when the K9 is attached to the handler by a long lead, the K9's offensive and defensive capabilities are completely nullified and the handler cannot draw a weapon and engage effectively while trying to manage the dog. If the handler gets surprised at the end of the track by a suspect intent on doing them harm, it means the handler got too close and probably did not read the proximity alerts the dog gave before they got there. Because the handler is attached, the dog cannot react fast enough to save either and they both may become victims. The best tactic is to learn and train for proximity alerts, stop; and plan before approaching the suspect. See *Tactical Tracker Teams; Coverman.*

The ultimate and major problem with always running into a bite at the end of the track is that it usually becomes what the handler and trainer are concentrating on and not the subtle body language clues that the dog throws when they begin to get close to the subject. If we only concentrate on the conclusion then we miss the components of the trail that might just save our lives; because we will always have a tendency to rush head long into threats. Trailing/tracking is muscle memory training just like any other form of physical training. If we rush in at the end of the trail in training, we will rush into the end of the trail on a felony search.

I recommend using a tug, ball, or simple praise as the reward. Concentrate on rewarding when a successful call-out is made after a good proximity alert in training. The reward, if thrown, should be in such a way that the dog dos not concentrate on the handler and lose focus on the subject of the trail. In essence, the source pays off in a similar fashion to detection training: Pay on sniff, or in the case of the proximity alert, pay on alert, and later "pay on alert" with call out.

Of course, training will have to incorporate K9 deployment for an apprehension, but this type of training should really be done once the K9 team is very proficient in all other forms of the felony trail.

Reality Based Scenarios

If the K9 team is working on felony trail training, then basic trailing and scent discrimination should already be solid. It is at this time that we begin to introduce scenarios and conditions that mimic real cases. This is really rather simply and a matter of imagination more than anything else. The handler/trainer must only consider the cases where the K9 might be deployed for trailing/tracking: Car bailouts, burglary suspects hopping fences, robberies, etc. Try to mimic the conditions and potential suspect actions for the training. This takes time, planning, and usually several people to properly organize, but I am telling you: a little extra work with reality in mind now will stock pile the suspects caught on the street later. In urban environments a good number of suspects don't simply hide in some bushes somewhere. They climb on roofs, break and enter into other houses, run home, or call friends and wait for a pick up. It is crucial that these types of conditions enter into the training set-up.

Some of the best training areas for these types of scenarios are abandoned military housing areas, defunct subdivisions, and abandoned warehouse areas. If you take the time to look in your beat, you might be surprised by what you find. Take the time to meet and talk to property owners/managers about what you are training for and how it might benefit the community; and perhaps the property itself one day. I've found the vast majority of property managers and owners tend to be very supportive of K9 efforts, especially when they find out that it might translate to a reduction in trespass and burglaries due to suspects being captured more often.

I will outline a scenario that I use often for our police training here and abroad.

Attempted Burglary

This is one that happens all the time and in just about every beat in every city. The usual suspects looking for a quick way to make ends meet by entering into someone else's property when they are not there. These crimes, though often opportunistic, often have a small amount of pre-planning. The suspect will usually case the joint for a little while to see what the general activity in and around the area might be. This usually involves walking the perimeter, checking darkened areas and places most passersby cannot view. This translates to scent pools and contact odor in and around the scene other than just the point of entry. This is significant because many handlers do not take into consideration all of the contact and scent pool odor of the subject prior to the crime taking place. They often misinterpret the dog's interest in such things as distraction and thus correct them off the odor in the process. A burglar trail is often far more than running immediately from the scene to a completely new area. If they spent a lot of time around the scene prior to the burglary or attempt thereof, the dog will have interest in that odor and those places where it might be found in concentration. In other words, it may take a little time to get out of the scene.   You won't know what your dog will do until you practice it.

Have a good trail layer go to a predetermined house, warehouse, or business suitable for training, and have them go through the gyrations of casing and hiding in darkened areas around the location while cars drive by, manipulating windows and doors, etc. Once they have laid enough cover scent in and around the area, have them choose a point of entry and make it as real as possible. Simulate the "suspect" being scared off by security or patrol and then age the trail out to a typical response time for K9; ten to thirty minutes or so.

When you run these scenarios for the first few times, run them like the "Tiered Ladder of Progressive Training" cited above. The first scenarios should be relatively simple, with low contamination, no distractions, and be relatively short in distance. We need to pay the dog fast for good work to help build familiarity and commitment to the trail. Slowly increase the complexity of the scenarios as the dog gets better at the job.

When the K9 is brought to the scene for the first time, I advocate taking the time to let your dog take a break and familiarize itself with the scents and things in the area of the immediate crime scene. I call this a *scent inventory* and it should be done with your Coverman (armed back-up) in tow and ready to go. I have jumped many suspects who were hiding in the perimeter when I was in the process of getting my dog ready. There is nothing worse than having to manage the dog when not being ready to deal with a suspect. The scent inventory is usually nothing more than a short walk around the outer perimeter of the activity at the scene that allows the K9 a moment to catalog al of the things in its work area prior to a start. This time is very important and I chalk it up to one of the cornerstones of my trail starts. Not only can the dog empty itself and be ready to work, but it can stretch its legs a bit prior to a big work out and because it was not rushed into the job, it will, perhaps, perform just a little bit better.

I like to have the trailing harness already on the dog as it exits the car and my trailing long lead in hand so the only thing I must do to go to work is switch from collar to harness with the trailing lead. Make sure that you stay alert to the dog's body language on that perimeter. As you move around, your dog may wind the subject or catch the trail scent out of the area and react to it. If you are unprepared for this, you may miss it completely or worse, correct your dog for a perceived distraction. Do this too much and your dog may leave that trail when you start it later.

The trail of a subject spooked from a scene is usually fear based, and those pheromones create a brighter scent picture for the K9. With or without a scent article at the start, these trails are attractive to patrol dogs and they can detect them from quite a distance. The physical reaction to such a trail is often a strong pull to source and an attempt to follow above and beyond what the K9 might normally do. Simply put, the drive for the trail is more single minded and stronger.   If a patrol dog detects such a trail and really wants it, it may be best to buckle the dog on the harness and see what you get. Fear and other emotional scents appear to be fleeting and do not last as long as the actual human trail. Take advantage of it if you find it.

If my K9 walked his perimeter with no fanfare and we are ready to work, I bring him back to the location the suspect was last known to have been and control my scene. If there are people milling about, I like to manage their sight, sound, and scent picture as much as possible for the K9's sake. If there is too much activity it may be too much of a distraction and the K9 may have a tough time isolating a suspect trail. The way I manage the scene is to put all of my people at the scene in the area of what I call the "Path of Most Resistance", or the place a suspect probably could not have gone, such as through a wall. I do this because when too many people stand on top of your suspect scent trail the dog may have difficulty finding it. Getting people out of the way helps immensely.

The next thing I do is "walk" my dog by my officers and people at the scene so he has an idea that they are there in the first place. This helps quite a bit when these people have been walking outside of the start area and have created their own scent trails that are now fresher tails on top of the older suspect's. The thought process being that if the K9 knows the person is present in the area they are less likely to follow that improper trail. This style of start has been coined "Missing Member" and was first written about in 1950 in a *Boy's Life Magazine* article written on police bloodhounds by Jim Kjelgaard. It does not always work but it does enough that I use this step every time.

The last step is crucial and timing is very important. This is the start of the trail on the scent article. Now, some of you may be wondering what kind of scent article do I have if it was an attempted burglary and nothing was left behind? That's' easy actually, anything the subject touched or handled such as a windowsill, doorknob, or fence. Again, in reality-based scenarios we must run them like they are real so it is imperative to have your Coverman ready to go and at your hip and prepared to defend you.

As mentioned before, fear scent or any emotional scent is a stronger target odor for dogs than any other, and if your timing to the scene was good, there is a great chance that the K9 will be attracted to the potential entry points for the burglary with no prompting. Your entry point, tool marks, etc. is now your scent article. The other scent factor that comes into play here is simple human contact odor. If the entry point was not handled by anyone else, the mere presence of the suspects scent from the hand, with or without gloves, is more attractive to the dog's nose than human blown odor in the area from simple proximity. The dog should naturally gravitate to hand odor.

So, the key to the "scent article" start in this type of scene is to have the dog harnessed and ready to go when you approach. Watch the dog's nose and if it appears to be suddenly interested in something and moving towards that location, be prepared to give the start command to trail as soon as it hits it. I do not like the downing at the start of a track in the immediate vicinity of the article or start point. Nine times out of ten, the K9 has the trail when you get into the area. Stop your dog at this point and you may be correcting them off the trail and the scent article. It is important to understand that dogs process odors as fast as we can define colors with our eyes. Dogs catalog every odor present at a scene in a matter of seconds. When we spend too long preparing them for a search in the presence of such odor, we are actually demotivating the search.

When the dog begins, it will usually want to canvas the immediate starting area quite a bit. The handler must be prepared for some starts and stops in the immediate vicinity. Everything the suspect touched or handled may become a target for the dog and you have to be

A red lens is a good option when using a head mounted lamp on real deployments at night.

patient enough to let this happen. The K9 may also want to cruise the perimeter of the site or building and if you pay attention, you may see that is closely resembles what a person might do while casing the joint. Again, be patient and take your time. If you rush your dog or tell them to get to work, they may do just that... right onto another track... not your suspects'.

The entire time the handler is working, the Coverman should be at the non-gun hip of their handler and within arm's reach. This distance is crucial for non-verbal communication, and in case the Coverman has to pull the handler out of a danger zone—in an emergency. If it is a felony search, I recommend gun(s) drawn and ready to use. Depending on the ambient light conditions, I do not advocate the use of flashlights at this point. If the handler can read the K9 well enough, then the light will only serve to target the team from a distance and destroy the night vision of the handler. Night vision can take up to twenty minutes to return. The vast majority of the bad situations that I got myself into were when flashlights illuminated my presence and let the suspect know I was coming from a long distance. Now this may be a matter of departmental policy and personal choice, but consider keeping the Streamlights holstered unless they are really needed. If a light is absolutely necessary, try using a Petzel head-mounted, low illumination read light in LED. This casts a very casual light—usually only enough to read the dog at a lead length but confusing to people seeing it from a distance. It is not expected and still may allow you to surprise your suspect if he happens to see it.

Once the K9 has processed the scene it will usually work toward the fringe of the pool scent of the suspect in order to locate an exit trail—if one was not readily scent visible. The handler will know this has occurred because the dog will want to speed up and the meandering and checking of different things in the area of the crime will have slowed or stopped altogether. It is important that you do not speed up too fast as you want to. The dog will be taking up at least 50% of your load allowing you to run faster and easier. Your Coverman or supporting people will not have that luxury. Furthermore, speed may get you killed by running right into the lap of the suspect; because you were too busy trying to keep up, and not observant enough to see a proximity alert from the dog; signaling that you were close.

When trailing on a felony suspect I do not worry about each and every nook and cranny along the trail that might hide a suspect. A trail/track is not like a building search; perhaps with or without a scent trail. In a building search, you are clearing room/area to room/area and the dog often does not have anything to work with—right off the bat. This type of start and stop work is manageable with the dog because it does not have a clear target yet. A trail or track, on the other hand, does have a clear target and the dog knows where it is. If you constantly stop the dog for every perceived threat, your dog will quit or find something else to conveniently search for; each and every time you restart after a stop. If you start and stop on each and every potential threat location, you will demotivate the dog significantly. The dog, if trained properly to this point, will let you know when you are close. You simply have to have trained yourself to read the alert and react accordingly. Tracking a trailing is very dangerous for just this reason. Once the K9 is a solid trailing dog and scent discriminates well, these trails may become fairly easy and the dog can literally drag you into a firefight if you are not prepared for it.

The juxtaposition is that, on one hand, you want the dog to find the subject and on the other, you have to do it safely. This may not be low and slow, the way the human sight based mind normally needs to operate. There is a fine balance point in this endeavor and the handler has to be very savvy at reading his or her dog in order to allow it the proper speed to work unencumbered, but in such a way that the suspect does not have the advantage of an ambush or surprise. The dog is the great equalizer but it is up to the handler to be able to utilize the tool properly by reading it well.

Through all of this, the Coverman or cover officers must be able to work as team without shutting down the dogs drive for the trail. This is like a choreographed dance and if you do not practice it with scenario-based training that is lifelike, you will not be prepared for the dance. If you are not prepared for the dance then you will step on toes. Stepping on toes on a felony track might get you or others killed. It's time to practice.

As the trail goes on, it is important that the Coverman or some other team member be able to call out the direction of travel, interest points, and things that might have to be checked later. This also takes practice and if a team has not worked together before, communication is often the first thing to suffer. If real time GPS devices are available this is one of the best ways for a command post or dispatch to track the K9 teams progress.

The last part of a good scenario-based practice trail is the ending. The ending should be creative, and by using past cases as examples, it is possible to really put together some interesting problems that require team work and coordination in order to gain an apprehension without incident.

Several Potential Endings

1. Proximity alert to a hiding location such as a shed. Stop on the proximity alert, call in a quick perimeter, and engage with a suspect call out.

2. Trail to an apartment complex and a door of interest. Call in reinforcements and conduct a knock and talk.

3. Trail to a hiding spot where the suspect breaks and runs into a loose perimeter. Switch from trailing to open area off lead—air scent search if safe to do so.

4. Trail to an ambush that was set up in advance to sorely tax the dog's ability to detect proximity and hash out the consequences. I like to do this with Simmunitions or paintball guns for realism.

The key here is to vary the trail and the ending. Challenge the dog's nose as well as the team's ability to coordinate the search and respond to the threat if one is encountered. If you do not train this way, you will not be prepared for the real thing and that could be tragic.

Lastly, try to video record these practice trails with a Point of View, (POV), Camera system. GoPros are great and unobtrusive when mounted on the chest of the handler. There is also a great video glasses system, (PivotHead) that incorporates different lenses coupled with an 8 GB, 1080px video camera. It is impossible to clearly remember every subtle nuance of a search, and the beauty of POV video is that you can record the event for later dissection in a similar way to how professional sports teams go over games and practice. If you have several videos going at one time: Handler, Coverman, suspect, then you have the ability to put together a very informative training session that could prove invaluable to your department later.

A different type of recording system that is chest harness mounted on Frank Wagner at a training course in Dusseldorf, Germany.

The author wearing a pair of video recording glasses prior to a training trail.

The Tao of Trailing

Chapter Twelve
The Trouble with Age

"If the dog has trouble with another dog, behind a fence while trailing past it, switching from grass to concrete, or choosing the person that matches the scent article, does age of the trail really matter?"

Think of scent as varying shades of grey mist. The fresher the scent, the blacker the grey mist. With your eyes, the black appears easily but as the shade lightens; it becomes more difficult to isolate what you are trying to see. If there is glare or worse, other colors of mist mingling with the grey, focus becomes difficult. How soon one locates light grey mist is directly proportionate to how badly one wants to find it and the ability to think through distractions.

If while you are looking diligently for a light shade of grey, a colorful butterfly flits past your field of vision and you stop to look because of its beauty, you may have difficulty returning to your search for grey or forget about the grey altogether. This is what separates those who are focused from those who are distracted. Those who distract easily will at times never find the grey, and the times that they do are often those times when there are few to no distractions. Old scent is grey scent in the dogs mind. In order to find the grey, the dog must have low or no level of distraction. Low to no level of distraction is related to how we maintain dogs and their natural mindset.

Ultimately, this is not so much a training problem as it is an acquisition issue. This boils down to proper testing of the puppy or dog before it is purchased. Too often in the trailing world, puppies and dogs are chosen based on the following wrong reasons:

1. Breed "Bloodhounds are the only dogs to follow a two week old trail."

2. Emotion "Oh! That puppy is the cute one and he has to be the best because he was the first of the litter to come to me!"

3. Choice of the breeder "This breeder really is the best in the world and she knows her stuff. She promised me she was picking the best dog for me!"

4. Appearance "I always wanted a bi-color!"

5. Last pup in the litter Enough said.

Number three gets my goat pretty badly... In November of 2013, I was working on arranging for the testing of some hound puppies in Europe. One of the long distance problems I encountered was that I just had surgery and could not do it myself. I asked a couple of my trainers in Germany if they could test in my stead and they agreed. The arrangements were being made with the breeder over the course of about a month, tons of emails and calls, when one of my trainers detected storms on the horizon. He told me he did not think the breeder was going to have any puppies for us to test other than perhaps two of the original seven. I contacted the breeder myself and she emailed me something to the effect of this: "I have two that I think are the best, and anyway, you should know that all puppies of this breed are suitable for work: it's just getting the right personality for the right person". This is breeder speak for: "I really have to make sure I sell all my puppies and people already put money down." I see this issue with far more hound breeders than GSD or Malinois. I think this is because there really are no professional hound breeders who specialize in police, military, or SAR work. Ultimately, the primary goal is homing the puppies. This same thing happens to a lot of handlers looking for their first really good working dog. They do all the right things and research; but because it is their first working dog, they often fall for this line rather than walking away from the litter. When in doubt, and if the breeder insists that any handler buy what that breeder picks, rather than allowing testing, my advice is to walk. Ten years of doggy baggage because of a bad breeder pick is not worth it. Avoid this trap.

This may seem like a strange issue when talking about how well dogs follow aged scent but as far as I am concerned, it is probably one of the least thought of issues, but the number one reason: dogs can be genetically predisposed to distraction.

I prefer buying all working dogs as puppies simply due to the fact that any adult dog or green young dog may have social and potentially bad handling baggage that is going to come with it. Any social or handling mistakes will be part of the green or adult dog and nothing will make those problems go away completely. Yes, training and management can make things better, but this is a just a mask and the problem can appear again later, and if that is during work, it is a big problem.

The usual baggage I see with adult and green young dogs are:

1. Kennel syndrome—the dog is concerned about everything because it never made it out of the kennel while growing up

2. Fear of people, places, and things due to poor exposure and socialization.

3. Too much attachment to just one person

4. Possession aggression issues over food, people, and things.

99% of these issues are all related to breeders or vendors who really do nothing with the dog other than the bare minimum. This is definitely not indicative of all breeders and vendors. There are really good people who sell adult and green dogs and have done all of the necessary socialization and environmental exposure before they sold the dog. In my opinion, there simply are not enough of these good people.

On the other hand, if I buy my dogs at seven to eight weeks of age after careful testing, the adult dog is really going to be a mirror of those early tests and ultimately the socialization and environmental exposure I did with it. In short, the pup if genetically sound, and having passed all my tests, will be a very focused dog for work and not subject to distraction in any significant way.

Testing puppies includes reactions to all manner of stimuli and in particular, hunt and prey drive.

Genetics, health, nutrition, and proper social and environmental upbringing are the determining factors when it comes to the level of focus the dog will have when working; and ultimately how it deals with aged trails. These same issues will also make or break a trailing dog in all conditions. My bottom line is buying the right dog: first and foremost. If I have the right dog, I have a better chance of following an older trail.

To begin with, I never concentrate on aged trails with our working dogs anyway; if they have any problems at all with surface transitions, animal or human distractions, or scent discrimination. I want a dog that ignores distractions, seamlessly works from soft surface to concrete and does not switch to fresher human trails. Even a very focused, single-minded pup will have problems with distractions if it has not been exposed to them. If the dog has any problems with any of these training elements at all, an aged trail is irrelevant because the training deficiency will now simply be exacerbated. If anything, concentration on aged trails occurring with these problems still in effect will create worse problems. The handler will create a dog that will pay more attention to the guidance of the handler versus really working the scent. When there are distraction and focus problems, aged trails will only become more difficult. Solve the basic problems before moving on to the most difficult one of them all.

As I wrote in *K9 Trailing; The Straightest Path*, human scent trails that age are stressed, moved, and destroyed by many natural and environmental conditions that vary each and every day, without consistency. No two days, let alone two hours, are alike. This is one of the problems I have with trailing/tracking certifications that push the age envelope too much: it is impossible for humans to determine what a viable age is from condition to condition. This is because we can't detect our own scent and we cannot know how long it lasts—no matter how fresh it is. We can only go by what we see in the dog. If the tests or methods used to determine viability of age are known trails, then it is very possible that the dog was guided by someone who knows where the trail or ending is. If this happens, then the perception of trail age viability will always be skewed or incorrect. Unfortunately, it is just this issue that leads to trail certifications and tests to qualify working handlers that are not reliable, let alone possible, in most cases.

My process for determining the age that is viable for testing or certification is based on averages and double blind trails. When I started this business, I believed that dogs were very reliable for trails over twenty-four hours. Life on the street with my first working bloodhound, working hundreds of real cases led me to question that position. When I began to embrace double blind testing, or testing like real deployments, I learned that my expectations rarely if ever met my new test results. Over the course of about eighteen months I whittled down my expectations to average results that I was seeing in average dogs across the board.

After testing my own dogs, I tested and worked with other dogs all over the US from the west coast to east coast, and also now, dogs in Europe. I found that none of the dogs EVER were able to do what their handlers expected in trails over eighteen hours old; much the same experience that I had, personally. Some handlers were humbled by the tests and actively sought ways to increase their ability through better testing, adopting double blind testing standards, while an equal number ignored the results and simply adopted the phrase "Double-Blind Testing" and continued to say their dogs could reliably run trails in excess of twenty-four hours in age. These handlers, rather than recognizing the truth and adjusting accordingly, decided to lie about it. This is a shame and very self-serving. Their own personal situation is apparently more important than the public they profess to serve

At this stage of my career, November 2013, I think I can honestly say that there is not another handler/trainer who works with more trailing dogs around the world than I do. I am not bragging, I am just stating what I think is a fact. The trailing world is relatively small in comparison to the rest of the dog world and it is easy to see who is doing what and where they are doing it, especially in today's digital world. My opinion is not based on theory or simple personal experience with one dog. My opinion is based on working and testing hundreds of dogs.

My testing standards were very simple and straightforward for most age related issues. I did not even throw urban conditions into the mix for reportedly advanced teams. I must say that my tests were never meant to be part of a thesis or scientific experiment. In hindsight, my tests evolved with time and I did not keep the records that I should have. Now, I wish I had standardized my process better and documented everything with a higher degree of detail and accuracy. I truly hope my amateurish approach might be an example for someone with real scientific experience: to honestly test the aged trail phenomenon that so many in the SAR world embrace. Should this come to be, I also hope that the scientist or researcher who tackles this project is completely unbiased and has nothing to do with the dog world or dog community. I believe this is the only way to maintain any degree of objectivity. I have discovered that even scientists, like every day people, can be prone to finding the answers they wanted in the first place.

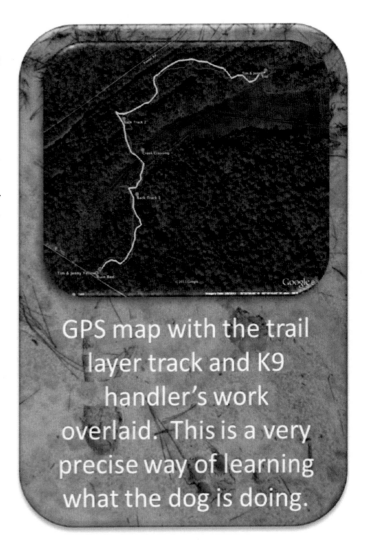

GPS map with the trail layer track and K9 handler's work overlaid. This is a very precise way of learning what the dog is doing.

My Evolving Testing Standards

1. Soft surface such as woods and grass, with little to no human contamination. Four-hour-old tests had one surface transition and a human or animal distraction.

2. The trail layer carried a GPS and one was assigned to the dog team. Many of the trails were video recorded—but not all.

3. Nobody on the trail with the dog team, including the evaluator, knew the direction of the trail, the route, or the end point. All trails were a minimum of one-half to two miles, dependent on the age of the trail.

4. Most trails were run in the evening or early morning to provide the best scent trail conditions possible for the dog. An average of one hour to two hours was allotted for completion for all trails six hours and older.

5. Trails at four hours had a thirty-minute to one hour time limit at a distance of ½ to ¾ mile.

6. Trails up to one hour old were all no more than ½ mile in length and had a twenty to thirty minute time limit.

7. Distances were all approximate because it was impossible for the evaluator to monitor the trail layer and maintain a double blind condition. Similarly, all times could not be exact.

8. All tests were evaluated by other trainers or myself.

9. All handlers who attempted trails in excess of twelve hours old were experienced handlers certified elsewhere for trails of twenty-four hours.

Test Results

1. Trails forty-eight hours in age could not be proven at all and not a single handler has ever passed this test. As the years have gone by, fewer handlers agree to take this test; however-word has spread that the chances of passing it are slim to none. Other less than scrupulous handlers, who don't know this test or me, have falsely stated that someone did pass it and that I refused to publicize it or pay the price of success. Of course, these people could not name the handler, date or time of the "successful" trail.

2. The price stems from my 2.2 and 2 Challenge that goes back to 2004, when I first thought to make a public challenge to any handler to try a 48 hour old trail, two miles long, and win two thousand dollars. The rules were simple, GPS of both the trail layer and the dog team and the test is double blind. The handler or anyone with the handler could not know who the subject was, where the trail was, or where it ended. The conditions were super easy for normal trailing, primarily soft surface of woods or grasslands.

3. I proposed this challenge because of the sheer number of handlers in the USA, and now abroad, who routinely report and brag about their dogs reliability on trails even older. Some handlers professed reliably working trails out to as many as ten years! This professed success created intrigue and envy in the hearts of many new handlers. Worse yet were a few people in the scientific and law enforcement community using less then solid testing standards that backed up these claims. One trailing expert, who also happened to have a PhD, stated on her web site home page that bloodhounds were capable of following trails ten years old! Lo and behold, everyone back in those days was running trails at least three days old.

4. When I put out my challenge on the World Wide Web, I had many handlers who promised to take me up on the test—even going so far as to set the appointment date and time. Almost every one of these people backed out in the end and did not make their appointment. Not a single handler has taken the test in the last two years. I had even more handlers who denounced me as a pariah and harbinger of shame to the Search and Rescue world for extolling such obvious blasphemy. Needless to say, I was not popular and still am not in many circles; simply for my insistence that dogs are not reliable on trails over twenty-four hours or that their dogs cannot do what they are reported to be able to accomplish with relative ease.

5. In the early days of my lonely, conservative position, I had few trailing SAR friends. On the other hand, most handlers in the military and police world supported my position completely and were pleased that someone in the trailing world was finally challenging all of the hype. Happily, I can now report that times are changing and the numbers of SAR people who support my theory are becoming far more numerous. This is due to several reasons, but one of the most important is the dismal performance of many trailing teams working cases of extreme age. Not only did they fail in the vast majority of cases where they were deployed, but they also, in many instances, led investigations 180 degrees the wrong way on life and death cases. There were even a few cases where "suspects" who were convicted of murder or other high crimes were later released because of advances in DNA evidence.

6. Instead of a magical K9s solving crime and saving people after all other means of investigations failed, we have seen that in most instances, these old trail dogs were just... dogs and what they were reportedly able to do was outrageously overstated.

7. Since 2005 only one dog team has passed one of my trailing tests over twelve hours of age. The GPS trail of both the dog team and trail layer were almost a match. This trail was approximately ¾ of a mile, and uniquely, primarily hard surface. The weather conditions were misting rain for the entire 24 hours prior to the test. Over 98% of the GPS trails of other dog teams never came close to the subject GPS trail.

8. Trails over six hours old and one mile long: Only two teams have passed this test since 2008. These trails were almost all hard surface and run after 10:00pm in very humid, cool conditions. All trails in soft surface over 6 hours were not successful.

9. Trails at four hours, ½ to ¾ of a mile approximately. Mostly soft surface with at least one hard surface transition and at least one fresh human or animal odor distraction: twelve handlers have passed this test.

10. Trails at approximately one hour old. All soft surfaces such as woods or grass, no known human distractions. No known domestic dog distractions: Fifty-seven dog teams have passed this test since 2009. Roughly one-hundred-twenty since 2005. I say roughly because my record keeping was not good in the early years. Interesting, the success rate for this test is about 50% for first time applicants and about a 80% success rate for those who took the test a second time.

Unfortunately, the aged trail syndrome seems always to be the determining factor when so many evaluate trailing dogs. This is very discouraging for many handlers who honestly suspect that dogs may not be reliably capable of the elevated time frames, and who also have perfectly good working trailing dogs to begin with. These people, who selflessly slave away at producing a K9 that can perform in a variety of real world conditions, fall short when they are tested by others on trails in excess of twenty-four hours in age. Why do they fall short? Primarily because these handlers only follow the dog when it is truly working scent and not just running. They have really learned to read their dogs, and not simply follow because the dog is moving. They do not follow the dog when it is obvious it has no scent. When they encounter these old trail tests and fail them, they are told that they simply have not reached the upper echelon of "Trailingdom" and obviously need to work harder. The root of the problem is not the dog or the handler. It's the testing process that most organizations have, that test and certify trails in excess of twenty-four hours in age. The tests are not double blind, the evaluator or other people following the handler and dog on the test know where the trail is, or where the subject went to, and people who play the game pass the test. Those who don't, don't. It is really that simple.

Worse yet are the test trails that have the same subject trail and multiple trailing dogs running the test. The first dog has the hardest job and usually will fail unless guided by the handler, evaluator, or both. All of the subsequent dogs that run this same trail have an easier go of it and often pass. Why? It is simple, because they followed the dog trail that ran before in a completely acceptable age of trail time frame. I have had many trainers who practice this method of training and testing argue with me that because the test dogs are purportedly "scent" discriminating, they therefore could not be following the dog that ran before. The other equally impossible argument is that because the dog had a scent article, it had to be the person who is at the end of the trail. My question is: How can any human know this? What testing process proved it? How is it possible to know what scent the dog is following? To my knowledge, there is no man-made machine that can detect and quantify human scent on the trail. There is definitely not a human alive who can do this supernatural feat. My position is that this is simply human rationalization for an event that desperately needed rationalization to overcome the common sense that should have been considered in the first place. I have never understood why something so simple can be so incredibly distorted. That is until I realized that the root of the problem is: that to admit the obvious would be tantamount to admitting everything that had been trained and tested for before was false. This is not something anyone can do easily, especially if the falsehood had been lived, practiced, and taught for years. I know this because I was on this side of the ball field in the beginning part of my career. I had to have the same "Come to Jesus". If I can do it, so can others.

Currently, my belief is that the average trailing dog is most effective on trails that are under six hours old—in variable surface conditions. I believe that there is little to no reliability in trailing dogs working trails older than twelve hours in age. Yes, there are dogs that can do this and sometimes well, but the key word is reliable. If a tool is not reliable for the work it is used for, then it was the improper tool. Trailing over twelve hours should not be expected to be fruitful. I think general deployment history over the course of the "trailing aged trail" phenomenon fad reflects my statement quite well. The fantastical stories of dogs finding things or corroborating evidence a couple of times a year in the newspaper are not an argument against this no matter how passionate one might feel about trailing dogs. The truth of the matter is dogs are just not finding people or even evidence in most of the aged trail deployments we hear about. Corroboration perhaps, but who is to say that the trail was truly corroborated other than the investigators who asked for it in the first place? Was the dog simply used to provide another nail in the coffin of a suspect investigation? It is my opinion that this, indeed, is sometimes the case.

This chapter may completely deflate some who are reading anything like it for the first time. It may anger others and the-next home for this book might be the burn pile. Others may simply wonder why would we use trailing dogs then; if they are only good for a trail a few hours old when all of the call outs are for cases over forty-eight hours? Well, the issue here is the solution made the problem we face. It was not too long ago in the total scheme of things when nobody thought about trailing dogs finding people who had been missing for days let alone 48 hours. The problem occurred when a couple of sensationalized cases broke on international news of dogs purportedly trailing after these time frames had elapsed, and people were found. Nobody really looked at the root cause for the find and simply assumed it was trailing aged scent. I think in most of these cases it was simply the dog being in the right place at the right time and no trail at all. But, because there was a news story, suddenly everyone wanted in on the action and an entirely new field of K9 work was developed… that was completely ineffective. Unfortunately, it was this phenomenon and its related hype that created the confidence in trailing dogs following trails of this age. The hype really created the need, not the other way around. In other words, people called for the trailing dogs at these ages because they were under the false impression that the dogs were viable there. You ask just about any average citizen with no dog experience about bloodhounds and usually the first thing they tell you about is that bloodhounds are the only dog that can track people down after many days have passed.

My feeling is that the solution simple: Stop continuing to try and fit a square peg into a round hole. It just won't work. There is no training that I have seen that makes a dog reliable following these older trails. The solution is admitting the truth and then reducing the expectations of those who need the dogs. It also requires a large amount of proper training. Those who are in need of tailing dogs need to be taught that the reliability factors are not just age, but also contamination and distraction. The keys to maximizing the trailing dog's potential is to minimize all three: age, contamination and distraction. More importantly, is the fundamental knowledge of the resources that are available. Responsible agencies that call for a search and rescue or police-trailing dog to hunt for an abducted child should know how the dogs work and what they are truly capable of. Trying to learn about a resource during an emergency is the wrong time. It's really that simple.

The Tao of Trailing

Chapter Thirteen
Scent Pools: Drowning Prevention

"How can man know incorporeal scent when all of our senses are honed to vision? We cannot, therefore we must leave this effort to others creatures that do and harness their effort. When the dog looks like it is working, it probably is, let go..."

Scent Pools

As they relate to trailing, are concentrations of human subject odor in the form of blown human gas, sloughed skin cells, and contact odor of a subject body part to an object.

Scent pools have probably destroyed more finds of suspects and missing persons than just about any other trailing situation. I say this from experience of being thoroughly embarrassed while working my own dogs in real cases. In the beginning, I simply was unaware of the fact that I was being embarrassed!

Scent pools have the curiously disturbing ability to create immediate excitement in the handler's mind that they might be getting close and shortly thereafter be followed by depression, because the handler thinks it must have been a critter when they don't make the find in a short time or that they may have lost the trail. I kind of equate it to an addict's cocaine high; the initial hit might be great but the aftermath is a nightmare.

The problem is that the scent pools can happen in a very large area, often times far away from the suspect; depending on wind and other environmental conditions. The other factor is that while the dog is working on the fringe of a large scent pool, or before it even gets there, that subject could move at a significant distance from the subject of the hunt, further complicating the work of the dog. There are also different types of scent pools based on the activity of the subject. The key to all situations is patience and recognizing the body language of the dog and not interfering unless you absolutely have to.

I will describe the various scent pools I have experienced and attempt to provide a series of remedial actions to solve them.

Notable Scent Pool Types:

Subject Present
1. High find
2. Hidden, buried, or submerged find
3. Building finds
4. Distraction find; too many people present

Subjects Not Present

1. The Start Of The Trail
2. Large amounts of physical subject contact odor, Physical Evidence
3. Backtracks, cross tracks
4. Vehicle pick—ups

Subjects Present

1. High finds

High finds like trees, balconies, and decks are super easy and should be part of normal training and they really take no special tactics or effort. Very high finds, on the other hand, can and do create surprises. To begin with, depending on the height and the wind, a handler could trail right up to a building with a person on top of it and never find them. The handler also might get relatively close to a building a subject is hiding on top of and the handler would never know to look out and up. Why? Because of the nature of human odor on very high finds.

I will give you my training-altering real case scenario and then I will examine the problem in detail. As a young K9 handler with little experience, I chased a guy in a housing area with very large apartments with multiple stories. I had a great trail from out of the area in relatively open ground into the apartment complex area. As we approached the complex, my hound air scented the subject briefly and followed the air scent to the left and behind me. Not understanding what happened, I thought he was air scenting the subject from behind us and I followed him. After about seventy-five yards, Ronin's air scent body language changed to nothing. No trail, no air scent, nothing. Furthermore, he seemed pretty perplexed and started howling. Again, not understanding what he was doing, I took this for being close and started frantically looking behind buildings and bushes. Ronin eventually took me back to the area where he started the air scent and repeated the process but in a slightly different direction. This went on for about ten minutes until I pulled him off, now believing it was a critter.

As sometimes happened on real cases, another officer would collar the bad guy and we would end up empty handed. Not a big deal: I was used to that experience by this stage in my game and finally understood that every trail was not a great one like advertised at the seminars. Still, I was always curious as to what my suspect did to elude my dog and I would visit him or her in jail.

I always started out these interviews the same way because most bad guys are suspicious of cops asking questions. "Hi! My name is Jeff and I am a K9 handler for the City. You may have noticed me with the floppy eared hound at some point? Don't worry, nothing you say will be used against you and this conversation is off the record and I promise not to ever bring it up."

At times, the suspect would simply tell me to "F" off and the conversation would end, but at other times, I would have guys like the man I am about to describe who would have a major case of diarrhea of the mouth. What he said was painful, but necessary for me to hear:

He started the topic of conversation by telling me that I had the stupidest dog on the force and I should be embarrassed. He then went on to say that he was up on the roof of the apartment building looking back on his track when he saw everything we did. Because he explained it so well, I knew he was not lying. Anyway, he went on to tell me how at one point I was directly below him and he had been very tempted to try and spit on me from above because both my dog and I were so oblivious to his presence. The conversation digressed and at one point, I was ready to hospitalize him but left instead.

Rather than blow it all off, I tried to set up the scenario in training and later added it to my *California Peace Officer Standards and Training, (POST), Course Outline K9 Trailing Outline*. My course was the first of its kind in California in 1998 and this case had an impact on making the school a reality.

You may have deduced what occurred after seeing the pictures and reading what I have already written but I am going to bore you with it regardless. This could save yours or someone else's life one day.

At very high points, three or more stories, the wind can often be very different than on the ground. After experimenting with smoke grenades, I noticed that the smoke rarely hit the ground below the grenade when lit off on high. Like the first picture in this chapter, the smoke drifted almost horizontally until slowly hitting the ground at some amazing distances. This was my first clue.

The next clue was my dog's body language. I ran practice trails to the building and really watched the dog. If the wind was coming back to the trail from the high point where the subject was hiding, my dog would exhibit an air scent alert each and every time with varying degrees of distance from the building. Sometimes only fifty yards or so but at others, 500, 600, and 700 yards away! Nowhere near the building! Without fail, because of the strong scent cone, my dog would abandon the trail in favor of the fresh direct scent. The problem was the width and breadth of the scent. It was wind dependent and sometimes as wide as fifty yards and other times only a few yards. The other problem was the cone was angled from very high to the ground and it was not a direct course to the subject. It was almost like a constant puff of scent magically appearing in shifting spots in and around the same area. If the spot drifted far away from the trail, my dog would eventually forget where the trail was in favor of all the fresh odor that led nowhere.

Smoke bomb simulating human scent as it rises then drifts horizontally out across from a high find. This scent can drift hundreds of yards away to deposit randomly on the ground.

The solution was my dog recovering and locating the trail again, or more importantly, me remembering where the trail was and dragging his happy ass back to it if he would not leave the fresh scent. What happened in the real case I wrote about was that we struggled so long and hard and I corrected my dog so much that he shut down and the trail did not exist anymore for those reasons alone. I should have been spit on; I was so annoyed with myself!

The cool thing was that once I ran Ronin across these trails a few more times, he figured out that the air scent was cool, but he would go back to the trail and go to the place the subject went in or up. He learned through experience that the trail would be the path back to the subject.

I had to help a bit with the early trails, though. If he got too hung up on the fresh spot of air scent, I would drag him forward and away from it, and cast him in the direction of the trail he abandoned. Without fail, I could get him back in the area and he would recover. We simply had to practice until he figured out the means to the end. My hounds were rather dense with this training and the nose was very hard to override. A baseball bat would have not made them leave the fresh odor. The shepherds I have trained, on the other hand, generally figured it out after the first trail and never made the same mistake again. This is that cool headed calculation I like from the pointy eared dogs... I just wish they had the same patient nose! We need to breed more Shounds.

On the other hand, it is important not to help the dog too soon. There is a very fine line between helping and guiding when it is not necessary. The dog has to have a little bit of time to try and work it out. This is not an impossible problem; just a difficult one. I do not like to take the K9 out of odor right away; rather, I try to give them some time to solve the problem on their own. The element that you should be concerned with is the interest level of the K9. If the dog is frantically looking for odor and working hard, give them time. You might be surprised when they work the pool to the fringe and grab the trail again working out of the area. Remember, the dog knows scent better than you.

If you help a dog when it is working hard and take it off what it was working, your move is tantamount to a correction. In other words, you are telling the dog it is wrong. It will not understand that you are moving it to something better, (and mayhap, you are not even doing that), it only understands that you are moving it when it was on odor. Be patient and take your time. Observation of good body language indicators is your guide.

I often tell my students that the proximity alert from very high finds might be the last thing the dog finds on the trail. I do this for two reasons: One, the dog may never make it to the very high find because of all I have explained. Two, the handler or dog might get killed while they circle around providing an easy target directly below the suspect. Think about this and then train with it. You need to know how your dog works this problem. Furthermore, when working any case that might involve criminals and proximity alerts, a good back-up is MANDATORY!

The back-up, also known as a Coverman is the handler's eyes and ears; the person who can take care of the handler if the crap hits the fan. Do not fool yourself, when you are on the end of a lead managing a dog, you will be useless as a tactical asset. Leave it to someone else. A good Coverman who practices with the dog will quickly learn the proximity alerts and act accordingly. But that training is for another day...

Buried, Hidden, or Submerged Find

These can be a big problem, because again, the handler may not recognize the proximity alert and subsequent scent pool work when the object of the search is not found quickly.

This problem is almost always rooted in bad training habits of helping the dog when it does not need it, when the handler sees or knows where the subject is. In much the same way a handler might try to help the dog work a shifting high-find scent pool when it is actively engaged in the search and has not begun to become distracted. If a handler hurries or moves the dog when it is close inside any scent pool situation, the handler is correcting the dog and the dog learns nothing. It is always best to try and allow the dogs to work out problems on their own as long as they are actively working.

What I see often in training situations with a scent pool: the K9 is working it, and the handler, knowing exactly where the subject is, is a handler who has a tendency to lead the dog in the direction of the subject rather than remaining neutral. This is the double-edged sword once again. The problem is that we see the dog's excitement to the scent pool, observe the hiding spot of the subject because we have far better eyesight than the dog and then make a dumb move like a pull on the lead. Dogs have very limited ability to differentiate color and they have extremely poor depth perception. Their eyesight seems best geared towards moving targets, where ours is exceptionally good at picking out details of stationary objects.

So, when the dog runs into the scent pool and begins to frantically engage it, we start to look around and lo and behold, there lies the subject behind a bushy bush and a tree. We can see him or her well because of the color patterns that enable us to perceive the difference in the background. The dog is looking too, but instead of seeing something that stands out, because the silhouette is broken and fused with objects around and in front of the subject, the dog only sees a blob or an extension of the hiding spot. Dogs can rarely see the difference, thus continue to work the scent pool into stronger scent patterns, hopefully, zeroing in on the subject in the process.

Try to picture scent as color and the closer to the subject the dog gets, the darker the scent color becomes. I think, in a way, this is how the dog is working odor and it takes time to sort out all of the scent patterns and wind their way in. If we constantly drag them to the subject when they are working hard, we are effectively guiding them and they do not learn from the experience.

Hidden, walled, or buried subjects have a tendency to create a frantic circling reaction in the dog and depending on the wind currents and the terrain, the scent pools can be very large. The size and shape of the pool is also age dependent. Think of a can of Coke just barely lying on its side; the soda drips out of the mouth and pools at the base of the can. As more soda pours out, the can tips more and the entire process takes about thirty minutes. The direction, width, and breadth of the pool of soda will be based on several things: pitch of the surface, unevenness of the surface, obstacles in the way, breeze, and turbulence by outside influences, and ultimately age. As the soda spills onto the surface more and more, the pool becomes larger. The ultimate size is really limited by the source of the soda. When the can is empty or moved, the pool begins to settle and evaporate.

I think this is a really good way to visualize human scent production as it relates to a scent pool with a subject present. If the subject leaves, the pool begins to dwindle and evaporate. The bottom line is that the longer a person stays in one location, the larger the scent pool becomes and I have seen dogs hit on them from over 250 yards away. If a dog begins to work a 250-yard long scent pool, it may take some time to work into it. Patience is a must and if you take the dog out of it, and the dog reacts as if it is a correction, that particular subject will have to be found by someone else.

K9 reacting to buried scent pool to the left of source and then working into it.

In training, take care to remain neutral if you figure out the location of the subject before your dogs does. Pretend it is a game that you want to stretch out to the last minute and that all of that time is agonizingly delicious. Do nothing but follow and watch. If your dog wants to run to the furthest edge of the pool and work back in, let it and be happy that it is working. We do not have the nose doing the work so it is not a good idea to presume that we know more than the dog. There is a reason the dog ran back to the edge and started all over. Think of it like a particularly difficult knot you have to undo and then retie. It starts out very complicated and difficult to decipher by simply looking at it until you untie the first couple of lengths. But, as you do this, you remember that in order to retie it, you must remember each and every step you have just undone and what you untied must be retied later to complete your task. If you do not remember the technique you just destroyed, the root of the knot will remain a mystery.

I have watched dogs work scent pools and have seem the gears whizzing as the dog frantically circles to and fro. They start on the edge and try to work in towards the source but something may happen to the odor as it drifts from the subject, almost like a stream flowing around a boulder. As the stream rushes around the boulder, the water eddies and swirls in the little pocket behind the boulder, and new mini bodies of water are created. Scent swirling behind a building or large tree may create a similar effect and when the dog hits this pool, it may have some trouble leaving it because the pattern is so dissimilar to what was followed before. It is very possible for the dog to drop into this new pool, try and decipher it and then go back to where it came from trying to sort the whole pool out from scratch. Kind of like untying a difficult knot, getting stuck, and starting over. If the dog is working well, let it, enjoy it, learn from it and better yet, allow your dog to solve the puzzle. If you do this not quite so simple task, your dog will solve the next scent pool all that much faster. If you insist on solving these problems for your dog when your dog is working, please remove the harness from the dog and place it over your own shoulders and then do it yourself.

When there are barriers in place between the subject and the dog, the resulting scent cones and pool will create scent anomalies to which the dog may react in very unexpected ways. For example, the subject could be on the opposite side of a building and the dog alerts to the scent pool, works it in the front of the building and into a foyer or little pocket, jumping up onto the walls, trying to get scent drifting from above.

I had the pleasure of working just this problem in the spring of 2014, in Dortmund, Germany. The trail went to the front of a large, four story office building. As the dog circled, it suddenly lunged into the glass framed, stepped foyer and began jumping onto the walls trying to get its nose higher. The handler, seeing this behavior, was convinced the subject was inside and tried to open the locked door. When this did not work out so well, she was a little confused and started to exhibit stress. For whatever reason, the scent of the subject was circling around the building on high wind currents and was settling in the foyer. I counseled patience and told the handler to just allow her dog to work and do nothing more than try and watch without influencing. She settled back into her lead and did as I instructed. It took about five minutes but eventually, the dog worked to the back of the building and found the subject on a set of steps leading to the second story. If the handler would have succumbed to the stress of the problem in the foyer, and more importantly, the door was open, it would have been very easy to yank the dog off the problem and into the building where the ability to locate the subject outside may have been sorely compromised.

Submerged Finds

Submerged finds are particularly difficult; as any Human Remains Detection dog handler can attest, but they also produce difficulty for the trailing dog and handler from time to time. Fugitive cases have a propensity for water, it seems. I think it is because the suspect often feels that by treading through water he or she will trick the dog off the trail. I actually like that way of thinking because it can make my job a lot easier. Water attracts and holds scent quite nicely and the more a person uses the body of water the more attractive it is to the dog. The problem really is when he or she runs too far up or down stream and the handler does not have the patience or experience to work the edges and find the exit.

The other problem can occur when the person hides in the body of water or partially submerges themselves out of sight of the dog and handler. The K9 might work its way up and down the bank, constantly alerting on certain currents or the edges of the bank. The water acts as a physical medium for the scent to travel on and seems to thicken the scent like syrup. Rather than scent on drafts of wind, it remains more physical and strong on the current.

K9 working the fringe of a stream trying to narrow down the source.

Dogs have a tendency to focus where scent is concentrating in water and that is invariably downstream. For some reason, many dogs have trouble working into the waterborne scent stream like they might on a windborne scent cone. Perhaps this is due to the lack of concentration or narrowing of the scent cone on water. It may simply be too spread out with no clearly defined source even when very close to the subject. For whatever reason, the dog may alert very nicely to the nearness of the subject but simply not be able to close the gap; consistently staying in one particular place that holds the odor such as an embankment, rocky outcropping, or submerged tree. My experience in this situation is to look behind the dog and start manually physically searching areas on the upstream side of the dog. Specifically, look for thick water plants, trees and rocks upstream. This really has to happen if the dog begins to lose interest or gets distracted.

Building Finds

A building find can be really frustrating because many handlers simply did not know that it happened. The problem with most building finds is that they are often the stomping ground of the subject and rarely are they as simple as walking to the door and knocking on it. This is especially true of criminal cases. The suspect may commit a crime in an area away from home and then run back to it. If this is in an apartment complex, the problem is increased exponentially and directly relative to how much the subject walked around the rest of the complex. Here is the problem:

1. A fairly fresh trail leaves the apartment complex to the scene of the crime.

2. A fresher trail goes back to the apartment complex and perhaps not directly back to the apartment.

3. There are numerous older trails in and around the suspect's apartment proportionate to the activity of the subject.

The K9 works into the morass of odor and in some situations, may actually find the correct apartment, but due to the overwhelming odor and trails of the suspect, past and present, the dog continues to work the area versus stopping and alerting at the door. The handler, none the wiser, continues to follow the dog and perhaps misses the interest at the suspect's door.

Why does this happen? Really, it is a case of bad training techniques or stale ones. Most handlers set up their practice trails with success in mind and not really working out a problem. The training solution to finding the correct apartment rarely involves the trail layer in his apartment complex. Most of the time, the training is done in relatively fresh or sterile conditions where the door find is relatively easy. There are no old scent pools present and rarely any older trails. One fresh trail leads to the correct door and voila: success.

This might be a great way to introduce door identifications but does nothing to help the dog work through the human maze of scent in a suspect's home base. The best thing to do is work the dog into these conditions slowly, with varying degrees of old scent trails already in place. With each new trail, increase the level of subject contamination. Perhaps the first trails are single trails to the correct door and when the dog gets that, add in a single older trail that leads away from the door in an opposite direction. Once the dog nails that, add a couple older trails. Get it to the point where the dog can work in a busy apartment complex and breeze through it. Keep in mind that you are not really training the dog to do something more, you are exposing it to new conditions and allowing the dog to learn on its own through moderated exposure.

K9 reacting to scent at the base of a door.

As the dog learns subject contamination in these conditions, it is a great idea to strengthen the door ID. The problem for most people in training for the door ID is two-fold: first, most handlers guide their dogs to the door and do not let them show a responsive body language reaction to the door or door handle. They just drag them to it saying such things as: "is that it?" Of course, when the dog is offered such an easy way out, they will take it. I guarantee you the only thing they will learn is how to watch you closer for body language changes and the cue to react to the correct door.

The other problem is that the standard training regimen is often one small step; immediately jumping off to a giant step versus tiered training. And again, the dog often ends up being guided to the door. The dog must learn these things in small steps that are easy to digest. There must be a clear continuum of events that lead the dog logically to the correct conclusion without the guidance of the handler. So, how do we accomplish this? It is really quite easy if you have the patience.

Start by having the trail layer walk to the correct door and before walking in, take the time to rub hands up and down the base of the door, leading in a line to the door handle. Once at the door handle, grip and rub the handle with vigor. The idea is to impregnate the door with odor from base to door handle so in the dog's olfactory mind it appears as a beacon on a foggy night. Most dogs, when trailing past or near the door, will give a clear head pop in the direction of the concentration of odor. If the subject magically opens the door when the dog reacts to the odor, the dog learns that its reaction to the concentration of odor meant something. On the other hand, if the handler leads the dog to the handler and says, "Check it" and opens the door, nothing is learned other than the handler will always help. The next time you run this scenario with almost all certainty, the dog will react with more interest to the stronger odor.

An excellent example of a K9 reacting to venting human scent from cracks in a door and then narrowing down the source to physical contact odor on the door handle.

The reason for the stronger reaction is what I call glandular or contact odor of the trail layer. The trail odor, or the gas/scent that comes off the human body naturally, is one type of odor and frankly, it is often not all that strong. On the other hand, when the trail layer touches or handles something, the odor is much stronger and most dogs naturally react to it. The more one touches an object, the more it smells. So, layering a door, top to bottom with odor, can almost be construed as a scent magnet as long as there are not too many distractions when the dog encounters the mini scent pool. As the dog become more proficient at detecting and then focusing on door handles and entryways, it is time to start pulling back the layer's scent a little at a time. Get to the point where the dog naturally alerts on the door handle with only a single touch. What we are looking for is the dog detecting the mini scent pools that exist when people enter doorways in the face of older scent pools and trails in and around the area the subject calls home. This is not easy and can stump even the best trailing dogs. The better handler will practice for this problem frequently.

Distraction Finds

Distraction finds are generally related to the end of a trail with far too many people. Dogs have a very easy way of detecting and individualizing a trail, but when faced with a group of people at the end of it, many have a tendency to break down. The problem seems to be the subject's fresh scent pool in and amongst the fresh scent pools of all the other people. What once seemed easy to define and follow now becomes more difficult. This might be due to the sheer quantity of fresh human distraction odor accompanying the subject odor. I think many dogs get so excited when finding the fresh odor that they begin to alert on any nearby human. If a handler mistakenly encourages or rewards the dog when it makes the wrong choice, then the problem can quickly become a habit.

Again, I find this problem is often related to training that has not been tiered properly and false expectations that the dog will always scent discriminate correctly. The latter is what really creates the training issue. Many handlers think that as soon as the dog can start working moderately difficult trails that they can run into the city amongst many human odors. It is simply a matter of too much too soon. Build the basics in training and make sure the dog is solid on two people and making the right choice before moving on to three, four, or twenty.

One method that seems to work great for this problem is what one of my first students Kevin Baughn, now turned trainer, calls the human flag trail. This is nothing more than a firetrail with multiple human distractions along the way and in close proximity to the subject.

The way to set this up is to take about five to ten decoy people and walk them in a line along the projected path of the runner, dropping each one off at a spot approximately 10 yards apart and in a line. They can sit or stand as you see fit and they should all be out of sight of the dog before you go to the next step

Next, have a GOOD runner with a big article, such as a shirt or hat, and a big attitude get your dog revved up like when you first started with the first runaway firetrails when he was a puppy. The trail layer needs to flap the article up and down out in front of the dog by at least ten to fifteen feet and call to it excitedly with a good high-pitched voice. As soon as the dog's head is bobbing up and down with the flapping article, have the trail runner flee from the dog along the same path that the decoys walked, running right in front of them and to a spot somewhere at the end. As soon as the runner is stopped, release the hound.

In most cases the dog will eagerly accept the run and hit the trail with vigor, that is until it hits the first decoy where they generally stop and try to ID the person. I've run this exact trail with many students who swear their dog would not make this error but invariably, almost all do. Why? Because they get so accustomed to running up in the lap of the first person that they find, and because many handlers allow their dogs to veer off trails and check anyone within the dog's vision. The problem is the dog reacting by sight not scent.

As soon as the dog begins to alert on the first person they see, correct the dog and tell it to get back to work. Most dogs will immediately begin running down the line again at least until they get to the next person where they might try to do the same thing again though with a little less energy. Correct again and get the dog moving. Usually, by the time the dog gets to the third person they are starting to get the message and may only give them a cursory glance. By the time they get to the person they are looking for, the body language says that they are very happy all of that exercise is over!

Subject Not Present

The start of the trail is the most important part of the trail and it is probably one of the most misunderstood scent pools of all. This is primarily due to the fact that the average handler does not recognize that the dog is working a subject scent pool at the start of the trail. This is often due to canned training and the excitement of the handler to get going. Many times handlers do not want to wait while the dog works out the morass of human odor, subject and otherwise which often permeates the beginning of a missing person or criminal search. Why? Well, I think it is because most training scenarios are not scenarios at all and the average handler tells their training subject to go to a particular location and run a trail without doing anything at the beginning other than walking away.   What this means is the start of the trail is relatively clean from a pool perspective and the dogs race through the start because the exit trail is so self-evident.

When a dog runs trails that always start like this, they can be slower out of the gate when they encounter new situations with lots of subject odor at the start, or numerous other exit trails that might be a little older. The exit trail is not so clear due to the sheer amount of subject scent of various ages. Couple this with subject contact odor, or scent from objects the subject touched or handled, you have a recipe for slow starts.

Maybe the best way to understand this situation is through visualization. Think of a person's home and they have not been there for months. The person comes home for the first time carrying an ignited red colored smoke bomb, one of those really intense military types, the guy walks up to the front door, turns around, and walks away still carrying the smoke bomb. The smoke bomb is never ending and emits smoke wherever the person goes. You have a little pooled and blown scent at the front door but it is pretty obvious where the smoke went as the man walks down the street and away from his house. Pretend that this smoke lasts for hours and does not dissipate.

Now, let us add some scent pool to the situation. Instead of a man who has not been home in months, we have a normal home with normal activity. The man walks in and out of his house, each and every day for work, to fetch his mail or paper, visit with neighbors, mow the lawn, wash the car, and you get the idea. Think about all of the things that the man touched and handled that have strong contact or glandular odor. Everywhere the man walked, he carried his smoke bomb. Think of the smoke bomb as an all-day sucker. Instead of blowing away immediately, it remains and permeates the area with smoke color. Each and everything the man touched glows with more smoke color due to more smoke intensity due to the touch. Couple this with a new color smoke for each and every other human that walked through the scene and you will have nothing but a solid haze of grey smoke.

If a human had to find an exit trail visually through all of the blown and permeated smoke that surrounds the home, it would be less than easy; perhaps impossible. Imagine a K9 having to work through all of that to find the exit trail with its nose. It isn't easy visually and it definitely is not with a nose processing scent.

From the human training perspective, muscle memory in training takes over for the handler and if all of the training trails were easy outs, the handler's now expects this in all situations, especially on real searches. Why real searches more than training? Stress. The stress factor of having to perform puts the body into complete muscle memory mode in all things because the mind's eye has horse blinders on. It is difficult to see past the lead when we are under stress.

Fast forward to real searches after months or years of training, without contaminated start training, and you have a dog that has problems with scent pools at the start of all trails. This is because training did not include it and the handler has no patience for working through it. The muscle memory conditions the handler to guide the dog out regardless if that guiding is in the right direction.

If the scene of the training or the real search has been contaminated by many people or it is the home or workplace of the subject, there is a significant scent pool of old and new human scents. Some related to the subject and many not. There may be so much odor that the dog simply cannot process it all no matter how much exposure training they have. In this case the search for the trail must be taken to the perimeter of the perceived scent contamination pool.

Prior to starting the dog, consider what the subject of the search does on a daily basis and how far outside their dwelling or your trail start they conduct daily business. Consider well, what all of your other searchers have done in and around the area. In particular, try to find out where they went outside the immediate scene. Once you have calculated all of this information, bring the dog into the place last seen, perhaps the front door or a particular room, and try to start with a very good scent article.

If the dog has scent when you start a trail and it appears to be working with no dramatic change in behavior, it is very important to remain patient if the dog circles the area of the crime or missing person scene, even if you feel the time it is taking is too long. Keep in mind how difficult it would be for you to figure out the smoke trails visually while trying to gravitate to the most recent one while you are watching your dog.

Almost every missing person or crime scene is more than a place where the subject walked into and then walked out of in a simple linear track. 99% of real search scenes are from locations where the subject interacted with other people and created multiple trails. Most subjects also touched and handled physical objects at these scenes. They left substantial amounts of human physical contact scent that is far stronger than simple blown and drifting human odor. The longer the subject was at these scenes the more odors of all types will be present in varying levels of concentration. All trailing tracking dogs will be interested in this scent and will want to investigate it.

When there are numerous older subject trails present that move in and out of the start, the K9 will have to peel back the scent layers to expose the freshest trail. Kind of like peeling layers off the onion to get to the core. It is not immediately evident to the dog and the process takes time. Most dogs have a tendency to circle through this subject contamination, working in a similar fashion to a visual tracker working circles out from the start trying to find a visual track. The K9 must get to the edge of the scent pool in order to discover the fresh trail that leaves the area. During this process, if the K9 encounters strong odor from contact or multiple laid trails over the same path, it will without fail, check these things out.

This process can vary from seconds to several minutes and as long as the K9 appears to be working with no major change in body language, the handler would do well to let the dog work. Try to enjoy the moment by watching the dog doing what it was designed to do, in all its glory, without getting impatient. Impatient handlers cannot help but exhibit human body language and line handling cues that let the dog know the handler is anxious. If this happens too much and for too long, the dog might very well take the impatience for correction and come off the scent; settling instead, for something easier to follow; such as a fresher trail of another officer, citizen, or animal. Dogs do this in an attempt to please the handler and many handlers have difficulty understanding that the dog switched scents.

If no start is to be found or the dog cannot break out of the scent pool, begin to work concentric circles outside of the perceived scent pool contamination with the dog. Start in an area with the least possible contamination and circle around the area of the search. If you are lucky and, more importantly, you have practiced for just this eventuality, you may find an exit trail that was masked by the contamination and scent pools at the scene.

There Are Three Things the Handler Must Practice for:

1. Examination of scenes and interviewing persons therein prior to starting the dog on an attempted trail. The purpose of this examination is to determine the extent, width, and breadth of the contaminating scent pool of distracting people who have laid fresher trails over the top of the subject's.

2. Working the dog in ever increasing concentric circles within the dog's scent memory. The goal is to teach the dog to maintain the target odor from the scent article for a long period of time after the initial scenting, so if the dog encounters the correct trail after scenting, it remembers to take it.

3. If the K9 has subject odor and appears to be working it, don't interrupt! This is the most difficult thing to deal with.

Number one is not necessarily easy but it is really just a matter of learning to figure out who and what has been at your scene after the subject went missing. Once the handler has this information, he must determine the extent of that activity then try to get outside of it.

Number two can be a real pain because K9s have a predisposition to fresh scent. Even with much practice and a good scent article, dogs simply have a difficult time not taking a fresh exit trail out of the scene. This is what they are engineered to do. Breaking this instinct is impossible, but mitigating it, though difficult, is very possible. We do this through the use of tiered training cycles using drive and motivation to get the K9 through lapses of subject scent in the immediate area.

To begin with, no matter how great the scent article is and how well the dog can scent discriminate, there are times that it will ignore the scent on the scent article for that of a fresher trail. This is especially true when the scent of a familiar person to the dog, or training partner is part of the contamination. If a known person's scent is present from the onset of the search, the dog is probably used to following it due to past training. If that scent is fresher, the trailing dog has a huge chance of abandoning the scent of your missing person for that of the known person. The scent pools and trails of a teammate, possibly a fellow investigator known to the dog, are difficult to give up, if not impossible, when that dog has practices following these people in the past. This is why I highly recommend that professional trailing dog handlers **DO NOT** use teammates or beat partners as practice trail layers.

I cannot begin to tell you the sheer number of real searches that I have witnessed and been a part of where the dogs gravitated to a trail after being scented on a good article and that trail was definitely not the subject's. After reviewing the work of the dog in earnest, side by side with people who came to the scene after the disappearance, the dogs work often times matched one of those people.   It was just these types of events that began to make me seriously question the viability of scent articles.

What I did not realize at the time, fifteen years ago, was that the scent articles were indeed, excellent for targeting a dog but the dog's instinctual response to scent stimuli as it relates to the act of trailing was responsible for the scent article abandonment phenomenon. I wrote about this quite a bit in the first part of *Chapter Four; K9 Trailing, The Straightest Path,* and enumerated some of the reasons for it. Though *K9 Trailing* was written two years ago, I believe more wholeheartedly today about these natural instincts of dogs, and how these instincts account for, or discount, scent articles. I have not found a technique to train this instinct completely out of them. I found that it was simply better try to minimize the contamination; especially that contamination from known parties to the dog, and get the dog to an area with fresher subject scent. It also helps to make the scent article a surprise to the dog. In other words, make it possible for them to find the article themselves without actually being presented with it. I have discovered that dogs that "find" the scent article without assistance tend to gravitate to a matching trail better than those dogs that have article shoved into their noses.

I think the key to working out of contaminating scent pools is not so much trying to find a way to make the scent article work better but to minimize the contamination by working out of it. The problem is that this can take some time and may mean working in concentric circles outside the area. When the dog has only been scented once, we must consider scent memory. If we re-scent the dog several times over the course of this trail search, then we must consider that the dog may well be "feeling" forced to find *any* trail and not necessarily that of the subject. I find the latter to be very common for those who like to re-scent and it is one of the reasons why I don't ever do it.

There was a time in my trailing career when I used to take the scent article with me everywhere and scent my dog whenever I felt the chips were down. This usually meant that I was not confident in the dog, the trail, or both. I would resort to letting my dog smell the bag once again, and I would see this sudden surge of energy and maybe some trailing for a little while, and then it would end... again.   I did not realize that I was simply feeding my insecurity in the trail and that my initial doubt was probably correct. There was no trail there and that's why I was nervous. Feeding the dog the scent article again did nothing but encourage my dog to find a trail, any trail, and we were simply running ghosts.

So, I came to work with a method taught to me by an early mentor, Glenn Rimbey. Glenn worked in a large prison system and was tasked with locating escaped prisoners with the dogs. The scent articles were not a problem, but often finding the location the prisoner hopped the fence was. When there is a mile or more of perimeter fence and there is no clear exit point, the only choice one might have is to run the fence with the dog until it strikes the trail. Glenn told me the way he did this with his prison dogs was to start training the dogs right on top of the trails with the scent article and over time, slowly move the start point away from the trail in not only time but distance. The goal was to get at least a ¼ mile and twenty minutes post scent article out before the K9 seemed to lose memory. The whole idea was to build the dog's memory for the scent it was given. Dogs can be pretty amazing and I am often surprised by the time frames they remember the scent. Still, there are also dogs that forget within seconds and never seem to grasp the idea that they have to maintain the scent. These are usually very impatient patrol dogs that will follow anything and everything with the intent of biting it.

So, the key for me on breaking out of scent pools of the subject and contamination, when the dog could not do it on its own, was to work concentric circles around the area based on the scent memory of the dog. These circles are directly relative to how long the dog is maintaining the memory of the target scent, and that can vary based on any distractors present. When there is too much scent, sound, vision stimulation, then scent memory is adversely affected. Obviously, the key is to build the drive for the trail through all of this distracting stimulation.

When working the K9 in the concentric circles the handler is really doing nothing more than circle casting outwards in a controlled fashion. The dog should be to the outside of the handler on a relatively short lead: four to six feet. The lead is still connected to the harness; the difference is the handler is now directing the dog to what the handler might perceive as a productive source of target human scent. I use the trailing lead as a measuring tool when determining the distance to perform these circles. If I have a thirty-foot trailing lead, I start my first circle thirty feet away from the last place my dog obviously had scent and continue with 30' intervals until my dog appears done. Or it finds the trail. When the dog is "done" is directly proportionate to how well the dog was trained for subject scent memory. To me a dog is done when it begins to become distracted and looks to other things such as other animal scent or simply shows a lack of interest.

If the K9 remembers the scent of the subject after the start, through all of the concentric circles one might perform, and then strikes the matching trail, it is extremely obvious. The body language indicator is usually a very strong "head pop" or head turn into the direction of the scent trail coupled with a big change in tail set and intensity.

The bottom line is that every search scene will have varying degrees of subject and distracting contaminating odor and it is not easy for the dog to work through. It is especially difficult for the handler and the dog if neither has practiced for it. As with all trailing training for professional dog handlers, training trails should approximate what the handler might encounter on the street. If the training is not realistic, success rates on real searches will be severely compromised.

Emotional Scent Pools

One of the most difficult scent pool problems to work through is excessively charged emotional odor. Heavy fear scent, in particular fear scent from a victim of murder just prior to death can be terrifying to some dogs and they simply will refuse to work through the problem. We all know that fear scent helps to charge dogs up but depending on the type, it can also push them over the other edge to aversion. The emotion as it relates to the odor seems to be far more finite than human scent alone and it appears not to last for all that long. My experience has been minutes to hours depending on the situation.

I have experienced this phenomenon with actual homicide cases; usually of the most heinous kind. These include situations where it was clear the victim knew beyond a shadow of a doubt that they were about to be killed. In these cases it was clear by watching body language indicators from dogs brought into the scene early on that they were anxious. Some refused to be near at all. This response seemed to drop off exponentially with time to the point that the dogs worked normally as with any other case; however, I was unable to determine an acceptable time frame.

There is no solid way to train for this, at least none that I can discover. Some dogs never get over aversion to this type of fear scent. The only possible way to desensitize a dog to this condition is through motivational exercises near these types of scenes starting on the fringe of the possible scent pool and working closer to the center over a series of separate exercises and times. This means that the trainer must have access to quite a few homicide scenes of this caliber. That is simply impossible for most. I believe the most important thing to understand is that this phenomenon can happen and that the dog could potentially shut down. Pushing a dog into one of these scenes when it is obviously traumatized by it may irreparably harm all training to date. It might be better to forgo the deployment and use the scene as a training situation to help desensitize the dog through proper motivation and reward.

For those interested in this phenomenon, I wrote about this subject in detail in *K9 Trailing; The Straightest Path,* Chapter Four, pages 42-44.

Physical Contact Odor

Human physical contact scent is probably the best scent available for a scenting dog. This is the scent that is transferred from skin to object contact such as a hand to a doorknob. Depending on the amount of contact odor, there may be a relatively small pool but a strong one from the dog's perspective. Crime scenes, or locations where a person has been in contact with numerous objects, can hold a dog's attention for a long period of time. Depending on how fresh this scent is will often determine how much time the dog spends there. The important thing to consider from a handling perspective is to make sure that the body language is noted and that the dog is allotted the time to investigate.

Bumping a dog out of this type of scent pool prematurely can cause the dog to shut down, or worse, switch trails. The common reason for the handler error is the fact that many handlers misread the behavior as a distractor such as animal scent. Many handlers simply get impatient and can't abide the K9 circling or checking something out for any length of time. The overwhelming desire to continue the trail and find what it is they are looking for can actually cause the exact opposite to occur. If the dog gets pushed or yanked off something as important as human subject hand contact odor on evidence or something else such as a door, fence, or gate, the K9 could, depending upon sensitivity to the lead, quit the trail altogether and find something else to follow. I see this a lot with pointy eared patrol K9's that are hyper sensitive to line checks and obedience. The key is to make sure that the body language to the event is understood as contact scent pool, and the best way to see this behavior, better yet register it, is to record it on a video camera. Nowadays, there are many micro-cameras out there with superb capabilities that can be mounted on chest and head while trails are run. Use these and go over the recordings over and over again until the body language is burned in your brain synapses.

Why is physical contact odor the odor of all odors? I think it is because when the human body makes contact with a surface, and depending on the length of contact coupled with the intensity and surface porosity, a certain amount of oils and skin cells are absorbed or deposited on the surface. These oils and cells define us as humans and are stronger than the gaseous or cellular sloughing human scent that emanates from the body as we move about our daily lives.

There are certain places on the body that produce a larger concentrations of these defining odors, and the body language of the K9 when encountering them indicates that they detect a difference as well. The obvious locations, of course, are the areas housing expressive glands that often produce odor even we humans can detect; armpits, feet, groin, and orifices. However, there are other places that we often do not associate with strong human odor but nonetheless are attractive scents to the K9: Hands, head and hair. All dogs seem to have a unique affinity to the human hand and I have always noted that, in how my working dogs reacted to things touched and handled by people. These items can often be detected by the dog from incredible distances and over very long periods of time. My first K9, Ronin, in one of his last deployments, located a buried wallet that was under about 3" of dirt and knee high grass on a 40 acre parcel of land. I would have never expected it to happen after such a time frame, I think it was directly related to the ability of human contact odor; especially odor imbedded into fabric or other very porous surfaces, to survive very long periods of time. Survival far longer than the gaseous or cellular forms that naturally drift from our bodies.

I watched a PBS special that showed some of the differences between Canis Familiaris— our domestic dog—and the wolf, and was immediately struck by one of the studies. The researchers had tested domestically raised wolves and dogs equally on how they reacted to human hand stimuli. Interestingly, wherever the human hand went, so too did the dogs eyes. No matter where the human hand drifted or pointed, the dog's eyes and nose followed. The wolves, on the other hand, did everything they could to avoid visual contact with the hand, as well as the eyes of the human. What this study appeared to show was that the dog was very attuned to the human hand and that this attraction probably related to the human hand being the bearer of sustenance, in other words: treats!

Scent pool created by activity and contact at this drift wood.

If the eyes of our domestic dogs are so firmly attached to the activity of our hands so too must be the nose and the olfactory system. It simply stands to reason as the dog's nose is the number one receptor for all things in the K9 world of identification. I believe that my observation of human hand contact odor generating a strong dog reaction when encountered is probably due to the co-evolution of dog and humans, with the latter becoming providers over millennia. I believe the human hand is probably one of the best identifying odor sources for the trailing K9 and dogs in general.

There is no exact body language of ALL dogs that reads human contact. Each and every dog has varying degrees of reaction and each reaction of each individual K9 can also change with the degree and type of contact. To quantify exactly how a K9 reacts to human odor, and put a description on that reaction will automatically qualify the description as false. There are degrees of similarity but no two conditions are alike; therefore, no two body language reactions will be alike. I believe the key to interpretation is an understanding of the averages of similarity through constant practice and exposure. As the brain is a muscle, there is muscle memory in the reading of a dog and when practice and repetition wanes, so to do true interpretation and subsequent understanding of the dog's body language.

Therefore, it is difficult for me here to place words in descriptive form that will help the student of trailing understand their own dog. In order to understand one's own dog's body language to all things trailing, not simply contact scent pools, one must be incredibly attentive and in tune with his own dog. It is a waste of time to internalize what others might say about what their own or ALL dogs might do, because none of those dogs are ours. Practice, record, and analyze over and over and then the puzzle begins to come to together.

I will go over a few items that occur naturally on many trails and that create a reaction in many dogs when encountered that often create confusion in the handler's mind.

Probably the first and foremost is the bush or branch that is thought of as a dog distraction but is actually contact odor from the subject of the search. The reaction of the dog is usually because the amount of contact was significant, and not simply a swipe of the leg or the hand. It often incorporates broken branches or leaves that double the scent picture in the dogs mind. What separates the dog distractor from the human contact scent picture is in the way the dog reacts to it and the associated body language. This is something that should really be recorded so that aspiring handlers can review the body language over and over again to increase familiarity.

When trailing dogs encounter broken branches or stems of plants, they normally do not react to them in a similar fashion to markings of dogs. Bushes are generally considered pee spots and that is usually the first consideration of the handler when they see the dog investigating the bush; but consideration must also be for the manner in which the dog peruses the bush. The pee spot generally gets a waving head that narrows to the spot, usually low on the bush or plant, followed by a nose plant on the splash spot. There is usually a corresponding tail set change with other dog marking as well.

When a super-dominant K9 detects and locates a pee spot in their own territory, they may become more rigid in body posture as well as display a taller tail set as if to say: "See! I'm here and I'm going to mark your mark!"

The alternate tail set is usually related to unfamiliar territory or dogs that are a little bit less confident. This tail set is usually dropped or drooping with body posture less rigid. The dog is not sure what marked the spot and not exactly sure if there could be an aggressive response to the trespass. Thus, the posture becomes a smaller silhouette to attract less attention. There is still in interest in the spot and the dog will still investigate, and if a male, still mark. In this case, the mark is somewhat surreptitious; kind of like a kid stealing a cookie from the cookie jar when he thinks nobody is looking. The dog has a desire to add his mark to the spot but also afraid of the consequences.

This body language is very severe compared to trailing behavior as it relates to human contact odor. Trailing behavior relative to contact is really nothing more than an extension of trailing, and the best possible description I have is almost an "afterthought". Kind of like, "Oh, here is something but I have to keep going." The K9 reacts, investigates, but usually without stopping or hovering for too long. They may even pass the spot initially and quickly make a U—Turn for a quick investigation. The tail set and body silhouette does not change much. The biggest indicator however, is based on deduction. The spot the dog hits is usually much higher up than another dog can pee and there might be a broken leaf or branch related to it. The way to find out exactly how your dog reacts is to set up physical contact odor on the trail in predetermined locations and film it.

Again, the key here is to not correct if the detection is based on contact. If the handler corrects the dog at a difficult juncture of the trail because he or she perceives a distraction, the trail may now be over. It really depends on how much obedience the K9 has and how sensitive they are to the lead. A soft dog will come off and possibly lose the trail. A hard dog might care less. The bottom line is that we need to truly understand what the dog is detecting whenever possible and apply handling techniques accordingly.

Gate handles, fences, door handles, etc. all usually have a very similar reaction to each other with a slight difference. Often the dog may detect the contact odor from a distance and circle back or off trail to investigate. When they do, it is usually nose down, panning up to the location of contact, such as a door handle. A follow-up behavior change to strong odor might be a slight to hard tail wag as if to confirm, "Yep, this is it!"

Dogs that react naturally to this type of odor are great because they can be taught easily to have an alert for the contact. This helps to identify doors that the subject got through. It is important to understand that subject contact odor reaction is trailing behavior of a slightly different kind.

K9 body language reaction to contact is similar but more intense than reaction to trail odor and the time spent on it might be longer. When the behavior is accompanied by a tail wag, the savvy handler will do well to allow the action and perhaps follow up on it.

It is quite simple to train for contact odor to understand how a dog reacts to it and more importantly, train for a reaction to it. A good identification of human contact to an object can pay off dividends in any investigation. If a handler can identify door handles or objects that the subject may have touched, and then fingerprints, DNA, fiber evidence etc. may be discovered.

To begin with, set the contact odor in stages of concentration and type on a variety of surfaces. The first one I like to do is a door handle as subjects frequently enter into a variety of homes and businesses as a normal circumstance of missing or criminal suspect type behavior. It is not as easy as having the subject simply walk up to the door, manipulate the handle, and walk inside.

The problem with this is the scent picture to a moving dog may be relatively small and the minor scent anomaly as the dog passes the door is rather innocuous. It is such a minor blip on the scent picture radar screen that the dog simply moves past it without much if any visible reaction. We must increase the size of the blip so it is more noticeable and the dog can't help but react to it. Understand that you are not teaching the dog "how" to react to human subject contact odor as providing training conditions that allow for the dog to naturally increase its own skills of detection without influence. The trick is in providing the conditions for self-learning.

With this K9 work, as with all K9 work, imagination is truly the key. Couple good imagination with the ability to see things from the dog's perspective rather than the human one, and a handler will create an environment ripe for doggy learning. The cool thing about it is the handler becomes more of a scenario builder than a "trainer." The K9 trains itself, and honestly, I feel that this is the best way for a dog to learn. I have found that every time I show the dog something to do that the effect is far less than when the dog discovers the "thing" on its own and has a natural response to it. I think the human training aspect of it all can be the final alert to the scent. Initially, we want the dog's reaction to be natural and the source odor to "pay" the dog with some semblance of a reward. Generally a little praise is all that is necessary. In other words, the dog reacts to the odor with some body language we recognize, we recognize it because we set it up in advance and know it is there, and it is immediately rewarded with praise.

So, to begin, we must set up the scenario ripe for learning. I do this with doors by having the subject of the trail walk up to a door that is not too far off the actual track and then manipulate the scene with his or her hands. I like the trail layer to start by taking their hands and starting at nose level, wipe them around and upwards toward the door handle. Once at the door handle, the subject must really work their hand oils into the surface. Not simply turning the handle once or twice, but really working it until it is warm to the touch.

This type of scent picture is overwhelming and the vast majority of trailing dogs that are really trailing, not just running to an air scent, when encountering this odor, will have a visible reaction to it. The reaction is normally a head pop to the initial contact at nose level on the door. This is why this first contact location is so important to the learning process. The contact at nose level attracts the dog to the scent anomaly and once close to the door, the handle scent picture takes over and the dog naturally gravitates to it. The handler must react quickly to this by not only observing the reaction but being prepared to reward at the source with praise. Timing is critical.

Sequence of Events

1. Head pop to the door (nose suddenly switching to the side off the trail)

2. Handler observes and prepares

3. K9 head pans upwards to the door handle and checks it. (there may be a tail wag associate with this behavior)

4. As soon as the handler sees a visible body language reaction to the door handle a praise reward must be given.

5. If the dog pans away from the handle and back to the trail, and a reward is given now, it will be too late and is completely irrelevant in the total scheme of things. It is best to recognize missed timing and set the scenario up again later. If the reward is given as the dog leaves the contact odor it may interpret the praise for leaving the odor and we do not want that!

If the timing for the reward is correct and the dog understands that its handler is happy with the discovery, the next time the dog detects the same condition; it will react more overtly and with more speed. Timing is probably more crucial with the second go-around because the dog will do it fast. Do these a few times and we are very close to developing a final alert to the contact odor. The most natural alerts seem to be jumping on the door and sitting at it.

Real search conditions will rarely, if ever, provide for such a scent picture as the subject walking up to the door and rubbing all over it. This is simply the beginning of K9 awareness to the scent picture anomaly. The trail is "small" odor and simple contact odor on a door handle is often only slightly "bigger" from the dogs' perspective. The importance lies in teaching the dog that it is important. That begins with making it big accompanied by a paycheck. Big scent, easy awareness equals pay check. It's that simple. Once the dogs understand the game and more importantly, the productive source of subject contact odor, they will naturally gravitate to these things on the trail.

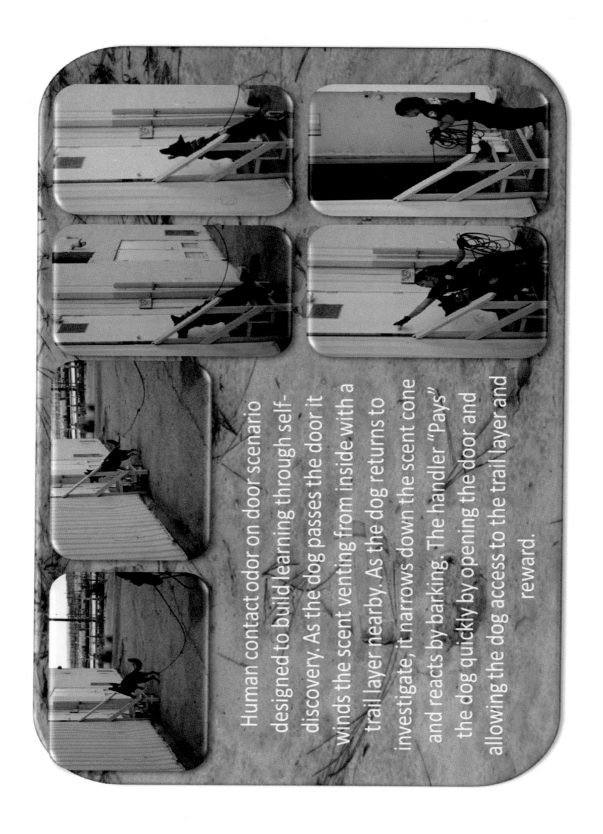

Human contact odor on door scenario designed to build learning through self-discovery. As the dog passes the door it winds the scent venting from inside with a trail layer nearby. As the dog returns to investigate, it narrows down the scent cone and reacts by barking. The handler "Pays" the dog quickly by opening the door and allowing the dog access to the trail layer and reward.

Once the handler sees that the dog is naturally gravitating to these types of scenarios, set up in advance, it is now time to start reducing the level of the scent picture. Start by reducing the amount of time on the handle and then slowly take away the rest to the bottom of the door until the only thing that is left is the simply turning of the handle.

The same training regimen may now be incorporated for any other type of contact odor such a fence climbing, car doors, picnic benches, etc.

Back Tracks and Cross Tracks

Back tracks and cross tracks of the same human subject can be very frustrating for the dog; primarily due to impatience on the part of the handler. Back tracks, in particular, have a habit of slowing green dogs down to a crawl, comparatively speaking, and many handlers can't take the delay without throwing out a "Get to work!" The reason for this is very simple. The average handler rarely sets up cross tracks or back tracks in their normal repertoire of training to see what it looks like. If one does not apply the training condition to training, then the K9 reaction to the condition will always remain a mystery and perhaps be mishandled.

Both conditions are scent pools in their own right. Anytime there is more of concentration of subject scent in one particular area, it must be considered a pool. The depth, intensity, and diameter determine the dog's reaction to it. Back and cross tracks have a tendency to put a wrinkle in the program because they not only add more scent to the condition, but they also add misdirection. These small "false" trails, if followed too far, can put the K9 into hunting mode. Hunting mode is a behavior that many handlers confuse with trailing and happily follow. Happily follow the false direction of a back track and the handler will simply be running eventually with no scent. If the handler went too far to remember where all of this went down, the trail might very well be over.

A back track is a trail that begins in one direction, and then, at some point in the original trail, the subject walks back on top of the same track; reversing direction and then peeling off towards an entirely new direction somewhere in the middle and often on a 90 degree tangent to the left or right of the original path. The more the subject walked back and forth on the original direction of travel, the more complicated the scent picture for the K9 to work through.

No two dogs work back tracks or cross tracks the same, but they all seem to try and orient to the freshest scent in the pool in an attempt to get the trail out. The speed and degree of efficiency in solving the backtrack puzzle is really related to the dog's natural ability but also to the amount of exposure in this particular condition. I believe that dogs are genetically wired with the ability to figure out back tracks and cross tracks as both of these occur naturally when hunting game. This ability is no different than a human child's propensity for a particular physical ability such as walking. The child is genetically hardwired to walk, but if the child spends his or her life sitting on the couch playing Xbox, he or she will not only walk poorly but be pretty darned uncoordinated at everything else as well. The dog is genetically hard wired to trail scent in all conditions, but the quality of the trailing will be related to condition exposure and ultimately repetition. Kids are genetically hardwired to walk and the Xbox is another story!

As I mentioned above, each dog may have its own separate body behavior change in reaction to back tracks, but I would like to enumerate a few based on my experience working with a wide variety of K9s.

My favorite style of dog is the dog that can whip through a back track like a red-hot knife through soft butter. Natural trailing dogs with the best genetic trailing markers are always these dogs and they can handle most back tracks with relative ease. The key to the technique is for the dog to immediately realize the scent picture conundrum and work toward the edge of the pool, scenting for the fresh exit trail. Believe it or not, there are some puppies that do this automatically and without much exposure to the condition at all. But these dogs are rare. Generally speaking, the dog will hit the back track and often time run all the way to the end where the scent ends. The really good dogs will immediately recognize the scent pool problem the back track presents, slow down, reverse, and start working the fringes of the scent looking for the exit trails.

The average dog without much exposure to this back track will often times get stuck in it and not get out, especially if it has had no training exposure to the problem. The body language indicators are when the dog encounters the back track, works to the end or the point where the person turned around, and then to the point where that leg of the back track ends. Many times the dogs seem not to recognize the fact that the trail may have peeled off somewhere in between both or more legs and instead of working toward the fringe of the pool, they have a tendency to get stuck in the section of the trail with the much stronger scent. Here is the issue: the dog may detect the exit trail somewhere on the fringe or in the middle of the back track, but they have a lot of trouble leaving the extra odor of a double, triple, or quadruple laid track. The sheer amount of odor in one spot is too appealing and the lighter scent picture of the exit trail seems to be less enticing. What a handler might see is a dog that literally keeps going back and forth from one end of the back track to the other frantically looking for more scent.

The key to this problem will be the drive of the dog. If the dog has super drive and appears to not be losing any interest in the work, the handler needs to let the dog work and not assist. But at the first sign of a little distraction or slowing down, it is time for the handler to start working concentric circles outside of the perceived scent pool. The circles are meant to cut the fresher trail out and it is crucial that the handler move far enough from the initial back track scent pool so that the dog is not dragged back to it like a bee to pollen. If the handler tries to work the fringe too close to the pool, the dog will simply be attracted back to the pool. The first circle should be at least 30' away and done in a concentric fashion. If the handler starts the first leg of the circle too far away from the pool, the other hand of the problem and a fatal one at that, will be loss of the trail.

Ultimately, the solution is training. It is important to make trailing training real and back tracks are part of real missing person and criminal trails. I start this process simply and in a way that I can measure the K9 response to the pool. The first thought is often to mark the pool with flags so the handler can visualize the beginning and end of the back track. The problem with this is the flags add human contact scent to the pool; thereby artificially raising the bar of subject scent at the scene and this will skew the results of the test and perhaps exacerbate the intensity of the dog working the pool. This we do not want. We want to minimize the response and increase the ability to detect the exit trail. Still, marking visually is a great idea and an easy way to see what the parameters of the dogs scent canvas are. My method is to have the trail layer scrape the earth well enough that it is easy to discern from a distance. Now, ground disturbance in its own right will increase the scent picture and the dog may very well detect the scrapes that indicated the beginnings and the end of the back tracks. The handler may see this by the inordinate amount of time the dog spends working the scrape mark. However, this is still better than adding human contact odor to the scene because the latter is more intense.

The keys to the scrape marks are as visual markers to the handler letting him or her know what the back track started and where it ended. This now allows the handler to get a better mental picture of the trail geography thereby allowing for better ability to determine where to start concentric circles working outside the pool. As mentioned before, the first circle should be at least a full trailing lead length from the scent pool. If possible, I like to work the dog into the wind as they have an uncanny ability to detect trails from a distance on the wind.

Vehicle Pick-Up Scent Pools

Cases where the subject is picked up by a vehicle are a little unusual and perhaps not suitable for a generic scent pool chapter. However, they occur so much in real urban searches that I felt them relevant to go over. When I first encountered car pick-ups, I did not really understand what was happening, and frankly thought that my dog was distracted or lost the trail. Part of this was because I believed in those days that car trails were entirely possible and practiced them regularly. I did not understand, at the time, that I was deluding myself with poor training techniques that were, in essence, nothing more than me guiding my dog to a wind scent of a person in a car when we got close to it. Because all of my trails were known when I first started trailing, and I expected my dog to be able to pick up the scent of the person driving away in the car, I had a tendency to force my dog through the pick-up site and did not have the patience to allow him to work the problem.

Looking back on it now, as soon as we got to the pick-up spot, I would usually lead manipulate my dog into moving out of the area as quickly as possible if I perceived a slowdown. This guidance was directly proportionate to my impatience and ego. My ego would not let my dog "fail" because any failure was really a direct reflection on my own ability after all. This is very easy to see now, but back in the day, I truly felt that I knew where scent was and how the dog should work it. My arrogance for my dog's works was also directly responsible for many of the blown subject finds that we should have had.

In the case of criminal searches, most car pick-ups have scent pools that are a little off the main path of normal human traffic. They are in the shadows or places not exactly in the line of sight of drivers because the criminal who waited for the pick—up did not want to be seen while waiting. So the body language indicators for the dog might appear somewhat strange.

The first stage of reaction to the car pick-up scent pool will often be the dog appearing to overshoot what seems like a turn: but into the street. They may ignore the concentration of "waiting" odor in favor of the obvious exit trail. The dog may actually seem to trail nose down on the concrete for varying distances in the road or along the edge. Slowly, the dog may start to go heads up and start to look around with a tossing head; attempting to acquire an air scent. Depending on how long the scent lasted in the road, the dog may or may not be able to find a way back to the scent pool start. It really depends on how practiced the K9 is at losing scent and getting back to it.

The amount of time the dog follows this fading scent can really vary and is largely dependent on environmental conditions such as temperature, humidity and wind; but most especially other traffic on the road. High humidity with moderate temperatures, low wind, little to no direct sunlight, and most importantly, little to no other vehicular traffic, are the perfect conditions to follow odor emanating from a car. Couple that with open car windows and you have a recipe for a car trail. Yeah, I know, I don't believe in car trails. Well, that is the truth for the most part but every now and then, the planets will align and there will be enough of a trailing scent picture for the dog to follow scent coming from the car. The problem will always be the destruction of the scent picture and this is usually from other cars, wind, and bad environmental conditions that corrupt the direction of travel of scent in the dogs mind.

To begin with, I believe trailing dogs follow trails based on linear movement, older to newer, less fresh to fresher. The scent follows a path and the dog follows that path. The direction of travel from beginning to end is related to the age of trail in some semblance of chronological order. In other words, the portion of the trail behind the dog is older or less fresh than the trail in front of it. If dogs could not do this there would be no way they could determine direction of travel and if they could not determine direction of travel, this hunting trait should have been lost through evolution.

Wild canids rely on all of their senses to hunt and obtain a meal so their expenditure of energy is judicious. Wild canids will not be successful on the vast majority of hunts using only one or two hunting traits. Expenditure of energy in a less than useful way will lead to demise of the animal due to starvation. The demise of too many individuals of a particular species, due to traits that are less than successful, normally translates to an evolutionary change in that trait or its loss altogether. Consequently, I believe that if dogs could not determine direction of travel on a linear trail when encountering it from a perpendicular angle, the prey scent—trailing trait would not be there in the first place. Running into a prey trail from the side or perpendicular, is the normal course of business for wild dogs. They detect a trail and decide to follow it based on the calculated ability to follow that trail to fruition. Proper directional following is absolutely the most important part of that equation. If dogs could not do this then there would be little to no need for the trailing instinct. This is my rationalization of the subject. My experience based on observation of thousands of dogs in this exact condition totally supports. The vast majority of good trailing dogs I see when encountering a trail from the side, or perpendicular angle for the first time, almost always follow that trail in the proper direction. They may back track for a bit but ultimately always seem to self-correct. There are a few times that this may not be the case and car trails are one of them. Why?

A linear trail of scent emanating from a car through vents, windows, etc., is subject to wind, cross winds, and vortexes that make a chronological trail virtually impossible. The scent comes out of the vehicle with absolutely no pattern and is sent to every direction possible. Yes, there is absolutely scent along the path the vehicle moves on, but the "direction" of scent is really not possible to determine. Concentrations of scent will be in places often times off the track... up against buildings and sometimes hundreds of yards away. One simply needs to put a smoke bomb in the back of a moving pickup truck and watch where the blown smoke goes in order to get an idea where scent might be. And this is from the back of a truck and not an enclosed car with less airborne material. The faster the truck moves and the more cross traffic

The Tao of Trailing Jeff Schettler

from other vehicles interfering with the original contrail source smoke, the further the smoke drifts and the more confused/contaminated it becomes. Yes, there is smoke, but the smoke path is now missing. And therein lie the problem and the reason why car trails are always less than probable. I do not believe that trailing dogs can follow "car trails" reliably. I do believe that dogs can detect scent from cars.

It appears the issue with car trails is truly directional as scent following goes. There is simply no strong way for the dog to establish direction of travel with major scent vortexes and contamination on normal city streets. Ultimately, dogs require a linear/chronological order to the scent trail in order to follow it reliably for long distances.

Going Back to the Original Scenario

1. If the environmental conditions are perfect,

2. There is a lot of subject scent coming from the vehicle,

3. There is little to no conflicting vehicle traffic along the same path backwards or forwards,

4. And the subject vehicle is moving relatively slow, then the trailing dog may follow the subject scent trail from the vehicle for a fairly long distance.

The loss of the trail will occur when the speed increases, the environmental conditions degrade, and other vehicles mingle with the subject vehicle. There is absolutely no rhyme or reason to any of these "trails," therefore they are really impossible to train for or predict. Regardless, the vast majority of car trails will end in confusion at some point unless the driver parks close to the start point. When confusion happens it may or may not be possible for the dog to remember where the condition began, and the distance from the confusion back to the start point may be hundreds of yards. The handler must therefore have an idea to help the dog go back to the start, if necessary, and this must be done with quickly. The longer it takes to get back to the scent scene, the more distracted and unmotivated the dog might become.

As most vehicle trails go, the average dog will only follow the vehicle blown scent for a short distance, usually only a matter of twenty to fifty yards. When this is the distance to confusion or loss, a good dog will often bee-line back to where this all started, and that is the step off point from sidewalk to car. When the dog gets there, it will usually start to circle and gravitate to areas that have stronger scent pictures. These will be areas where the subject stood, sat or hid. Contact odor will be the most interesting and a handler may see the dog nose perusing things like bushes, benches, or anything else that might have been touched or sat on.

The dog may venture back to the road and the hazy scent there, or even perhaps back track a bit. But when this behavior is seen in totality, a savvy handler will put the pieces together and see this body language for what it is, a vehicle pick-up. The handler should not discount the ending here as a lost trail but refer the details of this ending to investigators to investigate. A neighborhood check of the houses and business in the general area may reveal a witness who saw the subject and the vehicle and if the planets are aligned, perhaps even a license plate.

K9 working a car pick up scenario. The K9 will often alert on the pick up point and trail past it.

Scent pools are by far the most misunderstood component of trailing for the average trailing handler. The confusion usually comes from impatience in handling; not allowing the dog enough time to properly canvas the location from an olfactory standpoint. In order to understand scent pools and how the individual trailing dog reacts to them, handlers must strive to observe as many dogs as possible working as many scent pool conditions as possible. I recommend that scent pool scenarios be set up in advance with a scent pool condition in mind and planned for. When the trail is run, it is crucial that the dog's body language be recorded for later reference and digestion. It is only in this way that the handler will learn what the dog's body language means in these conditions. This gives the handler the ability to apply this knowledge to real searches in the future.

Chapter Fourteen
What Stands Out? What Is Missing?

"The loss of a diamond is easy to discern at a glance when it is owned by us. As we are possessive and mindful of our belongings, so too are dogs as they relate to scent in their world. The new and the missing often stand out in stark contrast to the surrounding scent world of the dog. What we perceive as tenuous or mysterious, to the dog may seem ridiculously obvious."

The need for a relatively fast start on the trail is implied by the chapter title. And by fast, I do not mean a rush out of the scene. By fast start, I mean allowing the dog access to the scene with some semblance of urgency. In some ways, this counters all of my advice for patience, but only on the surface. We must always remain patient with the dog when working. The problem is the dog's lack of patience with us when it already knows what it is supposed to do. And this, my friends, is exactly what we have when a good trailing dog is brought to the start or scene of a search.

I have written a lot on how I believe dogs process odor, specifically with their unique ability to determine the presence of things in great detail by scent alone. The analogy I used was how the dog might process the smells from a burger joint in comparison to us. We may smell certain things that stand out in our minds based on our likes and dislikes, such as the hamburger grilled over an open flame, pommes frites in the deep fryer, or the fabulous smell of freshly baked buns exiting the oven. Just writing of these things brings the odor to bear by memory alone. I think dogs take this discrimination to a level we have not even begun to fathom. Not only do they detect the meat, the fries, and the bread, I believe they detect all of the ingredients that go into their making as well as everything and anything else in the vicinity such as the mouse making off with a bit of sharp cheddar cheese that was haphazardly dropped on the floor. They may not immediately know the exact location of each and every scent but they certainly seem to detect the presence of it all.

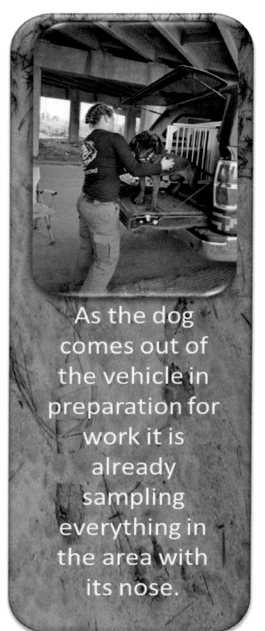

As the dog comes out of the vehicle in preparation for work it is already sampling everything in the area with its nose.

This, I believe, we can do with our eyes as well, but on a much more limited basis. Yes, the detail of things may appear more obvious to us without superior ability to determine detail by vision, but we are limited by cover and concealment. Dogs can smell right through the cover-up and immediately detect the hidden scent source.

Think about your own front yard that you have lived in, tended, and walked through each and every day for years. If the garden gnome that you so painstakingly placed, in just the proper spot, up by the fountain at the north end of the pond suddenly disappeared one day, you would know this loss at a glance. That is, unless your view of the pond was obscured by a tree or other covering object.

This would not be the case with your dog that has roamed the yard as much, if not more, than you. If the gnome had a scent or earth was displaced in its abduction, its disappearance would be recognized immediately regardless of a tree or any other thing that might block the dogs view. More importantly, the dog would IMMEDIATELY detect the presence of the thief who entered its inner sanctum.

Trained trailing dogs seem to be able to detect and determine what is present and what is missing at the start of many, if not all, search scenes. This ability is innate and natural with dogs; to catalog all odors everywhere. And, with the trailing dog that has run countless training and real trails from such scenes, this innate ability has now become enhanced through repetition and muscle memory. With each and every successful trail, the dog has become better at processing not only the trail itself and all of its subtle nuances, but also the complex nature of the missing person scene. In other words, the dog, through repetition, has learned to always be on the "lookout" for the scent of the missing person or the people not currently in the scent vicinity of the dog. The quicker the dog can isolate this missing person trail, the sooner it can be on the path to the capture.

I also believe that we have put too much stock in the scent article and how it supposedly marks the exact person the dog is supposed to find. The scent article is not natural in the dog's world, but the missing creature's scent trail certainly is. If the process of presenting the scent article becomes burdensome, too complex, or slow when starting the dog, I think the dogs will have a tendency to immediately switch to a natural scent response by deduction. In other words, find the trail that seems most obvious to them regardless of the article. To make the article important, it must be used in such a way that the dog not only comprehends but is comfortable— within its natural tendency of trail selection. The art of scent article production for the dog will be covered more in another chapter but it is important to understand the relationship to K9 detection of trails and why they follow them.   From an evolutionary standpoint, the reason why dogs trail is for life: food and reproduction plus identifying friends and avoiding foes. The need for trailing a scent is crucial for survival. So it must stand to reason that certain components of a scent trail will be more important to the dog than others. There was no place in the evolutionary ladder where the wolf was given a gauze pad in a bag and told what to search for. There was, on the other paw, a scent trail composed of certain indicators that told the wolf it would be worthwhile to follow: scent molecules that spelled young and naïve, old or wounded, fearful and alone. These concerns would hold the wolf's attention above and beyond others; in particular when the other trails smelled old, weak, or mundane.

When we formally discuss or teach why we, as a species, must reproduce or eat, we discuss the evolutionary need for the acts, and not necessarily the trigger for them. But, from an individual or personal standpoint, when we think of reproduction and sustenance in the form of food, we do not think that we must eat and schedule the events on a calendar. We think of eating based on the pleasure the act produces; we think of the taste of the chocolate sundae with the perfect whipped cream and cherry on top. When thinking of reproduction we do not think of the need for children to carry on our gene pool; we think of the appearance and the way our partner makes us feel.

So too with trailing, and when we think of why the dog takes one trail over another, we must think not only of the evolutionary trait, but the emotional response that triggers it. For trailing, I believe the ultimate trigger for the dog is prey drive and the excitement the thrill the hunt produces. This is actually the same for humans. As a species, hunting is not necessary to eat, but we humans are still attracted to the task due to the excitement hunting produces in us. Regardless of how we might rationalize it, it is the excitement of the hunt that is all consuming: not the need for it. When thinking of prey drive and the excitement of the hunt for dogs, it is not a pre-planned event that gets the dogs attention, it is the spontaneous rabbit that runs from the hollow into the open field

Couple quality indicators with the spontaneity of discovery and you will have a trail ripe for following. I think this is often the component of a traditional trail start that is often missing from the average handler's repertoire. And these two things spell the reason why many trailing dogs fail to follow the odor the handler started them on. The bag or bottle and the article therein simply do not trigger the correct evolutionary response in the dog, and the dog often takes trails that do not match them. If an article is used it must be in such a way that creates a natural, instinctual trailing response. Complicated, slow and cumbersome starts inhibit scent article use and increase the dog's propensity to slip back to the freshest trail out or the trail that is the most interesting or strongest.

My process of what I coin the "Scent Inventory" is nothing more than a preplanned method I use to allow my dog access to the scent scene in a circuitous fashion. I control the situation, giving the dog the chance to detect everything from a scent perspective without allowing following or investigation at that particular moment. Once I complete the inventory I prepare for scent article presentation at the PLS. My hope with the inventory is that my dog was able to catalog everything in the area; thereby knowing that some human scents are currently present and some are missing. With the aid of the article and the inventory, I found that my dogs had a tendency to adhere to the scent on the article better than using the article by itself without an inventory.

"What Stands Out" is also just as important as "What is Missing". This is evident in the beginning of the trail as it relates to suspect hand-touched objects at crime scenes. The physical contact odor of the hand is very appealing to the dog from the get—go, but contact odor from a suspect who is excited, or afraid, is like a magnet to the dog when it is smelled in comparison to normal human odor. The odor of a nervous suspect at the bank teller window will stand out more than similar contact odor of normal patrons, and almost all dogs will show a physical reaction to it. Police dogs that have experienced fear scent from the subject in apprehension situations will become very excited by fear scent on things that have been contacted by the subject at the start. These things will also stand out in the dog's olfactory system anywhere along the trail. For example, the suspect flees into a residential neighborhood and into a backyard in the hopes of getting out of sight from an oncoming police cruiser. If the suspect handles a gate handle or jumps a fence, the patrol dog will naturally react more strongly to these objects with physical contact odor. The reaction will almost always be stronger than the homeowner who may have touched or handled things in the same area. This contact odor stands out more than the homeowner odor, and most dogs, if truly working scent, will react and respond.

This condition is important to understand when working cases like this. I have heard many police K9 handlers, who found themselves in similar situations, start to discount their dog's insistence on smelling certain things non-animal. The FBI clue is the dog's intensity. When the dog reacts to a specific spot more than anywhere else and it is not an animal, then 90% of the time it is probably subject related.   When this condition occurs, the handler must not simply react in the negative, but be patient and wait the dog out. Pushing the dog past suspect contact odor may push the dog off the suspect trail.

Body Language Indicating Contact Odor

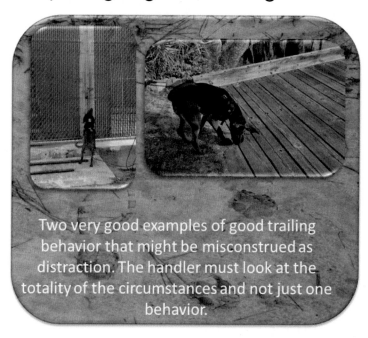

Two very good examples of good trailing behavior that might be misconstrued as distraction. The handler must look at the totality of the circumstances and not just one behavior.

1. Good trailing behavior to an area, house, or other location

2. During trailing, dog head pops to object; door, handle, wall, etc.

3. Dog's nose pans location furiously, up and down, side to side.

4. Dog may react more by sitting, pawing, barking or jumping.

5. Be patient and let the dog work or help it get into the area it wants to smell.

Animal Odor in Similar Condition:

1. Normal trailing behavior to a location.
2. Head pop **down** towards an object or spot.
3. Nose panning to place low on the ground
4. Tail drop or exceptional curling.
5. Nose plant without much movement.
6. Correct and tell the dog to get to work

Another condition that handlers face in the field is when they are working in natural, rural or wooded areas without much human scent traffic. When in these areas and the dog is trailing, any subject odor that is encountered—more than simple walking or running—will attract the dog, and the dog may show interest. These are things that have been touched or handled or where scent pools might exist. This interest level will be higher than when working in an urban environment with lots of other human traffic. As a matter of fact, the urban condition with its non-subject traffic will be grey scent in most cases where the dog is truly working. In other words, it does not stand out at all due to the number of other human trails and scents present.

There is also a condition where the dog may encounter a human object that was dropped or discarded long before the trail of the subject was run, sometimes many days prior. If there are tons of objects present, such as along a highway with lots of human trash thrown from vehicles, there will be little to no response. On the other hand, in the deep woods, where other humans rarely travel, if the dog encounters a discarded beer can or even a cigarette butt, the dog will probably hit on it and check it out. This will happen even if another, unrelated person tossed the can or butt. So, why all this interest now?

It's rather simple when we look at it from a similar condition viewed from a human perspective. I will use my homes front yards as an example. I live on an old sub-tropical plantation that cozies up to a tidal flat of the Edisto River in Coastal South Carolina. Our yard is very green with towering pines and ancient live oaks covered in Spanish moss. Everything looks like a manicured jungle. If a small section of an Arizona desert happened to be teleported to the middle of my front yard one day, even if it was only one foot square, it would stand out in stark contrast to my normal view. My eyes would gravitate to it no matter how much I might not want them to. I would look at this one-foot square patch of desert constantly until it became normal.

Different circumstances and different behavior could mean distraction.

Well, the same thing happens to trailing dogs in relatively clean areas devoid of human scent other than the subject's. If a new human odor on an object is encountered along the

The Tao of Trailing   Jeff Schettler

trail, the object will be so "scent visible" to the dog that it will almost have no choice but to inspect it. Most dogs that encounter such objects will leave the trail momentarily for the inspection, but once the object is discounted, the dog will get back on the trail. If the object were related to the subject, curiously, many trailing dogs, unless Evidence Identification trained, would perhaps pause momentarily in the area but usually simply keep trailing. The reason for this is the object is subject related and everything so far has been subject related. The object in the dog's mind, unless trained differently, is nothing more than a piece of the trail. It does not stand out as much as it would in an urban environment with tons of human odor. I understand this is a difficult to wrap one's mind around but it seems to be a fairly standard model with most trailing dogs that I have watched work over the years.

The question then comes to mind about how to handle a dog that inspects a new human scented object in the woods when it was trailing someone else. I suppose we can train the dog not to, but is this really worth the time? I will leave that up to the individual handler, but from my perspective, it is not all that big of a deal. I look at the new human odor as an anomaly similar to the patch of desert that I could not ignore in my Edisto Island front yard. I could not help myself; but would want to inspect such a sight. I do not think a dog can really be stopped from a similar condition from an olfactory point of view. In many ways, I think they have to check it out to satisfy not only curiosity but to make sure that it is not the subject's.

"What Stands Out" and "What is Missing" are big parts of the dog's olfactory world. Prudent handlers would do well by learning these conditions and how their dogs work them. Be observant but more importantly, be patient.

Chapter Fifteen
Trailing, Hunting, or Air Scent?

"Forward momentum does not equal trailing as it is only one element of many that complete this process. Lack of understanding comes from subscription to only one element."

The interesting thing about cases where many days have passed, or even weeks, months or years, is the amazing amount of faith people put up to support anything that a trailing dog might do. This, even when we look at similar deployments from a historical perspective. These very rarely, if ever, produce anything really concrete. I have found very few similarities with any other type of law enforcement investigative work. One exception might be mediums and psychics, perhaps. Usually when an investigative tool repeatedly fails, or sends an investigation the wrong way, that tool is discarded. Not to say that search dogs cannot be beneficial, because I am a huge proponent of search dogs.   The dilemma is when trailing dogs are used outside of their range of true efficiency such as a last ditch effort. Anything the dog does is grasped, rationalized, and used to support any theory or suspicion. This is the dilemma that occurs in the majority of ancient trailing dog deployments.

If anyone honestly looks at this type of case work with any degree of scrutiny, it is very easy to see that the dogs fail in the vast majority of deployments, and in many cases, lead investigations 180 degrees in the wrong direction in the process. I can say this based on personal experience with many such cases: in the beginning as a handler, and later as an investigator. Unfortunately, every now and then a trailing dog will trip over a find or make the scent in other ways than trailing, and the fantasy cycle becomes self-perpetuating. Rather than truly looking at the evidence of the case, the credit is simply given to the dog as a trailing find. A perfect example of this is when trailing dogs locate dead bodies or air scent a subject based on proximity odor. The trailing dog could have walked in circles for hours with nothing, but suddenly gets within an area where an air scent is possible and a find is made. Is the find any less important? Absolutely not. The dog did great but the method in which the dog worked is important to consider. Air scent of a dead or live body is fresh scent and not a six-month-old trail. Unfortunately, some handlers use any find in any fashion to bolster their position on trailing aged scent. They do this out of pure ignorance in most cases but sometimes pure fraud.

There is another problem with trailing dogs that must be exposed and considered carefully. This is when theory, suspicion, or evidence gathered in other ways is used to guide the K9 and handler to a find or evidence: simply to support prosecution. This fruit of the poisonous tree has become a thorn in the side of anything truly K9 over the last couple of years.

I highly recommend any interested reader simply Google search these subjects and names. I have seen very similar situations with really old/cold cases, where trailing dogs are used, when there is suspicion of location and suspects, but nothing concrete. The handlers are given tidbits of information about the case or have one of the investigators with the information on the trail with them, when, as if by magic, the dog arrives in the "vicinity" of the body, suspect, or other evidence. The trailing dog is now a hero, again.

Unfortunately, the familial and social anguish over such cases is what fuels the fire encouraging the use of any resource that might possibly produce a result. Any result is preferable to none. And anytime anyone petitions the viability of such a resource, like a magical trailing dog, this same anguish then fuels anger against the petitioner for posing any question at all. True dialogue and testing of the trailing tool is rarely offered because the condition is often simply too sensitive.

The truth of the matter is actually quite easy to discover. One must only use basic scientific testing methods on any age of trail to discover where said dogs are a viable resource. These results will be devastating for a few and it is why these few will never truly consider scientific testing.

I write of these situations in trailing—ignorance and fraud—for this chapter because they are so incredibly rampant in the industry. Anyone can be a trailing expert and often has no formal training. It is one of the very few "professional" K9 jobs that normal everyday people can get into and work real life cases without truly being educated. I know this because I was one of those people when I first started. My ignorance level was only eclipsed by my exuberance for the job. I had just enough success in the early years that it did nothing but fuel my irrational consumption of any crazy tidbit of trailing "knowledge" that I came across. If it sounded good, I went with it. What set me apart from many of my peers was the fact that I was also working a lot of cases. I wasn't simply training my dog and hoping I could work. I was able to test out all of my training on real life scenarios, sometimes on a daily basis.

What I discovered was that much of what I had been taught was bullshit: car trails, two week old trails, etc. I only had to work a few real cases to learn that we simply could not do those things reliably. As covered in an earlier chapter, the reason it did work in training was because I guided my dog to success. When the gloves came off and I had to go after real missing people and criminals, this stuff just did not work. Thankfully, it did not take long for me to realize that much of what I was doing and perpetuating was false. I had to change my ways. This was not an overnight epiphany; it was rather a slow, progressive kick in the ass. By the time I put all of the bad K9 work to rest, I had actually already retired. Along the way I caught a lot of bad guys but I would have caught far more if I had learned the right way from the beginning, and did not waste my time with training that did not work. In many ways, this is why I write now. To save others, in particular: the public and law enforcement, from the headache of misdirecting trailing K9's.

I know it seems strange that I am writing about fraud and ignorant dog handling in a chapter called *"Trailing, Hunting, or Air Scent,"* but it was important for me to set the stage to alert you to this problem. It is the incredible need for any break in an impossible case that often begins the vicious circle, but there has to be some shred of success in the past to warrant it. And there usually is and this is where the title of this chapter comes into play. In the vast majority of these crazy cases of days, weeks, or months-old-missing person investigations where the subject happens to be found by a trailing dog, it can invariably be chalked up to stupid luck of being in the right place at the right time, and **Air Scent.** Blind luck and being in the right place at the right time would not close the deal in most situations unless the dog simply tripped over the find. This happens occasionally, but usually it is a case where the dogs gets to the right general area by other investigative means or prior information, and upon arrival, detects the odor of a decaying human or in rare cases, a live one. It is not a case of the dog following a specific human scent over any real distance; it is a case of the dog being in the right place to air scent. The problem is that the dog is given credit for a trailing find, when in reality that is not how the dog worked and the trailing delusion of old scent trailing is propagated once again.

Some may wonder: why does this matter? The dog found the person and that is the most important thing. I would argue that though the find is important and cannot be minimized, the way in which the find was made should not be based on falsehoods. This is especially true when those falsehoods foster false hopes in future cases. False hope and blind faith in a tool that is not reliable often results in an inordinate amount of time and resources being applied to support it; resources that could better be used in other ways. In some criminal cases, this sheer effort has led to the arrest and conviction of innocent citizens. The trailing handler's first credo should be to do no harm.

A trailing dog that is an air scent dog is a human remains dog. Dogs can and do perform all of these tasks when working simultaneously. They can and do go back and forth from one method of scent detection to another, all based on the conditions that they find themselves in. However, when training trailing dogs, many handlers make the mistake of allowing a dog that is not actively following scent to get to the area where the subject of their search is hiding—to allow them to make the find. They do this because they cannot read the dog's body language that screams: "NOT FOLLOWING SCENT!" and they guide the dog to the end of the trail with imperceptible lead handling and human body language cues. Novice handlers, and many veterans, slip into this bad habit because of several reasons:

1. The human need to have a happy ending to the trail.
2. Practice trails that are too complicated for the dog.
3. Always running known trails.

The argument in support of this is that the dog has to get a positive in order to keep it motivated to work. Nothing could be further from the truth. Dogs do not need the happy ending, the human handler does. Training like this does nothing more than to make the dog dependent on the handler to get it to the right place in order to close the deal. The dog will learn a behavior that the handler unintentionally teaches it because it is a creature of habit and taking the easy path to reward. If the dog learns that when the chips are down the handler will lead it to the subject's location, it will learn to "not work" each and every time, and simply run. This is where the hunting behavior comes into play.

Hunting is often confused with trailing because the subtle nuance of true scent work is lost in the action of movement. This action really is nothing more than forward momentum. The dog learns that if it lunges into the end of the lead and simply runs, the handler will follow it. Following is a type of reward. When the handlers see the dog is running in the wrong direction and stops, the dog will circle and then run to a direction the handler feels is acceptable. This following at the right time is usually because the handler knows where the trail is and the location of the subject. Following a hunting dog not in scent is an extremely bad habit and one if done enough can ruin a perfectly good trailing dog.

Hunting Body Language:

Example of trailing to a condition of no scent. It is time to think about moving to a productive source or going back to where the trail was last known.

1. Head up and panning, eyes actively looking.
2. Ears laid back
3. Mouth wide open and tongue hanging
4. Lunging or just running

To me, the big indicator that the dog is not in odor is when there is a productive source close by and the dog does not use it: coupled with a heads-high behavior, mouth open, and eyes panning. It is clear to me that the dog is looking and not scenting. This is very common in many "urban" trailing dogs I see. They run without scenting until the handler gets them to an area where there is an air scent of the subject. There is no need to work when the handler does it all, and dogs, being creatures of the paths of the least resistance, fit into this mold naturally.

When I encounter dogs that work this way, the first thing to do is to shut the behavior down. That is not easy if the problem is a habit. The key to this re-training is working on motivation with drive and getting the dog back to basics where the scent is strong and easy to follow with the nose. I strongly recommend high drive trails with lots of fun and high reward. The second key is not allowing the bad behavior of running heads up and looking. As soon as I see this behavior and it is obvious the dog is not in scent, we stop and do not move again until the dog shows scenting behavior. If there is no scenting behavior in the area, then we shut the trail down and step back to something even easier.

I understand that dogs do not necessarily follow all scent on the ground and that there are times dogs follow scent at chest height and higher, but there are corresponding body language behaviors that shows this. The big difference in this heads up behavior is missing "gaping mouth with tongue flopping" and most important, eyes that are looking for something. When dogs are actively processing odor there is a direction and action of the nose and head that shows this.

Chapter Sixteen
Double Dog Dare Ya!

"Employ the natural instincts of the trailing dog and opportunities for success rise exponentially. Nothing Canid is more instinctual than pack hunting; two may be better than one."

Okay, Y'all, I'm going to kick off on a trailing/tracking tangent that I've broached in the past and written briefly about in my book *Tactical Tracker Teams, A guide to high risk manhunts,* Alpine Publications 2013. In this chapter I open the can of worms a little bit wider and let a few wiggle out. I want to offer a different way of deploying patrol K9s on the street in a hunt for fugitives. This is rarely thought of let alone considered with any seriousness. This manner of deployment is a Dual K9 Trail or Track; in other words, working two patrol or police dogs on one suspect trail. There, I said it! Digest this for a moment and then let's continue.

To begin with, why do we not consider this type of deployment in the first place? Often times the reason why something is never considered is because many feel that the "something" or idea simply cannot be done. Much the same can be said about sailing around the world when it was once considered flat. Likewise, heavier-than-air flight during the early years of the 20th Century as the Wright Brothers first took off from the sands of Kittyhawk, North Carolina. Sometimes something is not considered because it simply was never thought of. In the case of dual K9 tracks this is probably not the case. I know I've been on a number of searches where Patrol Supervisors or Watch Commanders asked about getting two dogs into the act at the same time; not necessarily on the same track but deployed in different ways on the same suspect. Generally speaking, the naysayers tend to be the K9 officers themselves and there are usually two reasons for it.

The first reason is because many K9 officers have a mistaken belief that their dogs will not tolerate another patrol dog anywhere near their search, and will fight given the first opportunity. The other issue, and the often times and exacerbating reason, is that some handlers don't want to share the limelight. Another dog and officer means sharing the spotlight and that's tough for some super-alpha handlers. Believe it or not, the attitude of the handler has a lot to do with how any patrol K9 will react to another K9 in its presence during work. We've all heard the old adage that everything the handler feels goes down the lead to the dog; and nothing holds more truth than this in the dual dog deployment. If the handler is hinked-up due to another patrol K9 in the vicinity, his or her dog will be too. There's just no stopping it. The key to the double dog deployment from the get-go is the handler controlling his or her emotions about it in the first place. If you don't want a dogfight, don't get so worried about it. More importantly, train for it so the chances of it happening are slim to none.

Dogs are pack animals by nature. The ability to work together is hardwired and can be trained for.

Our patrol dogs are remarkably capable animals that amaze us on a daily basis with their ability to comprehend our needs and work for us. If we want our dogs to work with other dogs, they will. We simply need to expect that cooperation from them and implement the training to support it.

To begin with, I think dogs naturally work together far better than we give them credit for. After all, they are pack animals and hunting for things from a collective perspective comes natural. Our K9s are not all that far removed from the wolf and I know they retain many of the hunting traits their wild cousins use to such advantage chasing game. Trailing, or tracking as we humans recognize it, is a natural component of collective pack behavior, and cooperation is a must for survival when on the hunt. We use the trailing trait to hunt for suspects who flee. It stands to reason that some of the collective hunting traits inherently tied to trailing will hold over in our patrol dogs, and just perhaps, we can utilize this trait in police K9 deployment.

My first experience with working two dogs on a single suspect trail was a foot bail-out from a stolen car in Alameda California. I started my bloodhound on the car seat of the suspect as his direction of foot travel was unobserved. Just for kicks, my beat partner, also a K9 handler asked if it were possible to run his German Shepherd in reserve on the trail. I had never done this before and could not immediately answer.

There were times in the past that suspects we trailed holed up in buildings or other areas not safe for me or my bloodhound to pursue on lead and the patrol dog option in an open area search was really needed. During those searches I always called for the patrol dog to respond and had to wait sometimes for an hour or more. It had never occurred to me to have the dog already available in back-up. Part of the problem back in those days is that I was a new handler and did not understand dog behavior or pack behavior as well as I do now. If the need was a quick area search off-lead that was not safe for the trailing dog on-lead, then the down time waiting for the second dog could mean the difference between catching the suspect or not. This is especially true when the subsequent area search proved unproductive and the trailing dog had to strike up the trail once again. Sometimes getting the trail again after so long of a wait just did not happen.

I had never really considered having the patrol K9 in back-up with me while I was trailing, so the first time my friend and beat partner asked if he could tag along with his patrol K9 at the same time I said... sure... I think so?! To be honest, I wasn't sure what to do and had no real reason to say no. I know my hound could be a jerk from time to time, but for the most part he never had any concern for other dogs on the trail when working or at home and he loved to play with other dogs, male, female, large, or small.

Though we had a felony suspect on the run, who was hopping fences on the West end of Alameda, we took the time to talk a little bit about how to do this thing we had never done before. We decided that the Shepherd would follow behind five to ten yards as soon as we started and would be in reserve should we have to work a yard or building search off lead. Ronin took the trail a lot stronger than normal on that deployment. I noticed that he would flash little looks back at his back-up K9 and was pulling on the long lead a lot harder than normal. Immediately I could tell it was a competition and he simply wanted to the get to the car seat before the other dog because he knew this is where we were going to start the trail. The patrol dog also seemed to be more animated and was simultaneously pulling into his collar in the exact same direction. It immediately stuck me that both dogs had already acquired the target and were competing to get to it first. I was also surprised that they seemed to be feeding off each other and not necessarily targeting each other.

Ronin hit the track of the suspect like the sprung bar on a rattrap. His head snapped so hard on the trail and direction of travel that the "dirt bag" had taken that I thought his lead was going to split. I had an extremely hard time keeping up with him; he was so hard on the trail. The back-up dog was equally motivated and I remember my partner saying that he swore his dog had the trail too and was working nose down. He had started the dog on collar but had to switch to the harness to too keep from choking his dog. Once the lead went to harness, his dog was trailing in almost the same fashion as mine and steadily getting closer to us.

The intensity of the dogs in this training photo show what the proximity to the subject can produce.

Both dogs had absolutely no interest in each other from an aggression standpoint. They got far closer to each other than we planned and in many cases swapped places when my dog paused in a scent pool too long or was slow on a corner. When the positions changed, the patrol dog became the lead man-trailer. We only swapped back because we thought that was supposed to be the way to do it. Neither of us realized at the time that changing point on the trail was common place for all pack hunters and the positions could alternate with wolves or pack hounds on a deer hunt in much the same fashion; albeit without leads, harnesses, and humans involved.

There was no doubt in my mind that both dogs were only feeding off each other and cooperating. They had no interest in fighting; they only had an interest in the target. My favorite part of the trail was when we entered into a back yard and both dogs hit the far fence line like demons, barking and howling. They immediately gravitated to the exact spot the suspect had obviously hopped over, and in their attempts to negotiate its six-foot height, broke several of the fence posts holding it upright. Though I think it was my imagination, to this day I swear I heard the suspect on the other side squeal in panic at the Hell hounds cacophony…. and I loved it! Both dogs were working with such teamwork that it was like they had been born and raised together to do just this work. And that my friends, is exactly what it was all about. Perhaps they were not born and raised to work together, but there is a strong genetic memory for pack hunting.

If anything, it is the singular method in which we hunt people now that is unnatural. There is nowhere on Mother Nature's chalkboard a formula for trailing dogs working for man alone, or wearing a harness connected to a long lead. The strongest genetic instinct is for dogs to hunt together; yet we spend so much of our time trying to teach them just the opposite.

That first double dog trail was one of the best lessons I ever had at allowing dogs to work in a natural way. It flew in the face of every modern formula for police K9 deployment that I had encountered and still does to this day. Since that time in 1997, I have deployed my dogs with many patrol dogs in back-up and also with explosives K9s. Never once did I have a problem with fighting or aggression while working. Not to say that incidents cannot happen. There are some dogs that will absolutely not tolerate other dogs in their space, but these problems were not really the norm we all imagined.

Now there is a lot of precedent for what I am proposing, and by all means, this is not my idea or invention. Dogs in packs have been used to hunt animals and humans for millennia. To this day there are prison systems that use pack hounds to hunt escapees and these dogs work seamlessly together with no real formal training other than exposure and association. I am not recommending that we use no formal training. What I am recommending is that we start pushing the envelope of K9 deployment and consider the multiple dog factor in ways we have not before. I also recommend that formal exposure of working dogs to other working dogs should be mandatory and a new part of formal training.

It is really this exposure and association that is the key to dogs working together and it does not take that much work. Dogs are not out to pick a fight with other dogs naturally, and high drive does not necessarily translate to not getting along. If fighting were the natural genetic response to every encounter with other dogs, then survival of the species would be threatened. The standard practice for many kennel facilities is to segregate the dogs and not allow for any social interaction. This philosophy revolved around the premise that working dogs would work better if separated from other K9s and the work ethic would be stronger if the dog was not allowed much activity when not on the job or training. I believe this philosophy is archaic and based on human rationale and not what necessarily works well for dogs.

On the contrary, we believe that when not working or training, our K9s should be socially interacting with our other working dogs—other dogs really are the best teachers of acceptable behavior—in large runs where they can exercise naturally and be mentally stimulated. None of our dogs are kenneled in anything smaller than zero-foot by forty-foot yard, weather permitting, when off duty. They are often given two fenced acres for more activity.

At our facility we routinely pair or group working dogs with other dogs with the appropriate size or demeanor when they are off duty. This social integration begins when the dogs are puppies and continues into adulthood. We do this in large dog runs where they can interact naturally and with plenty of mental stimulation. We do not believe in small ten-foot by six-foot pens with no stimulation and solitary confinement. Solitary management practices, in my opinion, actually foster more aggressive interest in other dogs—especially in the form of aggression.

The payoff for our philosophy is dogs that are socially easy going without undo interest or aggression towards strange dogs. This is very important because strange dogs are a big part of normal deployment in any urban setting. Because dogs are a normal course of daily business with our working dogs, they do not flip out if they encounter strange canines when working in public. The exercise our K9s get from constant interaction with other dogs far exceeds anything that can be provided by running behind an ATV on a dirt road. Our dogs are stronger, faster, and usually far more agile than the average working dog because of the constant play with kennel partners.

My point with the previous paragraphs was not to try and change an industry but to offer a solution for exercise, socialization, and mental stimulation that directly translates to multiple K9 deployment and better working K9s. Dogs can work naturally together without this process, with simple part-time training techniques, but I feel a natural acceptance of other dogs comes from better social interaction and training.

When considering pairing two K9s on a single trail for the purposes of having a back-up K9, off-lead area search capability, or apprehension/handler protection, it is important that the process begin in a controlled training environment. The K9 unit should practice everything that might occur in reality; so the handlers and dogs can be prepared for any eventuality. The simple act of repetition will go a long way to prepare the dogs to work together for a common cause.

For the purposes of this subject I am going to outline a two K9 deployment for trailing/tracking as the primary activity and patrol/off lead area search as the secondary; should a dangerous situation present itself and trailing must be temporarily curtailed. The first thought after reading the last sentence might be why not simply have one dog that can do both effectively? That might be the ideal solution but the problem is that there are many times that a dedicated trailing/tracking resource—that is very good—is also a rare commodity. Not all patrol K9s trail long range through many conditions effectively. A solid, long-range trailing dog that can negotiate all manner of scent and environmental barriers is really a special dog. There are also many deployments where the trailing K9 is not an apprehension or protection dog, and would be at risk if deployed off or on-lead on a suspect. There have to be some serious questions raised on sending any dog into these conditions, and the deployment edict should never be made lightly. The third issue is that two dogs working on one suspect trail really work better than one. The competition and pack mentality of the dogs creates higher drive for the catch and I believe enhances overall performance.

The first deployment consideration for a suspect trail is the classic single suspect with a single purpose trailing dog on point. In this scenario a dual purpose K9 with off-lead area search and apprehension capabilities is in back-up. The deployment option to be considered is a Military Style Bounding Over-Watch. In the case of military tactics, this means that a combat unit moves while another covers during conditions of imminent or possible contact with an opposing force. In the case of K9 deployment it is two dog teams moving in a similar style after one of the dogs' proximity alerts to possible suspect contact ahead.

To begin, the trailing dog should have primary access to the scene for a good start with the back-up K9 held back a few yards but prepared to move immediately. I recommend that the second dog also be in harness vs. a standard collar or choke style chain. As soon as this K9 sees that the first dog in on the hunt it will want to get involved and take the point position. The competition factor ensures that this will happen with the vast majority of dogs. If a standard collar is used to restrain the dog it will put too much pressure on the neck and wear the dog out. In the case of a chain there will simply be too much constriction around the neck damaging cartilage and muscle in the process. Constant strain on the neck with a chain collar or choke chain for long periods of time can create permanent problems for any dog. A harness allows for restraint without tiring the dog or physically interfering with breathing.

If a collar has to be used, I recommend a pinch or prong collar, which will reduce the dog's instinct to pull so hard, thereby reducing the chance for injury. The dog must already have experience with the prong collar prior to the two-dog deployment exercise. Some people are very much opposed to the use of a prong collar in any form and believe that they are inhumane. I beg to differ and believe that the opposite is actually true.

The prong collar is nasty in appearance but in practice the chances for injury are fairly slim especially in the hands of an experienced handler with a properly fitted collar. When the average, uneducated dog aficionado looks at the prong collar they generally assume the prongs are very painful. This reaction is why people are amazed at the Indian Fakir's bed of nails trick when the magician lays on top of a bed of deadly sharp nails without injury. The reason for the lack of injury is the entire weight of the body is evenly spread out across the entire bed. There is no direct pressure from any one particular nail. Though not necessarily comfortable, the bed is far from dangerous when laid on evenly. Much the same can be said about the prong collar. If only one or a very few prongs are applied with pressure they can cause injury. On the other hand, if the collar is properly sized with an adequate number of links, the application of pressure may create slight discomfort but like the bed of nails when laid upon, is very safe. I often demonstrate this by using the collar on my own neck or sensitive parts of the arm or wrist. Studies have shown that when used properly, the prong collar actually has far fewer long lasting negative effects than the chain collar.

Some may consider the use of an E-Collar for the purpose of restraint and better control of the second dog while the first is deployed, but I am not really a fan of this. Though I use E-collars, I do so in only certain situations where I am confident the dog will not be put into defense when it is applied. The problem with a two-dog deployment, especially during the first phases of practice, is that the second dog will have, at minimum, a competitive reaction to the first dog moving forward. Some dogs may have a slightly aggressive response until corrected by the handler. The key to the correction is that it must be done in such a way as not to amplify the "fight" response of the dog. If the second K9 views the first as a potential threat, electric simulation may cause an immediate fight reflex, and this reaction may be directed at the handler. The same can be said about the prong collar. This is very much like when trying to break up a dogfight. When a handler grabs one of the fighting dogs and surprises it, the dog may react by biting its handler.

If an E-Collar is going to be used, it must be used on a dog that has a lot of working experience with the collar. The simple fact that the E-Collar is on the dog may negate any negative response to the first dog, however, if stimulation must be applied, the experienced K9 may only require a vibration type application to stop any aggressive response.

I recommend that both handlers have some basic hand signals in place before real deployment. Hand signals allow for easy and fast communication with little to no noise. Light and sound discipline is crucial for high-risk tracks. Suspects already have an advantage if they believe they are being tracked and have an ambush location prepared in advance. The tables are turned when the K9 team is experienced, the handler easily reads the dog's proximity alert, and the team does not give themselves away because of noise or light. Hand and arm signals allow for silent communication.

The entire tracking team needs to be on the same sheet of music for basic signals such as:

1. Halt
2. Down
3. Danger close
4. Suspect observed
5. Forward
6. Slow
7. Assemble
8. Flank
9. Over-watch

The K9 teams should have their own special hand signals such as:

1. Trail starting
2. Scent pool
3. Proximity Alert
4. Take Point

At the beginning of the deployment the point dog may or may not have an immediate trail out of the area. This really depends on the size of the scent pool at the scene, perhaps complicated by contamination factors, and age of the trail. If the point dog must circle to find the exit trail, the second dog should be held in a down or sit position as quiet as possible. Once the exit trail is determined, the point handler should signal the team and especially the second handler to move out and follow.

Preparing for a dual K9 deployment with an appropriate interval between the dogs.

The "following" or second position really will fluctuate based on terrain features, visibility factors, and officer safety. The dogs can usually work together fairly closely with little or no issues. During the first few practice phases it is best to start with a ten-yard interval between dogs with small changes up to no more than a five-yard distance from the point dog. Ideally, we want to get the dogs to be able to work side by side and pass each other with no agitated response. It is actually easier than it sounds even with super high-drive, dominant dogs and only takes practice and repetition. The key to cooperation is the innate following/pack drive in both dogs for the subject of the hunt.

Nothing really special has to occur for the second dog to know who it is hunting. My experience has been that the second dog normally detects and follows the subject scent as soon as the point dog picks it up. There seems to be a natural form of communication between both dogs through body language or perhaps their own unique scent patterns. The second dog may want to smell the scent article the first one used to target the trail, such as a car seat or piece of clothing, but I find in most situations they have a tendency to bypass it as the target scent is already known. I do not recommend forcing the article or start point on the second dog with any type of command or hand signal. It is best to simply allow the dog to follow on its own, as silently as possible. If any commands need to be given they should be simple and short. Avoid constantly chattering at the dog as this can be a huge distraction for both K9s and increase the chances of the suspect detecting the teams' presence from a distance.

The point dog will invariably overshoot turns and have to circle back from time to time. It will also react and canvas any scent pools related to the suspects' passage; this often results in circling and slowing behavior. When this happens, handler two must stop and take a covering position with his K9 in a down or sitting position. Again, silence is mandatory, as the first dog may have to work hard to solve the scent problem. A barking back-up K9 is a huge distraction and can give away the teams location and give the suspect a chance to fight or run again.

Turns are one thing but large scent pools in the middle of a trail can be another. Not only will the trailing dog have to work out of the pool and find an exit trail, but depending on the situation might also indicate the quarry is fairly close. Big scent pools with a frantic animation change on the part of the trailing dog may indicate that there is fresh proximity scent from the suspect in the area and the dog may be actively searching for a scent cone and an air scent. If this is the case, the team must be extra observant in all directions. Instead of watching the first dog and handler, dog team two should be facing out with some cover and concealment: observing an assigned area of responsibility for signs of danger. The second handler must also watch his or her dog closely for reaction to suspect air scent. While the trailing dog may be hunting for the exit trail or scent cone of the suspect

The second K9 is also working scent. The handler must pay close attention to this dog's changes of behavior, as well.

inside the scent pool, the second dog may be in a better position for an air scent and may react accordingly. The second dog in these situations may actually have a very good chance of catching a fresh suspect air scent before the first dog. This is very important because of the second dogs positioning on the fringe of the pool. Worse, if the handler is not paying attention, a very important alert may be missed. The second handler really has a difficult assignment in this condition—in that he must pay attention to his own sector of observation while simultaneously watching his own dog for signs that it detected the suspect from a distance. The second handler must also be prepared to follow again if the first dog breaks out of the pool and continues the trail.

If the point dog gives a good proximity alert to an area that is too dangerous to trail through, the decision can be made to allow the patrol dog to clear it. The same option may be used for buildings and other structures. This decision cannot be made lightly. Even off-lead and operating at full speed, a patrol dog can be an easy target for a prepared suspect with a firearm. Just because we have the option to use an apprehension K9 does not necessarily mean it's a good idea to do so. The deployment of the area dog off lead is a Use of Force consideration that must be made on the fly but also made wisely. The following training tips are based on full consideration being made with regard to safety for all involved including the dog.

If the decision is made to clear an area with the second K9, then preparation must be made for that process and it has to be done quickly. First off, some consideration should be made for the areas behind the projected search area for the K9. It's always a good idea to have a mobile perimeter force ready and prepared to deploy as a blocking force. This force should be far enough behind the projected search area as not to impact the searching K9. This force is in the area to block escape routes as well as to act as reinforcements should more officers be required. All units involved in the search must be aware of the situation, and that the second dog is going to be deployed.

The point dog and handler are now going to assume the back-up slot and must take up a position of cover and concealment. The point K9 may be a little anxious when the second K9 moves forward especially if this movement is related to proximity scent. Both dogs will understand that the subject is close and both will want to get in on the find. It may be difficult to keep the dogs quiet, but now is the time for silence, if at all possible. Constantly barking dogs will pinpoint their positions and if the suspect is armed and waiting, it becomes more information that can be used against the team and especially the deployed K9. On that note, it may be wise to have the K9 announcement made from a location the K9 is not coming from. In other words the announcement comes from one location and if the dog is deployed, it comes from a different direction. When the suspect has a clear idea of the direction the dog will be coming from due to barking or an announcement, the suspect will have a better chance of hurting or killing the dog once it is deployed. Making a call out from a different location from that of the dog can be considered a ruse to confuse the suspect. If the K9 has a good scent cone on the subject and has pinpointed the hide, giving the dogs position away before deployment might be a very bad idea.

Often times there may be several proximity alerts from the point trailing dog as it gains ground on the subject. These alerts are degrees of increasing scent pictures that tell the dog that it is getting close. Each proximity alert will create ever—increasing level of body language response from the dog in the form of speed changes, intensity in pulling, head and tail set. The problem with these alerts is when the handler is not practiced at reading them. Handlers either do not recognize what the dog is saying and that they are getting close, or the handler is hyper-sensitive and over reacts to them. The latter can create a condition of distrust in the handler about the dogs' body language and there is a very good chance that he will not react to the very close alert because of what he assumed were false alerts. In the vast majority of trails I have run with other handlers, who react this way, it was the handler who was at fault due to major impatience, sometimes even after one early proximity alert.

Trailing/ tracking criminals is a very dangerous affair, and all too often I see handlers simply rush right into any spur of the moment decision they make: primarily due to the overwhelming desire to seal the deal. The problem with this mentality is that it will get you killed quickly. The reason why most police K9 handlers or their dogs are wounded or killed on felony trails is because they are too impatient. If a handler is surprised by an ambush, 99% of the time it is because he or she blew right through small alerts along the way that screamed proximity. Lack of alert recognition is directly tied to moving too fast and not paying attention to the dog.

Swapping dogs at the point position is often a matter of safety but it also can be to reduce the fatigue of one or both dogs.

To prevent K9 Fatigue over a long trail or a condition of increasing levels of proximity alerts, the team may swap dogs several times until the final alert is made. Depending on wind and terrain conditions, proximity alerts can come from hundreds if not thousands of yards away. It is a really good idea to practice several changes of dogs so a team can operate seamlessly over the course of at least a mile and six or seven changes. This sounds long and hard but it really is not. If the second dog does not pick up a scent cone or fresh air scent in the vicinity of the alert from the point dog, it will usually start following the trail on its own or show negative body language. If the second dog shows body language that it is now tracking or trailing, head down and actively following ground scent, the decision has to be made to either allow it to continue or swap dogs again. This decision should be made based on the quality of the first alerts, (if there were any), and how strong the second dog is at trailing.

Interestingly, I find the trailing response from the second K9 happens even with normally non-trailing/ tracking dogs that have had no formal training. All dogs can trail instinctively with absolutely no training. It is really just a matter of whether they choose to or not. Working with a second dog creates a competition factor that might just awaken the new job. Even though the work is instinctual, it may not be refined and this is where the decision to swap back to a more seasoned man-trailer might be a good idea.

The Tao of Trailing Jeff Schettler

A long lead might also be a very good idea for the second dog even if it is in area search mode. Depending on the conditions, it may not be safe for uninvolved citizens or perimeter officers to deploy an off-lead patrol dog without any physical control. With a thirty-foot lead, and if the handlers uses short, bounding techniques, a surprising amount of ground can be covered in a short time. The danger is really transferred to the dog in this condition; however, as the dog is being restrained. If the suspect is armed and prepared, the only advantage the dog might have had was speed and agility. This method must be used judiciously because the long lead negates the K9s slight advantage when free.

Two dogs can definitely be better than one but not without serious training. K9 units cannot expect to implement this style of deployment effectively without practicing it first. I recommend that all K9s in a particular K9 unit get in on the game. In the case of smaller departments, work out a training schedule with other agencies and invite their dogs.

Chapter Seventeen
Ending It

"Easily achieved endings are deceptive. Easy endings will also be forgotten"

The single component of trailing training that appears to me to transcend all styles or methods is that of the ending. The endings are always the same regardless of the age or the difficulty and it is this that often defeats us when reality differs from our training. What differs from training to reality in trailing training? Real endings.

By real endings I am referring to a myriad of things that normal people would do; whether they know they are missing or not, hunted or not. Normal people are rarely sitting at the base of a tree waiting to be found or singled out from the crowd; sitting at a picnic bench away from all the other park goers on a Sunday afternoon. When training, we always have a tendency to make the endings very similar in that the person is out of sight, around a corner, in a tree, etc. It seems to always be the same and we rarely deviate from the way we found the trail layer the last time and this is what can kill our efforts on a real search.

Before we get into what I think is the right way to train for real searches, I want to write about what I think is wrong with what is done—more often than not. Without identifying the weakness and understanding the reasons for it, it is difficult to come up with a proactive plan to correct it.

The weakness with training endings is that we have a tendency to place people in places, and doing things most lost people or criminals would not do. If the endings are all very similar, then we are teaching our dogs a pattern that is difficult for the dog and handler to break away from when running real searches. I wrote about this in the chapter about Walk-Back finds in *K9 Trailing; The Straightest Path*. In this chapter, I brought up the fact that most tailing dogs never encounter a subject walking toward them on the training trail and attempting to pass them with absolutely no acknowledgement. In other words, like a normal person might do in passing on a busy city street. Not everyone is going to engage your dog and squeal, "You found me!" and promptly hand over a treat or ball.

After testing hundreds of dogs with this ending, I discovered that the vast majority failed to engage the subject walking past them, and continued on the trail towards the scent pool the subject just left. Most seemed confused and always went back to what they were doing; even if they did head pop briefly on the subject. Very few stopped in front of the trail layer unless the handler cued them with a line check or some sort of verbiage.

The reason why almost all of the dogs failed to engage is because the ending did not fit their pattern of training, and the K9 became a creature of the pattern. In order to become a good handler it is very important not to become fixed in any particular pattern except when establishing the basics with the dog. Once the dog is trailing nicely and reliably, it is important to become chaotic in your approach to scenarios and endings in particular.

Walk-Back Find; One More Time

If you read *K9 Trailing* and tried the Walk-Back find, you may understand exactly what I am talking about. On the other hand, if you are new to my style and are reading *Tao* as the first of my books, then I suggest you try the Walk-Back before continuing with this chapter.

To begin, use a trail layer completely new to the dog. This is super important. Have the person walk to a predesigned hiding spot and stay there until they see your dog coming towards them. The subject should have a good fifty yards or more of visual on the ground the K9 will traverse before getting to them; in order to adequately prepare for what they are about to do.

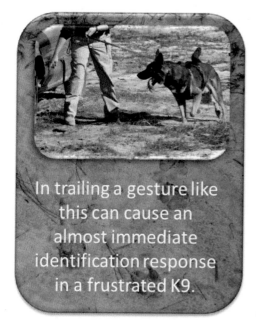

In trailing a gesture like this can cause an almost immediate identification response in a frustrated K9.

When the trail layer sees the dog coming, he or she should start walking back on the exact trail they walked in on: towards the trailing dog. As they approach the dog it is crucial not to look at the dog or the handler. As a matter of fact, if they can start texting on a cell phone as they are walking, or perhaps make a call, it will approximate what a normal person might be doing walking down the sidewalk. As the dog and trail layer pass each other, the trail layer should do nothing other than keep walking. The handler should do nothing that shows the dog the trail layer is recognized: such as a line check, stopping, or saying anything at all.

This is easier said than done as many handlers have a really difficult time not stopping in front of the trailing layer walking towards his or her dog. If the handler does anything in front of the trail layer at all, the dog will react to this person and have an interest thereby skewing the test. The handler usually has this reaction due to prior similar behavior, which has become habitual and the dog has learned that it means it has found the right person. The problems being most handlers never know they are cuing, or have no idea that they can be cuing the dog in the first place. The common misnomer is that because the dog is on a lead out in front; it is somehow free from handler influence. I have heard this many times in the past while teaching schools around the World, and it is usually from handlers with no other dog experience than owning a pet. Experienced handlers and trainers know how easy it is to cue a dog with something as simple as a change in head position or a look at the wrong time; especially on a lead no matter how long.

These handler behaviors usually include but are not limited to:
1. Line check
2. Stopping
3. Pointing
4. Body language change such as lifting up the lead over the head
5. Verbal cue such as "Is that him?!?"

Many dogs may give a little head pop as they pass, some may even wag their tails, but few will ever stop in front of the person and stop them in their tracks; which is what I would want if my dog was truly hunting for this person. In a busy environment with lots of other people, we need something definitive that says the person found is really the One. Head pops and a little wag don't cut it and this is really true if the dog seems to continue down the trail without looking back. And my friends, this is exactly what many dogs do... continue down the trail.

I find this reaction interesting even though I know programmed training is the culprit. This is because the subject's direct scent usually hits the dog full in the face and the trail is now a back track, which should, at minimum, slow the dog down in some confusion. Even with all of the "Here's Your Sign!" hints most dogs bulldoze on past. If programmed training is the primary problem then this exercise is really an indicator of how "bad programming" is for a working dog. The nice thing is this is a pretty easy fix as long as the handler's timing is good with some corrective countermeasures.

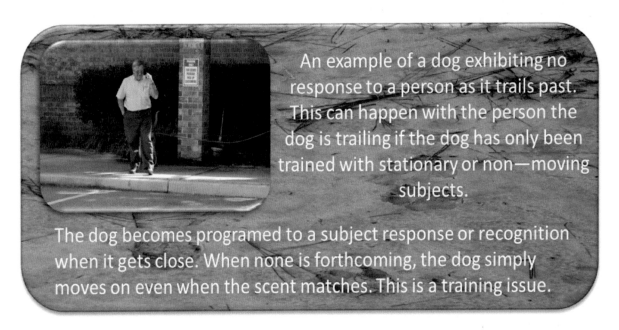

An example of a dog exhibiting no response to a person as it trails past. This can happen with the person the dog is trailing if the dog has only been trained with stationary or non—moving subjects.

The dog becomes programed to a subject response or recognition when it gets close. When none is forthcoming, the dog simply moves on even when the scent matches. This is a training issue.

Simply allow this exercise run its course the way it will the first time it is attempted. We really need a baseline to determine the extent of the problem; and any influence on the part of the handler or trail layer will not solve anything at this point. If the dog shows a glimmer of recognition such as a head pop and tail wag then it will be a little easier to solve than if the dog simply trails on past, with nose glued to the ground: with no other change of behavior. Don't worry about letting the dog finish with a positive on this, especially if they trail past the trail layer to the point he or she started walking from and then looks confused. It's perfectly OK to stop the exercise and put the dog up. Putting the dog up is a K9 Trainer term for putting the dog away for a time and stop training. Almost like a "Time Out" for the dog.

I highly recommend video recording this first exercise and viewing it several times before attempting corrective action. This will detail several factors that might help retraining. More than likely the handler will see that regardless of what he or she thought, some line guiding probably occurred.

Timing of certain stimulators and especially rewards will be very important. I highly recommend you read *Chapter Five Reward and Timing* in this book, prior to attempting to fix this. When it is time to run the exercise again and add some corrective counter measures, set the trail the same way and make sure to use a new trail layer.

This new trail layer should be a person who is very observant and has great reactions. Another experienced dog handler may be a very good option. This is because the trail layer will be doing much of the work retraining your dog. Have the trail layer wear sunglasses that make it impossible to see his or her eyes. When walking towards the dog, he or she should not look in the direction of the dog but instead look straight ahead and simply move eyes on to the dog.

As the dog approaches the trail layer he or she should pay particular attention to the dog's body language. You may have caught some things from the video recording that may help you quite a bit at this phase, so be cognizant of any new body language indicator that you saw in the video, and make sure the trail layer has seen them also; so he or she can react properly if they are manifested again. If the dog shows any indication at all that the person might even be remotely familiar, the trail layer needs to "Pay on Sniff". Pay on Sniff is a term detection dogs use when talking about the early detection training stages where the dog is learning to react to scent. When payment is made as soon as the dog detects the odor then it remembers the condition better the next time. If a handler waits until the

This is a good non—threatening posture for a trail layer to take that invites the K9 in. Of course, this is not appropriate with an apprehension K9. Waiting for the dog to see the ball before it is tossed underhand is important.

dog looks back at him or her, then the payment is connected to the handler and not the odor.

If the dog looks at the trail layer and slows or wags its tail, the trail layer should immediately stop, assume a non-threatening stance such as kneeling, and present the reward directly to the dog. If it is a ball, pay careful attention to the eyes of the dog and make sure the dog is focused on the reward. I like to present the ball in front of my body and move my hand holding the ball up and down until I see the dog focus on the movement. Once there is focus on the ball, carefully toss it underhand to the dog so it lands right in front of it. I prefer balls on ropes that don't roll much or bounce away when they hit the ground because I want the dog to have instant gratification and not accidentally lose sight of it. It is important that the reward and the trail layer are in close proximity—so the connection is mentally made in the dogs mind.

If food is used, the trail layer should immediately present the reward so the dog can see it in a low posture such as kneeling. The trail layer should not be too abrupt or aggressive with the movement because the dog may be alarmed by any major reaction. After the dog gets its reward: ball, food or whatever, make sure to ham it up with the dog and make sure it knows that what it just did was the best thing in the world. Tons of praise and love are appropriate at this stage. The more the dog feels good about what just occurred, the more it will remember the situation in the future. This cuts down training time dramatically.

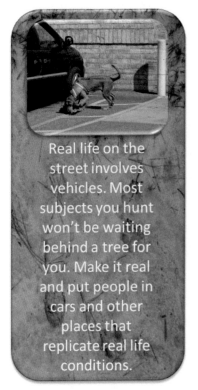

Real life on the street involves vehicles. Most subjects you hunt won't be waiting behind a tree for you. Make it real and put people in cars and other places that replicate real life conditions.

Generally speaking, most dogs get the game down quickly, and with only a couple of repetitions, as long as the payment is made on sniff or in connection with the trail layer.

Once the dog seems to have the game down, it is important to use multiple decoys with the trail layer to make sure that the dog is identifying the correct person and not just the first person it sees. Remember: bad programming can occur with the Walk-Back Find as well as with any other training method. Do not pattern your process. Patterns lead to programming. Programming leads to problems with a trailing dog.

Once the dog has the Walk-Back find down, other finds with unusual endings become a little easier so now it is time to add the unusual.

Car Find

Instead of the trail layer sitting at a bench or hiding behind a tree, try putting them in a parked car along the trail with the windows cracked. The dog may or may not have a scent pool or scent cone to deal with as it approaches the target. I like it better with the first few tries if the trail layer's scent is flowing past the car away from the trail. Ideally, the scent cone should hit the area a short distance from the end of the car; so as the dog trails past it quickly encounters the scent cone exiting the cracked window. As soon as the dog reacts with a head pop towards the cone, the trail layer should get the dogs attention by rolling down the window or making a sound.

Again, pay on sniff. As time goes on, we can roll up the window and rely solely on small drafts of scent exiting the cracks and vents of the car. If the dog understands that the fresh scent from the car means subject, it will quickly respond to the smaller scent cone and begin to detail the cracks or scent vents from the car with its nose. The payment can be delayed once the dog understands that the vehicle is the scent course. Even though the payment is delayed, I highly recommend that when payment comes, that it comes as the dog is focused on the car and not turning back to the handler.

Buildings

I wrote about human contact odor in various parts of *Tao* as well as in *K9 Trailing; The Straightest Path,* but it is important to consider this especially as it relates to subjects who have gone through doors and into buildings. The reaction to a door to a house may or may not be like a vehicle. It really depends on whether or not the house is breathing in or breathing out. When the house breathes out, the temperature inside is usually warmer inside than outside and drafts are sucked out. When the opposite is true, the house breathes in. When the internal air pressure inside the house is greater than that of the outside air, there will be leakage from every gap: around the doors, an open or slightly opened window, etc. This can be caused by a breeze against one side of the house: pressurizing through the soffit vents, the siding, the crawl space vents, or the vents in the roof. It can also be caused by a fan in a window, an air conditioner using fresh air, or an air make-up vent/fan for the furnace. On the other hand, a house with a furnace uses up a great deal of air to maintain combustion and the replacement air will be sucked into the house from the same locations. Now, barometric pressure and many other factors influence these conditions; such as how well the house is sealed and insulated. Temperature inversions are not the only factors that affect this breathing in and breathing out condition.

Ideally, we want to start building alerts when the breathing out condition is occurring. We can help to create this condition by cracking doors and windows to help increase the possibility of a small scent cone as the dog passes the location. Treat the house or building just like a car and you will have similar reactions. The dog will also react strongly to human subject contact odor on door handles and other locations, and one way to strengthen the response is to overlay more human subject odor on to the contact points. This will help the dog when a scent cone is unavailable due to the building breathing in such as anytime a furnace is on: fall, winter or spring.

If a door or window is the entry point, I like to have the trail layer just inside and able to react to the dog as soon as the dog's presence is detected. This is important for the pay—on sniff component of this training technique.

Groups of People

One of the most difficult normal conditions a trailing dog might encounter on a real trail is when several or many people are congregating and interacting in a relatively small space. In many of these cases the trailing dog will just mill around, getting excited without focusing on any one person. This usually happens when the dog has little experience in this condition or the handler is really running the scenario double blind and has no idea who the person is. Line checks and guiding usually don't happen in a double blind test and this is when the K9 will usually fail. They fail during the double blind because the handler in the past always had some idea who the subject was and usually manifested some sort of identifying behavior to the dog when it got close to the correct person. This behavior is usually the same as I wrote about above: line checks and verbiage, but also includes another that is a little different. This new behavior is letting the pressure off the lead when the dog is at the correct person. Almost all handlers practice this because the behavior has become engrained with just about every trail ever run.

The other difficulty is the sheer dramatic condition of the trail at the end. The trail, up to the ending, was relatively easy from a scent perspective because it is older scent and the dog is singularly focused on it. When the ending approaches with multiple people, the K9 will not only proximity alert on the subject but each and every person with the subject. The dog's excitement level will increase as it gets closer because the end of the trail means reward. This is also the time that the dog is most likely to false alert. Dogs, being creatures that always take the path of least resistance, will alert on the first thing they come across to get their reward if they think it will happen. This is why when we start working with groups of people at the end of a trail we don't start with large groups and some thought must be made with their placement when the dog runs amongst them.

Many people, when beginning this training, think that because the K9 can scent discriminate they will always default to the correct person in the group, but this is simply not true. Most dogs want instant gratification and because they are in source odor they will simply hit the first person they run into. Correcting the dog and showing it the correct person does nothing. This is because by the time the dog gets off the first incorrect person and goes to the second; it has forgotten the source odor and is focused on what it found. It now expects the reward. There is some argument that when the dog sits or does the correct identification procedure when it gets to this second "correct" person, that obviously the dog now knows it made a mistake. This is only because the dog will do anything now for the reward and it knows the procedure. It's now a procedure and not really identification. This happens because dogs think in the moment and do not have the linear-time way of thinking that we have. It makes sense to us but not the dog.

So, it's not really enough to correct the dog: because I do not think correction is really penetrating. What truly works is building the dog up for groups gradually in a properly tiered training style; starting with only a couple of people and then building to more—only as long as the dog is progressing without correction. We need self-discovery with the dog and not a guided response to the source. If at any time we start to line check or encourage, then we have lost the self-discovery. All that I wrote in the beginning chapters of this book about self-discovery and how dogs learn applies now more than ever.

The end of the first trails to groups should have no more than two people on the first few runs with the target person being part of the overall scent pool. The target person should also be the first scent cone the dog encounters. The other person should not have walked the trail with the subject. This means some thought must be given to the wind. I prefer that the wind not be blowing back onto the trail or to the dog from long distances. I want the cone to be perpendicular to the trail but in such a way that the dog detects the correct scent cone first. This should all happen out of sight of the dog. Therein lays a problematic component of the trail: simultaneously considering wind. This is because incorporating terrain features and using wind to your advantage can be difficult: terrain features bend the wind to often unexpected places and directions.

When the trail layers are out in the open when the dog detects the scent pool of both people, it will often gravitate to the first person it sees versus concentrating on the odor. This is why I like to run these with the people out of sight, such as behind a tree or wall. This forces the dog to follow its nose.

As with previous scenarios, I believe in paying on sniff when we are building K9 reliability. So when the dog detects and gravitates to the correct person, as soon as the dog is within range and focused on that person, payment should be rendered. We can work on the ID procedure, if there is one, later. Right now the dog needs to be paid as soon as it detects the correct person. This will insure that you have a dog working the person, and not the handler, for the reward.

Once the dog seems to be gravitating to the correct person based on scent, it is time to swap the condition so that the dog encounters the incorrect scent pool first. If the dog responds to this first odor incorrectly, then the handler should simply stop the exercise and start over with the first sequence of training. Again, I do not believe in correcting the dog once it has made a mistake. I far prefer to set up the scenario again, but do so in a way that we get the correct response. I also do not believe that the dog needs a reward every time it runs a trail: especially when it makes a mistake. It is far better to simply pack the dog up and do it the correct way later. I covered all of these training issues in proceeding chapters: so I will not go into their detail here.

Once the dog is correctly working two people with little to no trouble, it is important to add a third and then a fourth. Work up to a condition where you can have at least five people in a group relatively close to each other and the dog is successful 80% of the time.

Now comes the time when we start bringing people out in the open. But like before, we need to do it in steps from easy to hard. I would suggest going back to the two-person step and work up from there. The speed in progression will be faster because of the similarity in the games and the dog will remember the process as long as the process is not too complex the first few times it is attempted.

When the dog can work through a group of five people and correctly identify the correct subject, it is time to add some normality to the condition. By normal I mean people doing normal things when they are in a group such as talking, interacting, whatever. The more imagination you use, the better the dog will do in real situations.   A few things I can think of are a group of party goers having a good time at a BBQ picnic in the local park, a family fishing on a river bank, several people working on the engine of a broken down vehicle, or a subject hanging out in a homeless camp.

Active Evaders

Active evaders are those subjects who know they are being hunted and do not want to be found. These are the people who run again whenever the dog appears to be closing the gap. Contrary to popular belief, these people are not always suspects in criminal cases. They can just as easily be a suicidal subject in a Search & Rescue case or a missing kid who is actually a runaway. These things happen a lot, and in many cases, the SAR handler encountering it for the first time has no idea it is happening. If the handler does not recognize the trailing behavior indicating an active evader, the body language may be misconstrued for distraction behavior and the dog called off the trail. Therefore, police K9 handlers as well as SAR must train for this situation.

Active evaders provide the most exciting and the most difficult of all endings because the dog may be very close expecting the ending/reward, and all of a sudden, the reward is taken away and the trail begins again.   There are some dogs that are not really reward driven and seem to enjoy the trail more than the ending, and for these dogs, this is a miracle trail and they love them. The cat and mouse game simply ratchets up their prey drive and they get better with each attempted at evasion.   I love these dogs because when the cat and mouse game begins, the dogs just get better while the evader gets more exhausted and confused.   I worked such a case once over many miles and about eleven hours straight. The dog simply became better and stronger. The subjects on the other hand, were exhausted as was I!

As with all training scenarios it is best to work small and get bigger over time; aim small, miss small. I like to start active evader training with a single run from the anticipated finish for the first go around, and I like the trail layer to be in sight the first time when they run. This stimulates the K9's prey drive into a white hot frenzy and if the handler used firetrails as the first training technique, the K9 will immediately default to that level of trailing fanaticism. In other words, they will go nuts and that is what I want.

When the trail is about to end and the K9 is in strong air scent or showing a final proximity alert prior to anticipated capture, the trail layer should step out of hiding and flee in full view of the dog. The K9 should react to this by lunging into the lead and pursuing in full chase mode. The trail layer should have his or her escape route preplanned and preferably be out of sight shortly after appearing: making sure the K9 goes back into scent mode. I want that adrenalin rush to be scent based as much as possible.

As soon as the K9 is in adrenalin mode and back on the trail, it should run down the trail layer and be paid on sniff. Praise and reward the dog as much as possible making it believe that what it just did was the best thing in the world. Repeat this exercise several times. Eventually, the K9 will be expecting the trail layer to try and attempt to flee and its motivation will really increase at the end of the trail. This will increase the level of the proximity alert, and enable the handler to read this proximity from further distances.

Once the K9 understands the subject could be fleeing and does not show any surprise by this activity, throw in a runaway out of sight of the dog several minutes prior to its anticipated arrival at the initial hide. This gives the scent a chance to settle a bit, but more importantly, adds a dimension missing up to this point; a fresh exit trail from the hides scent pool. This can be a little difficult for the dog because there are two fresh scent issues that make it slow down and think about things a bit. The first is the massive fresh scent pool of the hiding subject. The longer the person was at this spot the larger and thicker the scent pool. Add the fresh trail out and you have a recipe for a little confusion. It's not as easy as it was before because there is no visual. The stimulation is still there because the dog knows the person just fled, but it will take some time to work through the problem. How long is really dependent on how much time the dog wastes running around in circles. This is where the slower, more methodical dogs will show a clear early advantage; because they won't waste energy moving too fast. Methodical dogs immediately slow down so as not to miss anything.

Super, high-drive crack dogs often start to spin circles sometimes running faster due to anxiety. This speed keeps them in the scent pool, but often causes them to literally run over the top of the exit trail without catching it. There are several problems with this, the worst one being that as long as the dog is running circles, the subject is making time on the dog and prolonging the search. The second is that the dog will tire far faster when it is anxious than when it is strong and confident on trail.

It is important with this condition, that the dog learn to slow down through self-discovery. In other words, the dog slows on its own and detects the exit trail, without the handler checking or communicating with the dog in anyway. The only way the connection is made is if the dog does this on its own. If we influence the dog's speed with interference, the dog's focus will now be partially on us and if the trail is caught it will not really understand that its speed created the problem in the first place.

When the dog learns on its own to slowly circle to catch the exit trail, it will remember this each and every time it encounters the condition in the future. The dog will also get better at the exit trail detection due to repetition. It will automatically gravitate to the fringe of the scent pool. This is where the "clean" area meets the human scent pool and any blip past the pool marks the exit in the dogs mind.

It really does not take much repetition with a good trailing dog to defeat these first, easy evasion tactics. The difficulty comes with multiple evasions from multiple hides. Like every other step of training with a trailing dog, it is crucial to start small and work big. A three mile escape and evasion course for a young pup that is unprepared for it will do nothing for your training program at all. When the dog fails at it, you won't even have bragging rights. It is far better to solve small problems and get larger with time.

The excitement and enjoyment is not in the end of the trail, after all. It is in each problem, that should the handler be aware, enables his deciphering of the body language: the nose wave into the wind, head pop to the turn, and the canvasing of the hip height grass blades leading into the forest. The poetry of the trail is to understand the tactics of your prey, and this is where success truly lies. The details are in the verses the dog is presenting to you, you only have to read them. If you only concentrate on the endings, you will miss all of the pleasure in between the beginning and the end, and in turn, miss the story that the dog is trying to tell you in its own way. The story is the key to the ending and until you understand with certainty what the dog is saying with body language, endings on real searches will remain elusive.

Chapter Eighteen
The Coverman

"The wolf pack hunts with single-minded purpose, but only through the singular abilities of each individual hunter, utilized with collective effort, will the elk be taken. Individually and regardless of ability, the lone hunter is not likely to succeed. Collectively, but without cooperation, success is similarly elusive. Only through the cooperation of the individual with devotion to the pack do they all flourish. Manhunters would do well to emulate the wolf pack."

I have often written on the subject of the Coverman, also known as the back-up or flanker to the K9 handler. The name is really not as important as the function of the person. The type of search—criminal, dangerous criminal, or missing person—will determine the number of people with the handler. The focus of this chapter is really the single back-up person who works with the handler on most searches: Search and Rescue or Law Enforcement. I like to use the term, "Coverman" because it describes the nature of this person whose primary job is to keep the dog team safe. The job of the back-up is to primarily watch out for the safety of the dog team while they do their job; particularly the handler who is often so absorbed in his or her job that safety considerations may be secondary.

A good Coverman is really a rare asset because few people take on the job as a primary duty. The average person running with the dog can rarely be called a Coverman because he is usually unfamiliar with the dog team and is doing just that... running with the dog. There simply are not a lot of teams that train and produce a specialized Coverman, but there should be. The Coverman is just as important as the dog and equally important as the handler. The Coverman can bring skills and ability to the hunt that would not be part of it if the person were inexperienced. Depending on the person placed in this back-up position, he could actually be a hindrance to the hunt, and if that is the case, the handler may be better off alone.

The Elements That Make Up the Ideal Coverman

The Coverman is responsible for the safety of the dog handler. He or she is the eyes, ears, ad if need be, the trigger finger.

Physical Fitness

The Coverman should be in better condition than the handler. This is because the trailing dog takes up a large percentage of the handlers load when pulling into the harness. A strong dog can make any handler look like an Olympian for a short distance, because the dog takes up so much of the total load. On the other hand, a strong trailing dog can increase a handler's speed by 10%-30% while leaving an out-of-shape "back-up" in the dust.

Even though the dog can make a handler look good physically, it cannot last for long. If the handler is out of shape or physically incapable of travelling any distance past a mile or so, even the strongest dog will eventually burn out if it has to pull a "giant sea anchor" for too long. Furthermore, if a handler gets winded after half a mile they are a danger to themselves and a detriment to the search no matter how good the dog is. As I wrote in previous chapters, a trailing handler has a responsibility to be in good physical condition. In my opinion, should be in better shape than the average person he might hunt. When not trailing, a handler should have a work-out program that keeps him continuously in shape. There is no slacking for this job. If one is obese or physically incapable of running a mile without stopping (not walking) without a dog, they should not be a trailing dog handler.

The Coverman needs to be in twice the shape than the handler. If an average handler has to be able to easily run a mile without stopping, then the Coverman should be able to run two miles at a similar speed. If the trail is several miles long and the dog is moving at a trot for most of it, the Coverman will have to run to keep up. If he or she is constantly falling back and struggling to maintain a good interval, then it will be impossible to perform other vital tasks that help with the mission and keep the dog team safe.

While the K9 is working the handler is reading and the Coverman remains watchful at all times.

Keen Powers of Observation

The Coverman is not there to watch the dog or point out things that the dog might do. The Coverman's role as an observer is to see all things that might impact the search and the safety of the dog team. The Coverman must be on the lookout 180 degrees in front of the dog team at all times, and occasionally 360 degrees.

Radio Skills

Radio skills and the ability to communicate over the radio to dispatch or a command post is critical. It is not simply a matter of talking; but listening as well for any updates to the search that might play out while the dog team is in operation. Radio skills are not natural but more a learned trait through lots of practice and experience. Police officers who are used to operating a portable radio as a regular part of their jobs have the ability to fulfill this role easily.

Part of using the radio effectively is knowing when to speak and when to be quiet. Not only is excessive chatter confusing to any listener, it can also affect the dog if it is too loud and constant.

The primary radio communications should be location updates if the K9 team will not be monitored with real time GPS, and also to communicate any major changes that the K9 handler sees in the K9 that might affect the outcome of the search, such as proximity alerts, scent pools, or air scents.

Geographically Competent

Natural land navigation skills, though initially taught, are also an acquired trait gained through experience and practice. Few people are natural navigators the first time out, and especially in territory that is unfamiliar. It takes lots of practice and it is definitely not all about GPS or compasses. The best Land-Nav guys are those who can remember, intimately, where they have been and can gravitate back to those places, even in the dark, without the aid of any device. A large part of this trait is the ability to memorize routes and directions of travel based on terrain features, and individual components of the trail that stand out in the persons mind. I find lifetime hunters are the best at this skill, especially those who grew up hunting and never used a compass or GPS.

My belief is that today we are too dependent on devices and are "dumbing" ourselves down. Rather than force our minds to remember what we have done and where we did it, we rely on machines to do the thinking for us. This is dangerous for the old-school profession of hunting people with a dog.

A good Coverman should be a good land navigator without a GPS or compass. Those items are a bonus that should not be relied on. The land navigator can help get the dog team back to key locations of the search in case the trail is lost somewhere in the field and the handler needs to get back to a place where he or she knew the trail existed.

The Ability To Not Be A Distraction

This is an element of a backup person that is rarely talked about, but a huge pet peeve of mine. I have worked hundreds of real searches and found a good number of people and evidence along the way. I can say with certainty that back-ups who are inept, or a distraction, have ruined a fair amount of searches. I know it sounds sacrilegious to say anything bad about a person who is there to help you, but if they interrupt the process of the dog repeatedly, they are not really helping at all.

The types I am talking about include the people who are so out of shape that they are gasping and puking after just a couple of hundred yards. If the handler must ask the back-up if he or she is OK right out of the starting gate, due to physical inability, then the person is an impediment to the search. Worse are the "announcers" or people who every time they see anything that might be of interest or personal concern, must peel off to announce it and distract the dog.

Examples of Bad Announcements are:

1. Alerts to things the Coverman believes the handler should show the dog.

2. Yelling "Car!!!" when vehicles are in the area but not a danger.

3. Stopping to look at something when the dog is working a scent pool or doubling back.

A Coverman watching for traffic as the handler prepares the K9 for a trail. The Coverman moves as normally as possible without bringing unwanted attention to himself.

The Announcers are often not malicious or so self-absorbed that they do these things on purpose, but usually victims of prior bad examples. There are rarely classes held by veteran trailing handlers who have truly been successful on the street. These handlers know the true value of a Coverman and what their purpose should be.

Dogs, when working with people on a trailing hunt, think of these people as part of the pack. When a member of the pack does something that is really loud or out of routine, it will get the attention of the trailing dog that is on point. The reason for this is the dog is wondering what all of the fuss is about and how it might relate to the prey. In essence, the dog thinks the new activity is related to the hunt and will often peel off what it is doing to concentrate on what the back-up is yelling about or investigating. This is damaging to the hunt and I do not believe a dog should be taught to tolerate it. If anything, it is the back-up who needs to learn how to work with the dog and not the other way around.

Some of the places where this seems to happen a lot is near roads with traffic and when the dog is in a scent pool or problem, circling, trying to find the exit trail.

Road with Traffic

Whether or not the dog is in danger or not, many people following the dog feel it is necessary to yell "Car!" as soon as one is observed and then attempt to run in front of the dog to block traffic. There are two problems here. The first is to yell when yelling nine times out of ten, is usually far from necessary. This yell is distracting to just about any dog and it is exacerbated if that noise is accompanied by the rest of the posse following up with their own screams of "Car!" in quick succession. Most dogs will, at minimum, stop what they are doing and look at the perpetrator(s). This is especially true if the screaming is followed by one of these people running out in front of the dog into the middle of the street.

In order to truly understand how this human misbehavior is understood by the dog, it is very important not to think about this from a human perspective. Instead, look at it from the dogs. Dogs are pack creatures and nothing is more pack oriented than hunting by scent. When the back-up runs into a traffic intersection, yelling "Car!" while simultaneously gesticulating hand and arm signals, humans might think: Great safety technique! Dogs, on the other hand see this activity and the sound that goes with it as a signal. Dogs may equate this activity the bark, howl, or yip of pack mates indicating a fresh scent and a change to the direction of the track. The focus is now off the trail that was being followed and onto the pack mate who apparently knows a better way to the prey. It does not take too many of these incidents to completely throw off a perfectly good trailing dog.

Now, I am not suggesting that we not be wary of traffic. I am not suggesting nothing be done. I am simply suggesting that whatever is done should be done in such a way as not to redirect the dog's attention onto the back-up people.

First off, cars that are far away really do not need to be announced at all. A vehicle should only be considered if the dog will be impacted by it in some way or if it is really a threat. In most situations, the average handler is well aware of most traffic because it can be such a threat. If he or she is unaware of traffic issues when working a dog near a road, then he is not really ready to work in an urban environment. The handler should practice in places with far less traffic until he develops some power of peripheral observation and learns how to anticipate and deal with such threats.

If an announcement must be made, it should be said quietly, and I like a cover man who is right on my shoulder; paying attention to things that I am obviously not. If the Coverman detects a vehicle that appears to be off my radar, I far prefer a little tap on my shoulder and a conversational voice that directs me to the potential problem. I also like it when my Coverman asks me if traffic should be stopped once I am aware, before running out into the middle of the road and assuming that is what I want. The yell and dash into the road should only be reserved for real threats and not for every car that comes by. What may be a threat, and what might not be, should be determined by the team well in advance through practice and discussion. The real search is not the time or place for practice and discussion.

Scent Pools or Places the K9 Circles to Investigate

Much of the same behavior at the street or intersection can also be seen when the trailing dog stops to circle back or investigate things. This is the absolute worst time to start to circle and investigate as a human back—up. If the back—up person decides this is the time to check behind garbage dumpsters and look into back yards, I can guarantee you that the dog will have an interest in everything that the back—up person is doing and will become distracted. The more the dog gets distracted, the better chance it has of losing the trail. Unfortunately, this kind of back—up behavior happens a lot. As soon as the forward momentum of the dog shifts or returns, back—ups will often then take the initiative to begin the search on his or her own; not understanding that this is distraction in the making.

It is best to simply understand that when the dog circles or backtracks, that the behavior means something, and the dog has a need to investigate whatever it recently encountered or passed. Perhaps a trail turn was overshot, perhaps there is a giant scent pool of the subject in the area— better yet— and maybe there is some physical evidence on the ground nearby. The savvy coverman will know that it is time to stand still, or kneel, and keep a roving eye on the surroundings. The coverman's job is not to watch the dog, but to watch what might affect the dog in the surrounding area, and alert the handler if necessary. The coverman knows that just as the dog is concentrating on what it is doing and being very careful, the handler is likewise studying the dog and being careful to interpret the dog's body language as accurately as possible. These situations can make or break a good trail and now is the time for the handler and dog to work together without any other extracurricular activity that might distract one, the other, or both.

During a scent pool or when the dog doubles back, the support team and Coverman must keep careful watch on their areas of responsibility while simultaneously keeping movement down to a minimum.

Visual Tracker

There are multiple human and animal tracks mixed into this trail and the handler has enough on his plate without trying to figure them out. This should be the job of someone in the support team, for the Coverman is there as only one person in support.

Visual tracking is probably one of the most under-utilized resources during a K9 trail. There are many times, even in urban conditions where there are multiple physical clues that the subject of the search left behind, and the team failed to notice. I teach all of my students to track as they trail; once they are past the basic stage of dog handling. There is nothing better for the ego of the handler on a real search than a boot print where one should not be. And, when that boot print matches one from the start of the trail, it is an extra special feeling.

Tracks not only give us warm, fuzzy feelings when we find them after a grueling two mile K9 trail, but they also help to motivate the entire team to a new sense of vigor. Tracks, depending on the quality, also can help to identify a suspect later on. And, it is not just tracks, we are looking for scuff marks indicating someone slipping or sliding, broken branches showing a route of travel, etc. etc. There is usually something left behind to read.

Tracks can also help get the dog back on trail if the handler and K9 lost the scent trail somewhere behind them. If the handler is geographically aware, he will always remember these locations, after only a glance; primarily due to the significance of the circumstances, such as K9 confusion, circling, excitement, etc. All of these things indicate a change in the scent trail like a scent pool, a turn, a back track, etc. Depending on how the team worked, the condition will determine if the dog loses or lost the trail in an attempt to work out of it.

Memory of key geographical places like these are imperative if the trail is going to be recovered once it has been lost; especially if that loss meant that the team moved far from this area in an attempt to locate the scent trail in the first place. The longer the K9 is away from the area where the body language changes began indicating a scent problem, the less drive it will have for the trail when it gets back. There may be absolutely no scent memory for the location at all due to the time away, and the dogs overall scent memory capability. Scent memory is really relative to the dog's genetics and training. Some very impatient dogs, when off scent for as little as five minutes, will not remember what they are looking for once they get back to it. They simply do not recognize that they are back into the scent they were recently following because too much time passed without it. Other dogs recognize it immediately but even these dogs can lose drive for that scent when gone from it for too long. There is no measuring stick for that scent memory time frame, as it is unique to each individual dog.

The other factor to consider is that diminished interest in the subject scent will also reduce the K9s ability to solve the scent problem. If it could not break out of the area then it first got into it, and then lost the trail because of it, scent memory reduction may only result in more confusion once the condition is encountered again.

Regardless of scent memory loss or reduction, if the team gets back to the place where it all went wrong, there is a very good chance that the dog may not be able to solve it. This is where the Coverman with good tracking skills can come in handy. By working concentric circles out of the center of the perceived scent problem in almost the same manner the a handler might, with a dog trying to catch and exit trail, the Coverman can look for sign or spoor indicating recent human passage. Once this track is discovered and followed for enough distance away from the problem area, the K9 can be restarted on the track. In this case, the track becomes a new scent article and the corresponding trail is also new to the dog.

A visual tracker as a Coverman is one of the best assets that a K9 team can have. Visual tracking is really becoming a lost art, and trying to do it while running behind a dog and pulling security for the handler is no easy feat. Any handler encountering a person like this would do well to make him or her partner immediately!

Chapter Nineteen
Trailing Physical Fitness

None of nature's hunters are physically unfit. Physically inefficient hunters do not survive in the field because they cannot compete with the prey that they hunt. Much the same can be said for human hunters. Though our modern world enables and rewards physical ineptness, the hunt for another man in the wilds does not. The human hunter has now become nothing more than another animal predator. The difference is that so too has the prey. Be inept at your own peril.
Find contour in Chaos!

Physical Training Disclaimer:

It is unfortunate that any time anyone has a recommendation for anything nowadays, there has to be some sort of disclaimer such as "Careful! The Coffee is Hot!" The days of common sense practice of anything seems to have disappeared. Because of this, we, as a species, in many ways have become soft, mewling, and ultimately more vulnerable to everything the disclaimers were supposed to protect us from. So in the spirit of Modern disclaiming: Trailing is a physically demanding job, and when done professionally the chance of injury is high. Physical fitness is a prerequisite for trailing but any physical fitness training should be done with safety and health in mind. If you are unsure of your ability to perform any of these exercises, do not do them. If you have any medical condition that may be exacerbated by any of my recommendations: seek advice from a physician before attempting any of them.

Trailing Physical Fitness Training

I have long been a practitioner of sports in the form of martial arts, bodybuilding, running, hunting, and anything physical. Though team sports eluded me, those that required constant study and commitment from a singular perspective enthralled me. From the age of eighteen, I stayed involved in one major physical activity or another. My preferences were the fighting arts as well as running and bodybuilding. Of these, I tended to stray away from the norm. The high-end karate schools with the GIs and fancy colored belts did not turn me on very much. On the surface, they were attractive, but once I delved into the nuts and the bolts of the product, I found most were made up of little more than the belts and GIs. Much of what I saw was nothing more than mechanical movement repeated over and over. There was form but no necessity to support the form. Instead, I gravitated to the small fighting circles in the beginning days of mixed martial arts fighting and the Pilipino martial art of Escrima. Escrima is a street fighting style developed when the Moro warriors rose up to fight the Spanish. Initially, the Moro tribesmen were savage fighters and known for their ferocity and skill with the long Moro knives and swords; the Barong and Kris. As the Spaniards settled in to rule, they forbade the populace the use and carry of edged weapons. In response, the people took up the use of rattan or bamboo in lengths similar to swords and knives. They used these sticks in dance forms in order to entertain the Spaniards while practicing their method of warfare at the same time.

It was not about a method so much as it was about survival. The people used anything and everything as a weapon and much of the style was based on learning weapons first and then transitioning to empty hands techniques. The thought process behind this philosophy in Escrima based martial arts was very simple: Why fight with a fist if you have a knife? The weapons style easily translates to the weaponless condition. More importantly, the Escrima martial art was developed for the street fighter with little in the way of pomp and circumstance. A major component of my Escrima training was massive leg, arm, and push up workouts, and the legs were by far the most brutal. My first few weeks found me soaking in ice water after workouts! The idea was to create lot of power between strikes and the legs were a big part of generating the energy for massive impact.

My style of dog training is very similar to Escrima in that it is simple, direct, and for one purpose only... to win. A big part of success in working a trailing/tracking dog professionally is being physically prepared for the demanding job that it is. No other K9 work is as long and arduous as trailing. It taxes every muscle of the body as well as the balance, endurance, coordination, and the wind of the practitioner. The K9 trails effortlessly and has the ability to run and work for many miles in a relatively short period of time. It is physically impossible for any handler to work with the speed and agility that the K9 possesses; but in order to follow without hindering the dog too much, the responsible handler must be in the best physical condition possible. In order to attain this condition the training must be outside the traditional physical fitness-training paradigm. I highly recommend that the handler consider the work they are doing and design a program around that.

Trailing in its own right is great training as long as the training is regular, at least five days a week. Most handlers do not work their dogs this often, and if they do not, I recommend supplemental training to reach that five-day minimum.

I have written down my workout program for any interested. It may or may not work for others, but I have found that it has served me well in maintaining health and preventing injury.

Running

Running needs to be the primary work out for the trailing handler. To avoid hindering the dog more than humans already do, we must have the wind and stamina to keep up with our dogs over long distances. We can never run as fast or for as long as the dogs will, but we can condition ourselves to say strong through most search distances. I have found, through experience, that the average handler runs trails under a quarter mile in length for most of their work. Of course, this is not every handler, but I have found it to be an average length. The problem with the quarter mile is that it is nothing when compared to manhunts that last many miles over the course of twenty-four hours or more.

The hardest trail I ran was with a seven-month-old pup named Kali. We ran two men down attempting to evade us for a TV program. They were given a one hour head start and twenty-four hours to accomplish the task and we almost ran them down after five hours of trailing. We would have; if not for being stopped at the last minute by the production company who needed more film time. We ran them down a second time at the eleven-hour mark. We traveled over eleven miles through incredibly difficult terrain; including river crossings and running in almost complete black out conditions. The thing that amazed me about this trail was that Kali looked like she could do another twelve miles and was not close to being winded. She had not eaten the entire time and barely drank water. At the time I ran this trail I was forty-nine years old and suffering the effects from major knee and abdominal surgeries: all within the preceding five years. I had conditioned myself for this work but was still physically debilitated after it. I had never run anything so difficult on my mind and body. I had always strived to say in as good of shape as possible, but I did not prepare myself properly for this and I paid dearly for it.

Normal running just does not cut it for trailing work: primarily because most people jog in the same locations doing the same thing over and over. They run the same path, over the same surface, at the same speed, at the same time, in the same weather, over and over. This type of training may be good for the cardio-vascular system as well as the muscles of the legs, but really does little to help the handler when it comes time to run a hound, in the woods on five mile trail, and in the rain. Jogging in shorts and running shoes around the block does very little to prepare for anyone to be dragged behind a running dog over hill and dale in a thunderstorm. I found very early on in my first days as a trailing handler that my normal running pattern of a two mile circuit in fifteen minutes, in my neighborhood, left me woefully unprepared for one mile behind my dog in uneven terrain in the woods. It didn't even prepare me for running behind him in the city. The problem is not in the distance or speed, it is the constant starts, stops, turns, bobbing, weaving, and simply trying to keep up and match the pace of the dog. Major changes in terrain and conditions aggravate the problems of following. If you add in darkness and rain, it can be a mess. I can jog a mile and not breathe hard. I can run behind one of our good trailing pups only six months old and have trouble after 300 yards. It is not distance, time, or speed that is the problem. The problem is attempting to keep some semblance of pace with the dog.

Running training for trailing must mimic real trailing if at all possible. The handler must choose the locations to run based on where he or she might work. If most of the hunts are in the forest, the mantrailer needs to run in the forest. The key to the running in the woods is not running on the trails. It is important to run off-trail, jumping logs, dodging vines and sticker bushes, mimicking the condition of a hunt.   If a creek crossing presents itself, run across it as fast as you can and climb the opposite bank in one bound. That will be how your high drive trailing dog might tackle it.

My injuries, aches, and pains over the years tended to be far less when I trained for running the off-trail way. Normal jogging simply did not prepare the secondary, and tertiary muscle groups like off-trail running did, and when I simply jogged in normal jogging gear, I would invariably twist or sprain something in my lower legs when I worked and trained hard with the dogs in the field.

Proper training gear is just as important of a training component as is the actual physical training. If the idea is to mimic deployment for conditioning purposes, one must also outfit himself in the appropriate footwear at minimum. Extreme reality training might incorporate every piece of clothing that a handler might wear when working his dog in the field on a real case. I honestly think this is probably the best way to train in order to reduce injury and truly prepare the handler for long hard trailing work.

The way I often trained for work was to run off trail in the footwear that I normally trailed in, along with a small pack with enough weight to mimic what I might actually carry with me: which was not much! Footwear to me is the most critical piece of personal trailing gear one can have. The shoes or boots must be lightweight, flexible, drain well, and have a better than average tread pattern that sheds mud and debris easily. And one must be able to run long distances in them—not just hike. The process of purchasing footwear for me was often trial and error. Nothing was ever quite right for much of my career. I ran through hundreds of boots and shoes and few really made me feel the love that I was always looking for. As my body aged, the footwear problem was exacerbated: primarily due to old injuries. Interestingly, my most comfortable boot for running and the one that fits all of my criteria of flexible, lightweight, easily drained on the run, and with a great tread pattern was the old-style Viet Nam-era jungle boot. By far the two most important parts of the boot are the Panama sole that sheds clay and mud like no other boot and the drain holes on the instep. I do not like water proof boots because in any real trailing conditions that incorporates jogging or running in extreme, wet terrain, the water often goes down over the top of the boot and fills the booty inside. Run long enough this way without a change and you have a recipe for blisters. The jungle boot on the other hand drains the water as fast as it comes in and it is not necessary to take them off to dry out right away. Running after emersion in drier conditions often results in the boots and socks drying on the fly. This is super important to me especially in my current training home area of Edisto Island, South Carolina. Few places are as wet and swampy.

Gear is a personal choice: I understand this. It is not necessary to do things how I do things. I am only offering some examples. I suggest that all aspiring handlers find gear that works for them all the time: gear that can take abuse and stay as comfortable as possible in all conditions, and for long periods of time. The handler must not only work with these articles of clothing and footwear but also train in them. The handler may go through a lot of equipment when using it: not only for work but also training, the financial trade off, however is really worth it.

I mentioned that I like to train with a pack on. This is critical because if the handler has not prepared for the weight of a pack on his back while running, it can quickly become debilitating. This is primarily because the body is not used to the chaffing and muscles are simply not prepared for the extra weight. I never opted for a large pack, as is often recommended for the average SAR deployment. They are usually too big and have too much stuff for any handler who is moving fairly quickly behind a dog: bobbing and weaving in the woods. Most SAR folks who are not trailing handlers do not have a good grasp of how draining a big, bulky pack can be. The vast majority of stuff in the standard SAR pack is nothing more than dead weight, and not necessary for trailing. My philosophy for all searches was to move light and fast. If I needed something bad enough, and the mission was critical enough for me to have to stay out in the field, it could be air dropped to me. A fifty-pound pack is just stupid for a trailing handler.

The trailing team is a rapid response search team designed to reach the target or establish a direction of travel as quickly as possible. It is not a unit meant to be fielded for long periods of time: simply walking. The dog needs to move at a relatively fast pace that allows it to work as naturally as possible and with as little resistance as possible. Carrying seventy-five pounds of extra weight is too hard on the dog not just the handler.

The ideal pack for me is a Camel Pak Hydration type multi-purpose pack. It should hold at least 2 ½ liters or three quarts of water and have a couple of other compartments for necessary gear: not too much, but important stuff only. I like padded shoulder straps and also a waist belt. The military grade or MilSpec packs are absolutely the best way to go, and by all means do not cut cost on the water bladder for this pack.

Here are the items I carry while training and working:

1. Ibuprofen, aspirin, or Tylenol
2. Couple of power bars or other similar high—energy small food
3. Small first aid pack for dog and human
4. Collapsible dog bowl
5. Lighter or matches in a Ziploc bag
6. GPS or compass
7. Small LED flashlight or headlamp
8. Hat
9. Light weight rain jacket
10. Knife
11. Paracord or light weight rope
12. Extra pair of socks—Put them in the bag with the matches
13. Gloves
14. Radio, The Garmin Rino is a great lightweight combo GPS and radio device that gives the handler some excellent land navigation and communication abilities.

The key to training for reality is understanding what those realities might be. A good wilderness trail where the subject has been missing for at least four to six hours can be ten miles or more. I have discovered my mean average for hunting people out of a city environment was three to five miles: so I opted to train for the latter.

When preparing for an ultimate working trail of five miles it is really smart to start slowly and work up to the distance. Not only with trailing dogs but the human handler. In my opinion, before we start training for a long event, we must have a very solid dog that can easily handler trails of four to six hours, and up to a mile long. If the dog does not have the endurance yet, then anything out to five miles will be less than reliable. If you have read *K9 Trailing The Straightest Path* and subscribed to some of my trailing philosophy, then one mile should be no problem.

Start with trailing trails from ¾ to one mile over varied terrain in a rural environment with little to no distractions in the form of other humans or dogs. Try to include conditions that will tax your muscles to varying degrees in almost a chaotic pattern. I like multiple surfaces such as sand, loam, and plain dirt or clay, coupled with varying degrees of elevation changes in no real set pattern. I also like the conditions to be relatively trail-less. I like to encounter the fallen logs, brambles, and vines in order to negotiate around; through, or over them without knowing they are coming.

As with my trailing philosophy of double blind testing, double blind physical training also has its advantages. The uncertainty of not knowing disallows the muscle memory condition and negates spontaneous reaction to obstacles and barriers. This is truly a training situation that trailing handlers must prepare for. It is far better to be prepared for anything and react quickly than preparing for a few known problems. The latter will only create minor conditioning for those problems and a slow reaction when outside the normal training box. This type training will help with endurance but not true conditioning and safety. The beauty of trailing in ever-changing conditions is that your body and mind will assume a high degree of this spontaneity while working the dog.

The constant twisting, jumping, slowing, stopping, sidestepping, bobbing and weaving will work many small muscle groups that are normally not conditioned in the gym or running roads or paths. It is these small, oblique muscle groups that help to prevent injury when busting all of the above mentioned moves in real work. Of all the training I have ever done, nothing has conditioned me better than trailing training and I believe it is because of the high degree of spontaneity in response to ever changing conditions.

Once I can comfortably handle trails up to a mile in ever changing environments, then I bump up my training intervals by half miles; adding a half mile every week. The goal is to get to five miles in eight to ten weeks.

Upper and lower resistance body workouts should not be neglected. Hanging on to the end of a well-worn thirty foot lead has a tremendous impact on the human body while trying to keep up with a powerful dog; in particular the Latissimus dorsi or broad portion of the back muscle group, as well as the biceps, shoulders and the legs. This comes from constantly reining in the dog by pulling and keeping the arms in a raised position when handling the lead and trotting or jogging in an attempt to keep up with a good, but moderate pace.

I believe building up leg strength is also vital for mission performance but that leg strength must be very usable in the form of strength during chaotic movement. There has to be a focus on flexibility as well and fast firing muscles. The typical but slow, heavy body building style workouts with an emphasis on squats do not work for a mantrailer. The legs simply become too heavy and lack the required flexibility for long range running. I believe in squats and many of the traditional workouts but with a style relative to our mission; long range endurance.

When working out, I spend a fair amount of time on my Lats and Biceps as well as all fast twitching chest, shoulder and leg workouts. I do not go for big, heavy weight programs like I did in my early years, but rather fast ones with little down time between sets and a concentration on more reps with light weights. I want strength without the bulk: more importantly, I want a fast reaction time to a variety of conditions over and over again.

Typical Weight Workout for Back and Arms

Arms: Reclined Bicep curls and reclined overhead Triceps extensions, six sets at a fast pace, eight repetitions, pyramid weight from lighter to heavier. Start with a Bicep set and immediately go to the Triceps upon completion with no down time. Thirty-second rest time between sets. Repeat.

Back: Three Phase Seated Lat Pull downs, six sets, eight reps, no down time between phases. Start with the traditional behind the neck Lat pull-down with a wide grip and full arm extension at the top. Make sure to touch the back of the neck on the downward stroke and extend all the way up on the return. Immediately switch to a frontal Lat pull-down to the top of the chest after the first phase, making sure to touch and extend on both directions. The last phase is the classic pull-up or chin-up with a shoulder width grip while seated. At the full extension from the second phase, switch to the shoulder-width grip, palms facing in and slowly pull down until the bar is under the chin. Slowly extend up fully. This is a single repetition of the three-phase seated Lat Pull-Down.

I recommend a slow pace with concentration on good form, full retractions and extensions. Lightweight quickly becomes very heavy with a two second complete stroke rate for each repetition of each phase. The total time for each phase is approximately fifteen seconds or forty-eight to sixty seconds for all three. Extreme weights are absolutely not necessary when good form and a slow pace is employed, and believe me, you will feel the burn as much as any body builder with tons of weight. The other key component of the exercise—for me—is keeping the rest time between sets to thirty seconds or less.

Chest and Shoulder: Incline Dumbbell Press with chest flies. (A chest fly is a movement where the dumbbells are held above the chest and lowered slowly to the sides of the body with elbows slightly bent.) Again; go light and slow. I begin with a moderate incline to focus the upper chest and some of the shoulders. Extend all the way to the top from a wide base and pause at the top. Do not raise straight up but more in a pyramid angle and touch, not bang, the dumbbells together at the top of the extension. I do eight reps of presses, and without a rest, move to flies using the same pattern of movement, slow with good form. Make sure to keep the elbow slightly bent and try your best not to move your arms much on the stroke. The key for me, and I know I am doing it right when I feel a tightening or pinch at the top of the stroke when the dumbbells connect at the end of the movement. Pause and return to the open fly position. I do eight reps and then start the entire press/fly cycle again for a total of three to six sets depending on "how into it" I am feeling. As with all of my exercises I rest for only about thirty seconds.

Five-Phase Shoulders: These are one of my favorite groups of exercises. Nothing I have ever done has helped me more with combating rotator cuff soreness and injury. I blew out a rotator cuff in my early body building years during my mid-twenties. My idea was to get big and cut so I went big with the weights. At one point in my training career I got up to fifty-pound dumbbell shoulder presses. My shoulders were twice the size they are today but they were also very inflexible. And, while trying to break that fifty-pound dumbbell barrier, I blew out my rotator cuff and had to rehab it for almost a year. I never did completely get over that injury, and because of it, decided that big was not always better. That injury actually set the stage for my conditioning program today.

The focus points of my shoulder workout are:

1. Low weight
2. Lots of reps
3. Slow pace
4. No down time between sets
5. Very good form
6. Full range of motion

I start my five-phase shoulders with a relatively low weight such as seven pounds per dumbbell. All movements are for a "one, one thousand" count. I bring the bells to a boxer's stance with my left leading and my right cocked. The bells/fists are in a natural boxing position or slightly angled. I slow punch to a full extension while shifting my weight to my left leading foot and rotating my hips to the right. As I bring my left foot back to the loaded position, my right foot fires out straight slowly, while I shift my weight from left foot to right foot, then rotating my hips to the left, until my right foot is at a full extension. Both strikes are one repetition and I repeat for a total of eight.

Immediately go to the next movement. Spread your legs so your feet are in line and at shoulder width. Bring the dumbbells to the front position, dumbbells touching, palms facing each other, elbows slightly bent. Raise the arms laterally until the dumbbells are just at shoulder height and pause. Lower the dumbbells to the start position and repeat for eight reps.

Immediately go to the next movement. Dumbbells forward and down palms facing the body, knuckles out, arms slightly bent. Raise your arms forward and pause at shoulder height. Lower your arms to start and repeat for eight reps.

Immediately go to the next movement. Keeping the same foot stance, raise the dumbbells until they are in the classic shoulder press position with palms or grip facing forward. Slowly press the dumbbells upwards in a classic press pyramiding the motion so the dumbbells touch without banging. Try to keep a slight bend at the extension. I avoid hyper-extending the elbows as injury can easily occur this way. Hyperextension seems to happen when the movement is too fast. Keeping an "on, one thousand" count seems to always keep the movement correct while reducing the possibility of injury.

Immediately go to the final movement. With arms hanging to the sides with palms/dumbbells facing the thighs, slowly raise your shoulders attempting to touch your ears... that probably won't happen for the average person, but you get my point. This movement works the trapezius muscle group and though the weight is very light, most people will feel a slight burn with this exercise due to all of the previous movements just completed. It is not the individual exercise that has the primary effect. It is the combination of movements done with proper form, at a slow pace; and low weight. The combination of five movements for one set takes approximately forty-eight to sixty seconds to complete. Each movement is full range and helps to build overall muscle strength while maintaining a high degree of flexibility. I try to complete three to six sets of this combination; adding weight for each set, e.g., 7, 10, 12, 15, 17, 20 pounds. Downtime between sets should be no more than thirty seconds.

Legs: Magic 30's: This is by far one of the best leg workouts I have ever done and I learned this during my Escrima training. It works so well that I still do them to this day. I do not have the full range of flexibility and ability due to numerous knee surgeries but I have discovered that the exercise dramatically reduced my residual knee pain and arthritis.

1. Begin in a standing position with your feet slightly angled out, shoulder width apart. Keep your head, neck, and back straight, arms bent and in front of you with the left hand clasping the right fist at chest level. Slowly squat to a ¾ position with

legs slightly bent. Pause and rise to a standing position then repeat for a total of thirty reps.

2. The second phase is a slow squat past the ¾ position to until the thighs are parallel to the ground and pause. Slowly rise to a standing position and repeat for a total of thirty reps.

3. The third and final phase is a squat until the back of the legs are touching or almost touching the calves. Your butt should end just off the ground and pause. Slowly rise to a standing position then repeat for a total of thirty reps.

This exercise may sound easy but believe me, it is crazy difficult and the burn is dramatic. I would recommend for those not used to squat type exercises to start with sets of ten to fifteen and slowly work up to sets of thirty. Do not be surprised if you are so sore you can't walk well the first time you try this work out. It takes a few weeks to get used to this program but once there, your flexibility and leg strength will be off the charts.

Squat Kicks with Push-Ups: This is another combination exercise that works many muscle groups quickly, with an emphasis on strength with flexibility and no bulk. It also increases the practitioner's overall coordination in a very big way by developing fast-twitch muscle response simultaneously with eye/foot coordination. Balance is a crucial part of trailing because the handler is constantly reacting and responding to the dog's movement as directed by body and line language. The faster the footwork, the better the movement and less drag on the dog. Martial arts and boxing footwork has made a big difference in my trailing and I practice it to this day.

The kick sets are based on my Escrima work out and my style is simply an example. Any style of martial art kicks can be employed. If you have never performed any martial arts kicking movements, I recommend one-on-one training with a martial arts trainer before attempting these exercises.

Squat Front Kick: Begin in a bladed stance: with the weak leg trailing behind the front, feet shoulder-width apart, while balancing on the balls of the feet. Hands/fists should be in an "On Guard" position with the weak fist leading and the rear fist blocking the head. Slowly squat to an upper legs parallel position to the ground and rise. At the top of the upward motion, cock the rear foot and strike the ball of the foot forward at just below waste level while simultaneously keeping a good guard position with the hands. Visualize targeting an opponent's upper thigh or groin. Pause at the end of the kick and slowly drop the foot to the ground directly below the kick- again, at a shoulder width stance. The rear foot is now leading. Repeat the exercise with the other foot. Repeat the two repetitions for a total of five squat kicks per leg.

Immediately drop to a push up position with hands at shoulder width and break out ten, two-count push-ups; one thousand one at the downward motion, one thousand two on the up.

Squat Side Kick: Upon completion of the push-up set, immediately take on the bladed kick stance above and prepare for the squat sidekick. Squat in the manner above, and on the up stroke, launch a sidekick below an imaginary opponent's hip or thigh. The kick should be in a slow whip like motion with the front of the foot and shin following. Pause at the end of the kick and drop the foot to a bladed stance, kicking foot forward. Repeat with the other leg. Repeat for a total of five reps per leg.

Immediately drop down to a prone push—up position with a wide, past shoulder width, hand position and knock out ten two count push—ups.

Squat Knee Strike: Immediately rise and assume a bladed stance. Squat as described above and on the upward stroke, bring the rear knee up and strike towards the chin of an imaginary opponent. As the knee comes up, move the hands to a clasping position as if an opponent's head is in the hands, pulling the head downward. Concentrate on lunging the hips up at the end of the stroke. Power comes from the hips. Drop the striking leg down to a bladed stance and repeat with the other knee. Repeat for a total of five reps per knee.

Immediately drop down to a prone push—up position with the hands placed in a narrow stance, or less than shoulder width apart. Knock out ten two count push-ups.

Jumping Jacks: Jumping jacks are a hold out from my military days an absolutely no other exercise does more for building the calves. I prefer the four count jumping jack equaling one rep: for a total of one hundred reps. Start with the feet together and the hands at the side. Jump up simultaneously clapping the hands above your head as the feet land shoulder width apart. This is count one. Jump again to the start position for count two. Repeat movement one-count three, and repeat movement two-count four; this is one complete rep. Do this for a total of one hundred reps. This exercise is not easy and most people unaccustomed to jumping jacks will be lucky to get out fifty without collapsing from calf burn. I highly recommend building up to the one hundred in increments of twenty-five.

I further build my strength and strength endurance by working out with a boxing routine on a speed bags. I find this workout further increases my flexibility while building cardio vascular fitness simultaneously. I also love the hand/eye coordination that boxing produces and this translates directly to better lead handling. A big part of trailing at a good clip in the woods is all about dropping the lead and picking it up as the dog negotiates trees and bushes or other obstacles. Nobody can keep up with a dog trailing without impeding it in one form or another. The key to doing this in a coordinated way is having superior hand-eye coordination and there is no better way to develop this trait then through the art of boxing.

Speed Bag Boxing: The art of the speed bag is very much an acquired trait. It is not easy and most people spend months perfecting it. The emphasis for me is not necessarily speed as it is form. Speed comes post form. Start with a good boxing stance and alternate the foot work with the firing fist. In other words, as you alternate from right to left, rotate the hips and put weight on the ball of the leading foot. I do three sets of three-minute speed bag drills alternating with the double end bag also for three sets.

Double End Speed Bag: The double end bag is not as fast as the speed bag but it adds less than predictable bag movement in all directions depending on the strike. I like this for developing hand-eye coordination in chaotic movement. The double end bag also allows for a lot of footwork, side-to-side, front to back and combinations of all of them. Couple the foot work with the boxing and you have a rich training environment for building hand-eye coordination and footwork at the same time you build your aerobic conditions and muscle strength. This has a direct bearing on catching a flying lead as it whips between trees and bushes on the wind. Of course, you can train for lead handling in a variety of ways but few training methods, for me, incorporate the necessary training components of aerobics, footwork, hand-eye coordination, and strength building.

Heavy Bag Boxing and Kicking: The heavy bag is normally a man's torso-sized bag filled with sand or other material that weighs it down; one hundred pounds is not uncommon for these bags and in the beginning, striking them may not be all that comfortable. The bags give, but not a lot, and it takes time to build up the physical tolerance to the impact. As with all physical training, heavy bag work must be done in tiers to build strength and endurance.

When working the heavy bag I specifically work on my footwork as it relates to my hand strikes and kicks. I usually have no exact sequence of strikes and kicks, concentrating more chaotic movement versus a standard routine.

My boxing workout is usually three sets of each bag, thus the speed bag, double end bag, and heavy bag. Each set lasts three minutes for a total of twenty-seven minutes or nine minutes for each cycle. There is no down time between sets and only a thirty second break between cycles. This is an extremely tough workout, and do not be surprised if one minute of each set is too much on the first go around. It may take some time to build up to three minute sets but once you are there you will feel the difference on hard, fast trails.

Physical fitness is a must with any physical job but especially professional trailing. There are no other K9 jobs that take as much of a toll on the human body as this one. If you have an interest in being all that you can be, more importantly, in allowing your dog to be all it can be, then you have to be fit enough to follow. If not, you have no business in the job and can actually be a liability. This is the hard truth nobody ever wants to talk about, but it is a fact. The dog can be fantastic, the best thing on four paws, but if the handler can't keep up after a quarter mile, then the handler just negated the dog's ability and created a problem for the investigation; especially if the handler is injured because of physical limitations. Now the focus is off the investigation and on the handler—in an attempt to remove him or her from the field in safety. If the investigation is a missing child or other person at risk, then any injury related to lack of physical ability preparation is simple irresponsibility. If a handler takes the job seriously enough to spend all of the time and money necessary to produce an exceptional mantrailer, then he or she should consider their own physical training in the same light. To do anything else is self-defeating.

Afterword

Trailing is very low on the totem pole of humankind's crowning achievements and not even on the vocabulary radar for most folks. However, early in my professional career, it became the focus of my life, my direction, my future, and ultimately the crossroads I think that each and every one of us is looking for in our lives. I was just fortunate enough to find my place. I had no idea at the time I first looked at the art of trailing that it would consume so much of my life to the point of self-definition and total expression. It truly became my reason for being.

I began my trailing journey a little late in life, and if hind sight was important, then an earlier age would have perhaps suited me better. Trailing is a young man's job due to the sheer impact the job has on the human body when working behind a high drive trailing dog. Very few other jobs can prepare the human body for the impact that trailing will have on it. Everything physically human is measured over and over and as the dog becomes better at its job, the human body becomes the recipient of all manner of physical abuse. In essence, what is easy and smooth for the K9 to negotiate is often difficult and painful for the human. The umbilical cord of trailing lead attachment to the human body is also the deliverer of punishment in forms only the manhunter can know.

As with boxing, the young man's body is molded by the profession to peak performance. The key to becoming a champion is truly the young man's body, for an older man can rarely handle the abuse. But really, I believe that it is not only the young man's body but especially the mind that is the key to becoming the best one can be. The body adapts to the punishment, but the newness of being what comes with the young mind allows for true expression of any art, and trailing is an art. To become good at something takes practice and commitment, but to master a thing requires an excitement for living that few other times in one's life can provide for; like the short years of youth. I understand now that greatness requires abandon and unfailing devotion to whatever cause ones calling or the art demands. Yes, we all can fall in love with abandon later in life, but perhaps not with the same complete lack of reservation and energy one has with youth.

As a teenager everything is possible and the newness of each day of life is truly excitement's spark. As a youth, I never thought of consequences of doing something the wrong way. I only thought of the doing or the being. Everything was possible, and sipping from the chalice of life was all that mattered. And this, my friends, is what is missing from the lives of most adults when beginning anything; the ability to abandon all for the cause. There is no consequence in youth and this is why the young truly are the best of everything we as a species wish to become.

I strive to always maintain a beginners mind in all that I do with trailing. I never want it to become the same old thing: mundane, or lacking excitement. And unlike any other undertaking in my life, trailing has always remained fresh; with each and every trail I have learned something new and have felt passion. Perhaps it is the nature of the hunt that thrills me. That ancestral, visceral blood pumping; longing for the chase that is never quite satiated. I have felt this at some level with other forms of hunting but never with quite the same intensity as I have for the hunting of man with a K9 partner. Honestly, it is difficult for me to put into words this passion, but I do know with certainty that I share it with other like-minded souls. We are not many but what we share is truly special. There is something ancient about the relationship with a Canid partner as it relates to hunting other humans and my peers know this intimately. To the average person this may seem insane but to other manhunters it is truly the spice of life.

My mentors who experienced it before me passed on this passion for trailing and my hope with all that I have written over the years is that I might in some way honor them by adding more hunters to the fold. Go forth and hunt!

Jeff Schettler

Jeff Schettler is a retired police K9 handler who worked for the City of Alameda and County of Amador in California and was attached to the FBI's Hostage Rescue Teams' K9 Assistance Program for two years. This program was designed to locate and apprehend high-risk fugitives on the run. Jeff has worked hundreds of trailing cases across the United States and is a specialist in the areas of tactical tracking applications.

Jeff was a certified military trainer, graduating from the prestigious US Army's Leadership Academy, also known as Drill Sergeant School. He currently trains police officers, military, and Search & Rescue handlers around the world in the art of K9 Trailing. Jeff raises and trains manhunter K9's that are working for law enforcement agencies across the USA. They are famous for their human find rates and are much sought after.

Jeff writes for Law Enforcement & Military K9 magazines: K9 Cop and Police K9. He is also the author of these popular books: Red Dog Rising: A K9 Trailing Autobiography; K9 Trailing: The Straightest Path A primer on starting a K9 team on human scent discrimination and trailing work; and K9 Trailing; Tactical Tracker Teams; A practical guide to surviving high-risk fugitive manhunts.

The Tao of Trailing

Bibliography

Wolf: The Ecology and Behavior of and Endangered Species. Paperback: 412 pages
Publisher: Univ. Minnesota Press; 1 edition (April 30, 1981) ISBN-10: 0816610266

Of Wolves and Men: Paperback: 320 pages Publisher: Scribner; Revised edition
(September 1, 1979)   ISBN-10: 0684163225

Bloodhounds and How To Train Them Publisher: Leon F. Whitney
1st Publication Date: 1937

Photography Credits
Lynn Cobb and Alis Dobler

The Tao of Trailing

Other Books by Jeff Schettler
www.JeffSchettler.com

Red Dog Rising

"Red Dog Rising" is now in its second edition and won The Dog Writer's Association of America's "Planet Dog K9 Service Award" for 2009. Jeff donates all his royalties from "Red Dog Rising" toward providing Service Dogs for Kids with special needs.

K9 Trailing: The Straightest Path

"K9 Trailing, The Straightest Path", is a no fluff, no fantasy, guide to trailing dogs and scent discrimination.

Tactical Tracker Teams-A Guide To High Risk Manhunt Operations

"K9 Trailing: Tactical Tracking Teams" is about teamwork and it should be required reading for any K9 handler – regardless of experience – who tracks fugitives with a police dog in a rural environment or wilderness area because doing so is arguably the most dangerous job in law enforcement today and a tracking team must be prepared to safely face the challenges to be successful with the mission.
~Sergeant Bill Lewis II (ret.)

The Tao of Trailing

Made in the USA
Las Vegas, NV
15 February 2022

43944647R00155